Taxcafe.co.uk Tax Guides

Using a Property Company to Save Tax

By Carl Bayley BSc ACA

Important Legal Notices:

Taxcafe®
TAX GUIDE - 'Using a Property Company to Save Tax'

Published by:
Taxcafe UK Limited
67 Milton Road
Kirkcaldy
KY1 1TL
Tel: (01592) 560081
Email address: team@taxcafe.co.uk

Ninth Edition, January 2011

ISBN 978-1-907302-33-6

Disclaimer

Before reading or relying on the content of this Tax Guide please read carefully the disclaimer on the last page which applies. If you have any queries then please contact the publisher at team@taxcafe.co.uk.

Pay Less Tax!

...with help from Taxcafe's unique tax guides and software

All products available online at

www.taxcafe.co.uk

Other popular Taxcafe titles include:

- *How to Avoid Property Tax*
- *Tax-Free Property Investments*
- *Salary versus Dividends*
- *How to Avoid Inheritance Tax*
- *Non-Resident & Offshore Tax Planning*
- *The World's Best Tax Havens*
- *Tax Saving Tactics for Non-Doms*
- *Small Business Bookkeeping, Tax & VAT*
- *Using a Company to Save Tax*
- *Selling Your Business*
- *Using a Property Company to Save Tax*
- *Master Property Capital Gains Tax in 2 Hours*
- *The Investor's Tax Bible*
- *Property Capital Gains Tax Calculator*
- *How to Build a £4 Million Property Portfolio*
- *How to Avoid Tax on Foreign Property*

Need Affordable & Expert Tax Planning Help?

Try Taxcafe's Unique Question & Answer Service

The purpose of Taxcafe guides is to provide you with detailed guidance, giving you all the information you need to make informed decisions.

Ultimately, you may want to take further action or obtain guidance personal to your circumstances.

Taxcafe.co.uk has a unique online tax help service that provides access to highly qualified tax professionals at an affordable rate.

For more information or to take advantage of this service please visit:

www.taxcafe.co.uk/questions

BUSINESS TAX SAVER

If you like this tax guide...

You will also like *Business Tax Saver*...

Our monthly guide to BIG business tax savings

You can try it for just £1

Go to www.taxcafe.co.uk/businesstaxsaver.html

About the Author

Carl Bayley is the author of a series of 'Plain English' tax guides designed specifically for the layman and the non-specialist. Carl's particular speciality is his ability to take the weird, complex and inexplicable world of taxation and set it out in the kind of clear, straightforward language that taxpayers themselves can understand. As he often says himself, "my job is to translate 'tax' into English".

Carl enjoys his role as a tax author, as he explains: "Writing these guides gives me the opportunity to use the skills and knowledge learned over almost twenty-five years in the tax profession for the benefit of a wider audience. The most satisfying part of my success as an author is the chance to give the average person the same standard of advice as the 'big guys' at a price which everyone can afford."

Carl takes the same approach when speaking on taxation, a role he frequently undertakes with great enthusiasm, including his highly acclaimed annual 'Budget Breakfast' for the Institute of Chartered Accountants.

In addition to being a recognised author and speaker on the subject, Carl has often spoken on property taxation on radio and television, including the BBC's 'It's Your Money' programme and BBC Radio 2's Jeremy Vine Show.

Carl began his career as a Chartered Accountant in 1983 with one of the 'Big 4' accountancy firms. After qualifying as a double prize-winner, he immediately began specialising in taxation.

After honing his skills with several major international firms, Carl began the new millennium by launching his own tax and accounting practice, Bayley Miller Limited, through which he provides advice on a wide variety of taxation issues; especially property taxation, Inheritance Tax and tax planning for small and medium-sized businesses.

Carl is a member of the governing Council of the Institute of Chartered Accountants in England and Wales and a former Chairman of ICAEW Scotland. He has co-organised the annual Peebles Tax Conference for the last nine years.

When he isn't working, Carl takes on the equally taxing challenges of hill walking and writing poetry and fiction. Carl lives in Scotland with his partner Isabel and has four children.

Dedication

For the Past,

Firstly, I dedicate this book to the memory of those I have loved and lost:

First of all, to my beloved mother Diana – what would you think if you could see me now? The memory of your love warms me still. Thank you for making it all possible;

To my dear grandfather, Arthur - your wise words still come back to guide me; and to my loving grandmothers, Doris and Winifred;

Between you, you left me with nothing I could spend, but everything I need.

Also to my beloved friend and companion, Dawson, who waited so patiently for me to come home every night and who left me in the middle of our last walk together. Thank you for all those happy miles; I still miss you son.

For the Present,

Above all, I must dedicate this book to the person who stands, like a shining beacon, at the centre of every part of my life: Isabel, my 'life support system', whose unflinching support has seen me through the best and the worst. Whether anyone will ever call me a 'great man' I do not know, but I do know that I have a great woman behind me.

Without her help, support and encouragement, this book, and the others I have written, could never have been.

For the Future,

Finally, I also dedicate this book to four very special young people: Michelle, Louise, James and Robert.

I am so very proud of every one of you and I can only hope that I, in turn, will also be able to leave each of you with everything that you need.

Thanks

First and foremost, I must say an enormous thank you to Isabel: for all her help researching everything from obscure points of tax legislation to popular girls' names in Asia; for reading countless drafts; for making sure I stop to eat and sleep; for putting up with me when I'm under pressure and, most of all, for keeping me company into the 'wee small hours' on many a long and otherwise lonely night. I simply cannot ever thank her enough for everything that she does for me, but I intend to spend the rest of my life trying!

Thanks to the Taxcafe team, past and present, for their help in making these books far more successful than I could ever have dreamed.

I would like to thank my old friend and mentor, Peter Rayney, for his inspiration and for showing me that tax and humour can mix.

I would like to thank Rebecca Benneyworth for her many truly unique and inspirational tax lectures which I have had the privilege of attending over the years, as well as her fantastic support at our Peebles conference. Get well soon Rebecca.

I must also thank Martyn for the EIS Pub Company idea.

And last, but far from least, thanks to Ann for keeping us right!

C.B., Roxburghshire, January 2011

Contents

Foreword   **1**

Chapter 1 Why Use a Company?   **11**
1.1 Introduction   11
1.2 Why the Government Likes Companies   13
1.3 Non-tax Reasons for Using a Company   15
1.4 Overview of Company Tax Pros and Cons   19

Chapter 2 Plain English Guide to Corporation Tax   **24**
2.1 What Taxes do Companies Pay?   24
2.2 Introduction to Corporation Tax   26
2.3 Corporation Tax Rates   27
2.4 Save Thousands with 'Marginal Rate' Planning   29
2.5 Future Corporation Tax Rates   31
2.6 Paying Corporation Tax   34
2.7 Cashflow Benefits of Using a Company   35
2.8 Company Tax Returns   37
2.9 Penalties   38

Chapter 3 Different Types of Property Company   **40**
3.1 Introduction   40
3.2 Property Investment Companies   42
3.3 Property Development Companies   45
3.4 Property Trading Companies   47
3.5 Property Management Companies   49
3.6 Companies with a 'Mixed' Property Business   50

Chapter 4 Property Rental Income and Expenses   **53**
4.1 Corporation Tax on Rental Profits   53
4.2 Calculating Rent Receivable   55
4.3 Expenses You Can Claim   56
4.4 Capital Expenditure You Can Claim   59
4.5 Furnished Lettings   70
4.6 Furnished Holiday Lettings   74
4.7 Interest and Finance Costs   76

Contents cont...

4.8 Tax Treatment of Rental Losses 78
4.9 Other Property Investment Income 82
4.10 Lease Premiums 83

Chapter 5 Property Trading Income and Expenses 86
5.1 How Property Trading Profits are Taxed 86
5.2 Trading Profits versus Rental Profits 86
5.3 Properties as Trading Stock 88
5.4 Work-In-Progress & Sales Contracts 94
5.5 Capital Allowances for Trading Companies 97
5.6 Trading Losses 100

Chapter 6 Corporation Tax on Capital Gains 105
6.1 When Does a Capital Gain Arise? 105
6.2 How to Calculate the 'Proceeds' 105
6.3 How to Calculate the 'Base Cost' 109
6.4 How to Calculate the Indexation Relief 111
6.5 Making the Most of Capital Losses 113

Chapter 7 Capital Gains Tax on Company Shares 115
7.1 Introduction 115
7.2 Capital Gains Tax Rates 116
7.3 Entrepreneurs' Relief 117
7.4 Entrepreneurs' Relief for Property Investment Companies 120
7.5 Entrepreneurs' Relief and Couples 120
7.6 Holdover Relief 121

Chapter 8 Stamp Duty for Property Companies 123
8.1 Introduction 123
8.2 Stamp Duty on Shares 123
8.3 Stamp Duty Land Tax 124
8.4 Stamp Duty Land Tax on Leases 126
8.5 Disadvantaged Areas 127
8.6 Zero-Carbon Housing 127

Chapter 9 VAT and Property Companies 128
9.1 VAT on Property 128

Contents cont...

9.2 Residential Property Letting	128
9.3 Holiday Accommodation	129
9.4 Commercial Property Letting	129
9.5 Residential Property Sales	131
9.6 Commercial Property Sales & Purchases	132
9.7 VAT on 'Build to Let'	133
9.8 VAT on Conversions	134
9.9 VAT for Property Management Companies	135
9.10 Interaction with Corporation Tax	136
Chapter 10 Saving Tax When You Extract Profits	**137**
10.1 Profit Extraction Principles	137
10.2 Salaries, Etc	138
10.3 Dividends	138
10.4 Income Shifting: The Gathering Storm?	140
Chapter 11 Personal vs Company Ownership	**148**
11.1 Introduction	148
11.2 Personal Tax Changes	149
11.3 Balancing Act	151
11.4 Rental Profits Kept in the Company	152
11.5 Rental Profits Extracted from the Company	154
11.6 Basic Rate Taxpayers with Rental Profits	155
11.7 Basic Rate Taxpayers Extracting Profits	158
11.8 Making the Most of the Basic Rate Tax Band	159
11.9 Investors with No Other Income	161
11.10 The 'Optimum Scenario'	162
11.11 Trading Profits	163
11.12 Traders with Rental Income	165
11.13 Trading Profits Extracted from the Company	167
11.14 Basic Rate Traders	169
11.15 Traders with Alternative Forms of Income	170
11.16 Traders with Employment Income	171
11.17 Traders with No Other Income	173
11.18 Capital Gains	175

Contents cont...

11.19 Summary 177
11.20 Older Property Investors 179
11.21 Tax Credit Claimants 179

Chapter 12 Making the Big Decision **181**
12.1 The 'Big Picture' 181
12.2 Types of Property Business Revisited 183
12.3 The Rental Income Position 184
12.4 Reinvesting Rental Profits 186
12.5 Capital Gains 188
12.6 Winding Up the Company to Reduce Tax 191
12.7 What if the Company Still Holds Property When Wound
     Up? 193
12.8 Long-Term Reinvestment 193
12.9 Retaining the Wealth 197
12.10 Long-Term Reinvestment Conclusions 201
12.11 The Benefits of Reinvestment for a Trading Company 202

Chapter 13 The Importance of Interest Relief **209**
13.1 Introduction 209
13.2 Who Should Borrow the Funds? 210
13.3 Borrowing to Invest in Shares 211
13.4 Borrowing to Lend to the Company 213
13.5 Corporate Borrowings 214
13.6 Deeds of Trust 217
13.7 Rolling Up Interest In A Company 218
13.8 Personal Interest Relief 221

**Chapter 14 How to Set Up Your Own
             Property Company** **223**
14.1 Who Can Help and How Much Does it Cost? 223
14.2 The Company's Constitution 223
14.3 Other Company Formation Formalities 225
14.4 Changing Your Company's Accounting Date 226
14.5 Dealing with Companies House 227
14.6 Statutory Accounts 228

Contents cont...

14.7 Choosing an Accountant or Auditor   229

Chapter 15   How to Put Existing Property
                into a Company   **232**
15.1 Introduction   232
15.2 Gifts of 'Business Assets'   233
15.3 Incorporation Relief   236
15.4 Which Relief is Best?   238
15.5 Pay Now, Save Later   241
15.6 'Trading' Businesses   245
15.7 Furnished Holiday Lettings   246
15.8 Tax Planning with Incorporation Relief   247
15.9 Turning Investment Property into 'Trading' Property   250
15.10 Property Investment Businesses & Incorporation Relief   253
15.11 Other Investment Properties   256
15.12 Stamp Duty Land Tax on Transfers   258
15.13 VAT and Business Transfers   261

Chapter 16   Some Other Important Tax Issues   **263**
16.1 Close Companies & Investment Holding Companies   263
16.2 The Dangers of Private Use   264
16.3 Selling the Company   265
16.4 Benefits and Dangers of Multiple Companies   267
16.5 Short and Long Accounting Periods   270
16.6 Becoming Non-Resident   273

Chapter 17   Specialised Property Companies   **277**
17.1 Property Management Companies   277
17.2 The EIS Pub Company   279

Chapter 18   In Conclusion   **284**
18.1 Weighing it all Up   284
18.2 Future Tax Changes   285

Contents cont...

Appendix A – Tax Rates and Allowances for Individuals **288**

Appendix B – Forecast Future Tax Rates and Allowances **290**

Appendix C – Marginal Corporation Tax Rates 2009 to 2015 **292**

Appendix D – Connected Persons **294**

Appendix E – Retail Prices Index **295**

Appendix F – Short Leases **297**

Disclaimer **298**

Foreword

By the author

People in the UK have invested in property for centuries. Substantial increases in personal wealth and disposable income over the last few decades, together with problems in other areas of investment and in the pensions industry, have, however, combined to make this an important new area of personal financial planning.

Despite recent difficulties in the UK property market, I personally believe that the property investment sector as we know it today is here to stay. Naturally, the sector will have its ups and downs, as any other sector does, but the philosophy of property investment as a 'career move', or a 'pension plan', is now so well entrenched that it is impossible to imagine that it could ever disappear altogether.

In 2002, in response to the huge demand for advice on property taxation issues which we had been experiencing at Taxcafe.co.uk, we published the first edition of *How to Avoid Property Tax*, the sister publication to this guide. In the following years, the demand for property taxation advice continued to grow at a phenomenal pace and this is responsible for the fact that our first guide is now in its fourteenth edition and this guide is now in its ninth.

But it isn't just the **quantity** of advice being demanded that we have seen increase, it is also the level or, if you like, the **quality** of advice being demanded that we have seen increase significantly.

We have also seen a huge broadening in the type of activities undertaken by the typical property 'investor', many of whom will now, at least partly, be classed as property developers, dealers or managers. This guide, along with its sister publication, has evolved in line with our readership and now caters for the whole range of property businesses which our readers undertake.

As I have already suggested above, a strong trend has emerged for people to enter the property investment business as a profession or as a means to save for retirement.

1

This 'new breed' of property investor is entering the market with a much higher degree of sophistication and is prepared to devote substantial time and resources to the business.

Almost every one of these 'professional investors' asks me the same question: "Should I use a company?" Very often, they are hoping for a nice, simple, single-word answer and, being the helpful chap that I am, I give them one: "Maybe!"

Being an accountant, you may think that my slightly evasive response is merely a ploy to enable me to earn more fees from consultancy work. However, you would be quite wrong, as "maybe" is the only answer that I could possibly give. This question is not an easy one to answer. There are a huge number of factors to be taken into account, not all of which relate to taxation, and it is therefore impossible (not to mention inadvisable) to simply give a straightforward "yes" or "no" answer. (And, in any case, I have plenty of consultancy work already, thank you!)

The first aim of this guide, though, *is* to answer that question, not in a single word, but in the many thousands of words that, in reality, the answer to this highly complex question actually requires. So, to provide you with a truly thorough answer to this crucial question, we will begin, in Chapters 1 and 2, by looking at the basic tax (and non-tax) implications of using a company.

The UK tax regime for companies is quite different from that applying to individuals, or indeed to partnerships, trusts or other potential investment vehicles. The company tax regime has quite a few quirks, which can prove to be costly traps for the unwary. It is therefore extremely important that any property investor considering the company route understands what they are getting themselves into!

In Chapters 3 to 10, we will move on to a more detailed look at the taxation of UK property companies. Here we will discover that there are several different types of property company and that each gives rise to a different set of tax implications which need to be considered carefully by the prospective corporate property investor.

Chapter 11 then provides a summarised comparison of the tax position of companies and individuals.

Following that, in Chapter 12, we will take a detailed look at all the factors involved in making the decision whether to use a company and their implications for the property investor. This is illustrated throughout by several examples designed to highlight the key issues.

In Chapter 13 we will begin to apply what we have learned so far by focussing on one of the most important benefits of using a property company: interest relief.

As most readers will know, individual property investors can only set interest costs against their rental income, often leading to rental losses which can generally only be carried forward and cannot usually be set off against other income or even capital gains on the same property.

One of the main benefits for a property investor in using a company is the ability to set interest on funds borrowed for a company's property investments against other income or capital gains within the company or even the investor's own salary or other income.

In Chapter 13 we will see the difference that this different treatment of interest costs can make to a property investor over many years as the economic cycle produces both short-term losses and long-term gains.

Reaching a Conclusion

In the end, only **you** can really decide whether a property company is appropriate for you - by undertaking a detailed examination of your own individual position and weighing up all of the factors involved.

My aim in this guide is to enable you to reach that unique individual conclusion and make a well-informed decision armed with a strong understanding of the many issues involved.

Whether you're one of those 'professional investors' whom I referred to earlier, or one of the many 'gifted amateurs' whom I also frequently meet; whether you see your property business as your pension plan or just a good way to supplement your income; whether you're developing, dealing, managing or just renting out your properties; whether you've always had a master plan or you stumbled into property investment by accident; in fact, whatever your circumstances may be, this guide will help you understand the questions you need to ask yourself before you can make a truly informed decision whether to use a property company or not.

And you may also find that "yes" or "no" are not the only answers to the property company question that you come up with. Many of my clients, with my guidance, decide that the answer for them is "partly" or "later".

There is absolutely nothing to stop an investor from running two property businesses in parallel – one as an individual and one through a company. Many investors also find that the best route for them is to start with a small property business owned personally and then to start up a second property business in a company later on.

Operating Your Property Company

Once you've made the decision to operate some or all of your property business through a company, whether with the help of this guide or not, you will then want to run your company in the most beneficial way possible.

The second function of this guide is therefore to provide the tax-planning advice and the warnings of potential pitfalls that you will need to know in order to minimise your tax burden as a property company owner.

Hence, as well as providing the overall summary of the property company tax regime in the early chapters of this guide, many more potential planning possibilities and possible pitfalls are covered in Chapters 14 to 16.

Chapter 17 then introduces some more specialised property company structures before lastly, in Chapter 18, at the end of the guide, our detailed findings are neatly summarised, giving you a final opportunity to weigh the whole thing up.

Tips and Warnings

Sprinkled throughout this guide, you will also find many **'Tax Tips'** and **'Wealth Warnings'** designed to highlight key points where there are extra savings to be made or traps to catch the unwary! Watch out for both of these as you read the guide.

Predicting the Future

In order to reinforce the issues discussed in this guide, I will demonstrate the tax implications of corporate property investment through the use of several worked examples.

In my examples, I have naturally had to make various assumptions about external factors beyond the control of the property investor, including:

- The growth of property values
- The future rate of inflation
- Interest rates
- The rates of return on property investment (i.e. market rental levels)
- Future changes to the UK tax system

I have made my assumptions as reasonable as possible, based on my experience of the property investment sector and the UK taxation regime.

However, if I can predict one thing with any certainty it is that the future will not be exactly as any of us may predict. Hence, whilst I believe that the conclusions that I have been able to draw in this guide are validly based on sound principles, the reader must nevertheless bear in mind that those conclusions are, to some extent, dependent on uncertain predictions about the future.

In preparing the examples in this guide, I have assumed that the UK tax regime will remain unchanged in the future except to the extent of any announcements already made at the time of publication and some purely inflationary increases to tax bands, exemptions and allowances.

As far as any purely inflationary increases are concerned, I have used the increase in the Retail Prices Index to September 2010 (4.6%) as the basis for the one figure not yet announced for 2011/12 and an estimated annual inflation rate of 3.5% for all future years. Subject to any announcements already made by the Government, I have then applied these estimated inflation rates to:

- Income Tax personal allowances
- The annual Capital Gains Tax exemption
- Income Tax and National Insurance rate bands below £100,000
- The rate of weekly Class 2 National Insurance contributions

The resultant future estimated personal tax rates for the tax years 2012/13 to 2014/15 are set out in Appendix B.

Most of the personal tax rates and allowances for 2011/12 were announced in December 2010 and these are included in Appendix A. The only estimate which I have had to include there is the annual Capital Gains Tax exemption and even that should now be reasonably accurate. Note, however, that the Government has not yet confirmed the Capital Gains Tax rates for 2011/12. In Appendix A, I have assumed that these will remain unchanged from current rates, but this cannot be guaranteed.

For later years from 2012/13 onwards, please remember that all of my assumptions are made simply for illustrative purposes and are only my 'best guess'; so some variation from my figures can be expected. The further we look into the future, the greater that variation is likely to be.

In reality, we are bound to see more significant changes to the UK tax system at some point in the future, especially following the recent change of Government. Whilst we have no idea when such changes will take place, they will almost certainly occur within the timescale which most long-term property investors are considering.

In Section 18.2, at the end of the guide, I have therefore attempted to analyse the potential impact of any further changes to small company taxation that we may see over the next few years.

Nevertheless, despite the ever-present possibility of changes to the tax regime, I remain firmly of the opinion that there will always still be a great many property investors for whom the use of a company vehicle to hold their investments will continue to be highly beneficial.

As with any other tax planning, my advice is this:

Hope for the best,
Plan for the worst,
Review your position constantly, and
Expect the unexpected!

About the Examples

In addition to the points made above regarding the future of the UK tax regime, please note that, unless specifically stated to the contrary, all persons described in the examples in this guide are UK resident, ordinarily resident and domiciled for tax purposes.

All persons described in the examples in this guide are entirely fictional characters created specifically for the purposes of this guide. Any similarities to actual persons, living or dead, or to fictional characters created by any other author, are entirely coincidental. Likewise, the companies described in the examples in this guide are similarly fictional corporations created specifically for the purposes of this guide and any similarities to actual companies, past or present, is again entirely coincidental.

Scope of this Guide

This guide is aimed primarily at UK resident property investors considering or using a UK resident company to run their property business (although issues facing non-resident investors or non-resident companies are covered briefly in Section 16.6).

The reader must bear in mind the general nature of this guide. Individual circumstances vary and the tax implications of an individual's actions will vary with them. For this reason, it is always vital to get professional advice before undertaking any tax planning or other transactions that may have tax implications. The author cannot accept any responsibility for any loss that may arise as a consequence of any action taken, or any decision to refrain from action taken, as a result of reading this guide.

Married Couples & Registered Civil Partnerships

Throughout this guide you will see me refer several times to 'married couples', 'husbands and wives' or 'spouses'.

Since December 2005, same-sex couples have been able to enter into a registered civil partnership affording them all of the same legal rights and obligations as a married couple.

This equality of treatment also extends to all UK tax law and hence, throughout this guide, any reference to 'married couples', 'husbands and wives' or 'spouses' should be taken to also include registered civil partners.

It is important to remember however, that unless specified to the contrary, the tax treatment being outlined will be available to legally married couples and same-sex couples in a registered civil partnership only.

Remember also that marriage, or civil partnership, is not always advantageous for tax purposes. It really is a case of 'for better or worse'!

The Last Word

Finally, to close this foreword, may I just say that whatever type of property investor you are, and whatever decision you reach about the possible benefits of using a company, I would like to thank you for reading this guide and wish you every success with your investments.

Chapter 1

Why Use a Company?

1.1 INTRODUCTION

Many UK property investors are currently being drawn towards the idea of holding their property investments through a limited company. Why is this?

Unlike most other types of business, it does not generally appear to be due to the protection afforded by a company's limited liability status.

No, this decision appears to be almost entirely tax-driven and is a direct result of the comparatively favourable Corporation Tax regime.

Corporation Tax rates fell steadily throughout the last two decades of the Twentieth Century until finally, in 2002, Gordon Brown shocked even the most veteran of professional Budget-watchers by introducing a 0% tax band for companies.

Many people dubbed this zero-rate band a 'personal allowance for companies' but, sadly, it proved to be short-lived and was abolished in 2006.

The short-lived zero-rate band represented the high-tide mark of the beneficial small company tax regime, as Gordon Brown and his successor, Alistair Darling, then went on to introduce a series of tax increases for small companies in 2007 and 2008.

Now the tide has turned once more. In June 2010, new Coalition Chancellor, George Osborne, announced a series of reductions in Corporation Tax rates over the next few years including, crucially, a reduction in the small profits rate back to 20% from April 2011. (We will look at Osborne's other proposed reductions in more detail in Section 2.5.)

At the same time, both the old Labour Government and the new Coalition Government have put in place a series of personal taxation increases, including:

- Withdrawing personal allowances from individuals with income over £100,000 from 2010/11 onwards
- Introducing a 'super tax' rate of 50% on income over £150,000 from 6th April 2010
- Increasing the Capital Gains Tax rate to 28% for higher rate taxpayers from 23rd June 2010
- Increasing all of the main National Insurance rates by 1% from 6th April 2011
- Increasing the Tax Credit withdrawal rate to 41% from 6th April 2011
- Freezing the higher rate Income Tax threshold at its 2011/12 level until at least 5th April 2014

Hence, with Corporation Tax rates falling and personal tax rates looking set to remain high for the foreseeable future, the apparent attraction of running any type of business through a company has been significantly increased.

For property investors, the relatively beneficial Corporation Tax regime looks extremely tempting. With Corporation Tax rates considerably lower than higher rate Income Tax at 40% or 'super tax' at 50%, many investors feel that using a company must surely be the easiest way to save tax on their investments.

Furthermore, the more beneficial interest relief regime enjoyed by investors using a property investment company (see Chapter 13) is often also an important factor.

With lower tax on profits and better relief for losses, using a property company does initially seem pretty attractive.

But is it really that simple? Clearly, the fact that we have published a whole guide dedicated to this question indicates that it is not!

Yes, at first glance, the Corporation Tax rates do look very attractive compared with higher rate Income Tax or 'super tax'. However, as we shall see, basing the decision to use a company on this one factor alone would be extremely short-sighted.

As we proceed to examine this issue in greater depth, we will see that the Corporation Tax benefits will not always be as great as they may, at first, appear to be. The advantage gained through the lower Corporation Tax rates is often eliminated by the problems surrounding the extraction of profits from the company.

Furthermore, with the wide range of Capital Gains Tax reliefs available to individual property investors, there is sometimes a danger that the long-term position, taking capital growth and the eventual disposal of investment properties into account, may be significantly and detrimentally affected by the use of a company.

Nevertheless, despite these drawbacks, there are still some situations where using a company can prove advantageous to the long-term property investor acquiring a portfolio of properties over time. Where the property portfolio is effectively regarded as a 'pension plan', for example, there may be substantial long-term benefits to be derived from using a company as an investment vehicle.

Furthermore, for those involved in property development, dealing or management, the way that these businesses are treated for Income Tax and National Insurance purposes means that a company can be even more attractive in these cases.

1.2 WHY THE GOVERNMENT LIKES COMPANIES

As we saw in the previous section, both the old Labour Government and the current Coalition Government have allowed a wide gap to open up between company and personal tax rates which has made companies very attractive to businesses in general.

Why?

The official story is that the Government is concerned to keep the UK as a competitive business centre within the global economy.

And unofficially?

While the official reason given is undoubtedly a major factor in the Government's thinking, there is an additional, 'unofficial' reason. Companies are subject to far more rules and regulations than individuals. Hence, the Government and its various institutions and departments have far more control over companies. This is useful for a number of purposes, including the ever-present need to police the so-called 'Black Economy' and fight tax evasion, money laundering and other criminal activities.

Hence, the Government has a very good reason to encourage businesses to form companies.

From time to time, however, Governments of all political persuasions seem to get 'cold feet' about just how much they have been encouraging small businesses to incorporate through the use of a beneficial Corporation Tax system. This, in turn, leads to some of the 'back-tracking' we have seen, like the abolition of the zero-rate band in 2006 and the Corporation Tax rate increases in 2007 and 2008.

The Government seems to swing from Corporation Tax cuts, designed to encourage the use of companies, to Corporation Tax increases, designed to tackle what they seem to perceive as tax avoidance (but which we would simply regard as sensible tax planning).

For several years the Government has been trying to find a long-term solution which allows them to 'have their cake and eat it'. Whether they ever will is far from clear, but we will return to this subject and look at some possible future scenarios for the small company tax regime in Section 18.2.

In the meantime, the key point for any property investor considering whether or not to use a company is to remember the lessons of the past and to bear in mind that Corporation Tax rates can go up as well as down!

Nevertheless, whilst the Government can be expected to withdraw part of the incorporation tax 'carrot' from time to time, the company tax system seems likely to remain considerably more favourable than the personal tax system for some time to come.

1.3   NON-TAX REASONS FOR USING A COMPANY

Before we go on to examine all of the taxation considerations behind the use of a company for property businesses, it is first worth having a brief look at some of the non-taxation factors involved.

There are many non-taxation issues involved in the decision whether to use a company or not. Some of these are covered briefly below, although this list is far from exhaustive.

Limited Liability Protection

Although this does not appear to be the major reason behind most property investors' decision to incorporate, it is still, nevertheless, a factor to be considered. A company is a separate legal entity and, as such, is responsible for its own debts and other liabilities. The usefulness of this, however, is often limited. Banks, for example, will often insist on personal guarantees from the directors or shareholders before they will lend money to the company.

Furthermore, modern insolvency law passes a large part of the company's financial responsibilities to its directors, who may find themselves personally liable where the company has been used in an attempt to avoid the payment of liabilities arising in the normal course of its business.

Nevertheless, limited liability is useful when the business faces unexpected losses or legal liabilities. This can be particularly important when the economy takes a turn for the worse!

Note that limited liability status can also be obtained by using a Limited Liability Partnership ('LLP'). For property investors, however, Limited Liability Partnerships suffer the major drawback that interest relief is not available for funds invested in a Limited Liability Partnership engaged in property investment.

Status

A business that is run through a company is generally perceived as having greater status than a business owned by an individual. For some reason, most people think that 'John Smith Investments Limited' sounds a lot more reliable than plain 'John Smith'.

This perception is, of course, complete rubbish, as is evidenced by the many corporate collapses which we have seen.

Nevertheless, the perception of companies as steady and reliable still remains and corporate property investors may find that they can use this to their advantage.

Flexibility of Ownership

Without the use of a company, it is difficult to involve many other people in the ownership of your property business. Joint ownership with your spouse or partner is easy enough to achieve, but later, as the business hopefully grows, you may wish to involve adult children or key employees.

It is far easier to spread small parcels of ownership of the business through the medium of company shares.

Separation of Ownership and Management

A company structure will also enable you to separate ownership and management. As your business grows and the years go by, you may eventually wish either to retire or to move on to other ventures. However, you may still have a highly profitable business that you do not yet wish to sell.

Using a company will enable you to retain ownership (as a shareholder) while passing management responsibility on to others (the directors). A company structure also enables this business succession process to take place at a more controlled and steady pace.

Tax Tip

Taking the succession planning idea a step further, a company is often a good vehicle for passing wealth on to your children (or other intended beneficiaries).

The problem with a property investment or letting business is that it does not qualify for business property relief for Inheritance Tax purposes. Hence, on the owner's death, the whole portfolio is exposed to Inheritance Tax.

What a company can provide in this situation is a means to allow the owner to pass on small parcels of ownership over a number of years, thus making use of the Capital Gains Tax and Inheritance Tax annual exemptions and avoiding both taxes.

A sophisticated share structure may also enable you to keep control of your company while passing on a significant proportion of the underlying value to your children.

Finance

Many investors wishing to hold properties through the medium of a company find it difficult to obtain the level of finance that they require. This problem seems to most affect those who are just starting their property business, or who only have one or two existing investment properties.

A 'Deed of Trust' arrangement can often be used to get around this problem. We will look at how this type of arrangement works in Section 13.6.

Conversely, for the larger portfolio, corporate status seems to become a positive factor in the eyes of many lenders, probably for the reasons explained under 'Status' above.

Additionally, where the investor is non-UK resident, but looking to invest in the UK property market, the UK's lending institutions actually seem to favour the use of a UK-registered company, as this gives the investor a presence in the UK.

Legal Rights

If you run your business through a company, you personally will no longer own property. Instead, you will own company shares. Legally, these are an entirely different kind of asset, giving rise to different legal rights.

What kind of difference this will make to your affairs will depend on your personal circumstances, as well as in what part of the UK (or other country) you and your properties are located.

As I am not a lawyer, I will not attempt to advise property investors on these issues, but the advice I <u>will</u> give is that you should get legal advice on the implications of owning your properties through a company.

Company Law

If you use a UK-registered company, you will be subject to the requirements of UK company law. This, for example, may restrict your ability to utilise funds from your business for private purposes.

Audit and Other Statutory Requirements

Larger companies require a statutory annual audit of their accounts. Even the smallest companies must file annual accounts, an annual return and certain other documentation with Companies House.

We will take a closer look at these statutory requirements in Chapter 14.

Costs

Inevitably, the additional statutory requirements involved in running a company will lead to increases in accountancy and other professional costs. These additional costs must be weighed against the tax and other benefits that incorporation brings.

Time

Running a company will take up more of your time. There is more bureaucracy, more paperwork and more administration to think about. Whatever you do, there are only 24 hours in a day, so the time eaten up by bureaucracy means less time to concentrate on your investments.

Hence, you have to ask yourself if the financial savings that the company brings are sufficient to compensate you for the time that the company takes up.

It's a question of how you value your time. If the company is saving you a large amount of money then obviously it is worth investing your time. But, in borderline cases, this could actually be the factor that decides against the company. Naturally, if the company saves you enough money, it will be worth employing someone else to do all that tedious paperwork. Then you can save money and time!

1.4   OVERVIEW OF COMPANY TAX PROS AND CONS

We now turn to the tax implications of running a property business through a company. As a broad overview, in general terms, it is reasonable to say that:

A company often produces a better taxation result on <u>income</u>
BUT
Personal ownership can sometimes produce a better result on <u>capital</u> growth

To illustrate this further, let's take a look at some of the taxation pros and cons of investing through a limited company.

Using a Company: The Pros

- From 1st April 2011, the first £300,000 of annual profit will be taxed at a rate of just 20% (the rate applying between 1st April 2008 and 31st March 2011 is 21%).

- Corporation Tax on any level of annual profits is charged at much lower rates than higher rate Income Tax.

- The maximum effective Corporation Tax rate for the year ending 31st March 2012 will be just 28.75%.

- By 1st April 2014, the maximum effective Corporation Tax rate on any level of annual profits will be just 25%.

- Companies still get indexation relief for capital gains purposes. This exempts the portion of any capital gain that arises purely due to inflation.

- The same Corporation Tax rates that apply to income also apply to capital gains made by companies. Hence, from 1st April 2011, most companies will pay tax at just 20% on their capital gains.

- Stamp Duty is payable at a rate of only 0.5% on the purchase of company shares.

- You may choose any year-end accounting date for your company that you wish (an individual's property letting business is taxed on a tax year basis).

- Company shares may be passed on in small quantities at regular intervals, thus utilising the donor's Capital Gains Tax and Inheritance Tax annual exemptions.

- A company may claim relief for interest and other finance costs incurred on borrowings for property investment purposes against any income or capital gains arising in the same period or against any non-trading income or capital gains of future periods.

- A company may also claim relief for other losses arising from a UK property letting business (excluding interest and other finance costs) against any other income or capital gains which it has for the same period or, in most cases, a later one.

- An investor may claim relief for interest costs on funds borrowed to invest in a property investment company against any other income, including salary, self-employment income or their own personal rental income.

- Only companies are eligible for up to 150% tax relief for the costs of cleaning up and preparing contaminated land for development.

Using a Company: The Cons

- Companies do not get a personal allowance.

- Companies do not get an annual exemption for capital gains purposes.

- Companies are not eligible for entrepreneurs' relief for capital gains purposes. (Individuals may claim entrepreneurs' relief on qualifying business disposals, reducing the rate of Capital Gains Tax to just 10% on up to £5m of capital gains. This relief will seldom apply to property investors, however, except in the case of qualifying furnished holiday accommodation.)

- Any personal use by the investor or their family of properties owned by the company may potentially have severe tax consequences. This should be contrasted with the Capital Gains Tax benefits of personal use when investing in property directly.

- Personal tax liabilities may arise when extracting trading or rental profits or property sale proceeds from the company.

- Company dividends may be subject to 'income-shifting' legislation at some point in the future (see Section 10.4).

- It can sometimes be more difficult to obtain relief for certain administrative expenses, such as 'use of home as office' and motor expenses, when investing via a company.

- The £1,500 per property Income Tax allowance for landlord's expenditure on energy-saving insulation is not available to companies.

- The Stamp Duty exemption for lower value company share purchases only applies to purchase consideration not exceeding £1,000 (compared with the Stamp Duty Land Tax exemption for property purchases not exceeding £125,000).

- Companies cannot have a principal private residence, and hence are unable to claim the principal private residence exemption, private letting relief or rent-a-room relief.

- UK resident companies face an 'exit charge' on emigration.

- Many other personal tax planning techniques, such as investing in Enterprise Investment Scheme shares, are simply not available to companies.

When it comes to the important issue of capital gains, we can readily see that there are more cons than pros here. This, however, is set off by the fact that companies are still entitled to indexation relief and the fact that a company could potentially pay tax at just 20% on capital gains of up to £300,000 per year.

Furthermore, the benefits of the lower Corporation Tax rates are highly significant, especially when combined with the more generous regime for relieving interest costs and other rental losses when using a company. As we shall see later in the guide, these benefits will sometimes be large enough to ensure that the company route does remain preferable overall.

The biggest 'con', however, is the potential additional tax arising when rental profits or property sales proceeds are extracted from the company. What this, and all the other 'cons' set out above, mean is that using a company is an extremely complex decision requiring some very careful consideration.

Chapter 2

A Plain English Guide to Corporation Tax

2.1 WHAT TAXES DO COMPANIES PAY?

In this chapter, we will take a detailed look at how Corporation Tax is calculated; sticking, as far as possible, to plain English!

First, however, it is worth summarising the different taxes that companies pay.

Income and Capital Gains

A UK resident company pays Corporation Tax on its total profits, made up of its worldwide income, profits and capital gains. It does not pay Income Tax or Capital Gains Tax. (You may have noticed in Section 1.4, that I referred to 'capital gains' for companies, but not to 'Capital Gains Tax'.)

Occasionally, a company may suffer a deduction of Income Tax at source on part of its income, but this can be deducted from its Corporation Tax liability for the same period.

Stamp Duty and Stamp Duty Land Tax

Companies pay Stamp Duty and Stamp Duty Land Tax on their purchases at exactly the same rates as an individual does. These taxes are covered further in Chapter 8.

Inheritance Tax

Companies are only liable for Inheritance Tax in the most exceptional of circumstances and, even then, the tax only arises as a result of external factors involving the company's shareholders.

A company does not die, so Inheritance Tax does not arise. Instead, companies are wound up and we will come to the implications of this later in the guide. None of this, however, alters the fact that, when a shareholder dies, the value of his or her property company shares must be taken into account as part of their estate for Inheritance Tax purposes.

VAT

Broadly speaking, a company is liable for VAT in the same way as an individual. This subject is covered in detail in Chapter 9.

National Insurance

If you employ anyone to help you in your corporate property business, the company will be liable for secondary Class 1 National Insurance, at the rate of 13.8% (12.8% prior to 6th April 2011), in its capacity as an employer.

The company is also liable for Class 1A National Insurance on any benefits in kind provided to employees and Class 1B National Insurance on any voluntary settlements negotiated with HM Revenue and Customs (e.g. on the cost of sandwiches provided at lunchtime business meetings).

Furthermore, like any other employer, the company has to deduct primary Class 1 National Insurance from its employees' pay and account for this through the PAYE system.

All of this is exactly the same as the situation where you employ someone to help you in your sole trader or partnership business.

The key difference, however, comes from the fact that National Insurance will also be due if you pay yourself a salary out of the company's profits, or provide yourself with any benefits in kind (such as a company car). We will look further at the implications of this in Section 10.2.

Apart from Class 1, Class 1A and Class 1B, however, a company cannot be liable for any other Class of National Insurance.

Unlike a sole trader or partnership, this remains the case regardless of what type of property business you have and there can never be any question of Class 2 or Class 4 National Insurance being payable.

2.2 INTRODUCTION TO CORPORATION TAX

All of a company's income and capital gains for an accounting period are simply added together and then treated as a single total sum of profits chargeable to Corporation Tax.

The starting point for establishing the company's profits is its statutory accounts for the relevant accounting period (see Section 14.6). Further, more detailed, accounts may also need to be prepared where the company has more than one type of income for Corporation Tax purposes.

Fundamentally, capital gains, rental profits and trading profits within a company are all calculated in much the same way as for individuals.

In the case of rental profits, however, there is a key difference arising due to the treatment of interest and other finance costs as general company overheads. We will deal with the implications of this in more detail in Section 4.7.

Further differences arise in the way that the income and gains are taxed, the reliefs and exemptions available and the rates of tax applying.

For capital gains, the biggest difference lies in the fact that companies continue to be eligible for indexation relief on their capital assets.

We will return to the differences between the corporate and personal tax regimes again in Chapters 11 to 13, where we will be taking a detailed look at their impact on the property investor.

2.3 CORPORATION TAX RATES

Officially, there are just two rates of Corporation Tax: the 'Small Profits Rate' (formerly known as the 'Small Companies Rate') and the 'Main Rate'. For the year ending 31st March 2012, these will be 20% and 27% respectively.

However, the Corporation Tax system does not operate in the same way as the Income Tax system. A large company, paying tax at the main rate, does not benefit at all from the small profits rate and will pay Corporation Tax at the main rate on all of its profits and gains.

The benefit of the small profits rate is progressively withdrawn through a system known as marginal relief. As a result of the marginal relief system there are, in fact, actually three effective Corporation Tax rates.

The effective Corporation Tax rates applying to profits for the year ending 31st March 2012 are given below. The rates applying for the previous three financial years (i.e. from 1st April 2008 to 31st March 2011) are given in brackets.

Corporation Tax Rates: Year Ending 31st March 2012
On the Company's Total Profits and Gains:

First £300,000:	20%	(21%)
From £300,000 to £1.5m:	28.75%	(29.75%)
Over £1.5m:	27%	(28%)

In practice, however, once the company's total profits and gains exceed £1.5m, everything is simply taxed at the main rate of 27% and the other effective rates can simply be ignored.

Example

Aaron Limited makes a total taxable profit of £500,000 for the year ending 31st March 2012. The company's Corporation Tax liability for the year can therefore be calculated as follows:

£300,000	@	20.00%	=	£60,000
£200,000	@	28.75%	=	£57,500

Total Tax Due: **£117,500**

The 'Official' Format

Note that when you receive a Corporation Tax calculation from HM Revenue and Customs (and perhaps also from your accountant), it will not look like the calculation in the example above. HM Revenue and Customs will follow the 'official' format using only the two official Corporation Tax rates, with a deduction for marginal relief where applicable.

Example

Aaron Limited's Corporation Tax calculation following the official format will be as follows:

£500,000	@	27.00%	=	£135,000

Less Marginal Relief:

on	£1,500,000	-	£500,000		
=	£1,000,000	x	7/400	=	£17,500

Total Tax Due: **£117,500**

For the remainder of the guide, however, we will stick with our unofficial format since it is by far the easier method to understand in practice and is also far more useful when we start to look at tax-planning issues.

2.4 SAVE THOUSANDS IN TAX WITH 'MARGINAL RATE' PLANNING

You will often see accountants refer to a company's 'marginal' Corporation Tax rate. For example, a company with a profit of £400,000 for the year ending 31st March 2012 has a marginal rate of 28.75% and a company with a profit of £120,000 for the year ending 31st March 2012 has a marginal rate of 20%.

The importance of the marginal rate is that this is the effective tax rate applying to any additional income or profit and also the effective rate of tax relief available for any additional expenses or allowances. In other words, a company with a marginal Corporation Tax rate of 20% will pay 20 pence on each additional £1 of profit. Similarly, a company with a marginal Corporation Tax rate of 28.75% will save 28.75 pence worth of tax for every additional £1 of expenses incurred.

To illustrate the impact of marginal rates, let's return to Aaron Limited once more.

Example

As we know, the company's taxable profits of £500,000 give rise to a Corporation Tax liability of £117,500 for the year ending 31st March 2012. However, let us suppose that this is before taking account of some extensive roof repairs that Aaron Limited carried out during March 2012 at a cost of £100,000.

After claiming the cost of the repairs, the company's taxable profits will be reduced to £400,000 and its Corporation Tax computation will therefore now be as follows:

£300,000	@	20.00%	=	£60,000
£100,000	@	28.75%	=	£28,750

Total Tax Due: **£88,750**

The tax saved is therefore £28,750 (£117,500 minus £88,750), which equates to 28.75%.

As we can see, the amount of tax saved by any additional claim or relief is based on the marginal rate and this is why this is such an important concept in tax planning.

Tax Tip

A company's marginal Corporation Tax rate will often change significantly from one year to the next.

For example, Aaron Limited might be anticipating a fall in its profits (to below £300,000), such that its marginal rate for the following year would be reduced to 20% (see Section 2.5 below).

In such a situation, a month's delay in Aaron Limited's repairs expenditure would have reduced the effective tax relief on this expenditure from £28,750 to £20,000. Hence, not only would the company have had to wait another year for its tax relief, it would also have been **£8,750 worse off!**

Accelerating tax relief is something that most people will be familiar and comfortable with, even without the impact of a movement in marginal rates. However, consider this:

What if Aaron Limited had a marginal Corporation Tax rate of 20% for the year ending 31st March 2012, but was anticipating an increase in profits for the following year, such that its marginal rate would increase to 27.5% (see Section 2.5)? In this case, the company would be better off to *delay* its repairs expenditure until *after* its year end (i.e. until April 2012).

Although this would mean postponing tax relief for this expenditure by a year, it would actually **save the company an additional £7,500!** The impact of timing your business expenditure carefully will be at its most significant when considering a movement in the company's profits from one year to the next which takes it from one side of the £300,000 threshold to the other.

2.5 FUTURE CORPORATION TAX RATES

Since 1st April 2008, the small profits rate of Corporation Tax has stood at 21% and the main rate has stood at 28%.

However, in the Coalition Government's first Budget on 22nd June 2010, new Chancellor George Osborne announced a package of reductions in Corporation Tax rates, commencing with the new rates applying for the year ending 31st March 2012 set out in Section 2.3.

The proposed reductions can be summarised as follows:

- The small profits rate is to reduce from 21% to 20% with effect from 1st April 2011
- The main rate is to be reduced by 1% on 1st April each year from 2011 to 2014

Financial Years

Corporation Tax operates by reference to 'Financial Years'. Just to make life even more confusing than it already undoubtedly is, the Financial Year is slightly different to the tax year ending on 5th April, which applies to income received by individuals.

A Financial Year is the year ending on 31st March in any calendar year but is officially described by reference to the calendar year in which it began. Hence, for example, the 2011 Financial Year is the year commencing on 1st April 2011 and ending on 31st March 2012.

It is important to be aware of this official terminology, as this is what is used on the Corporation Tax Return.

Corporation Tax Rates

As explained above, the June 2010 Budget included proposed reductions in Corporation Tax rates over the next four Financial Years.

Although not officially announced, the changes to the small profits rate and the main rate of Corporation Tax will also affect the marginal rate applying to companies with annual profits between £300,000 and £1,500,000.

The full range of marginal Corporation Tax rates applying in the next four Financial Years, are as follows:

Company Profits:	Year Commencing 1st April:			
	2011	**2012**	**2013**	**2014**
Up to £300,000	20.00%	20.00%	20.00%	20.00%
£300,000 - £1.5M	28.75%	27.50%	26.25%	25.00%
Over £1.5M	27.00%	26.00%	25.00%	24.00%

The above table is fine if your company happens to have a 31st March year end. For the rest of us, however, we have to look at the 'split year' treatment. In other words, the company's profits need to be split across two Financial Years.

The element of profit falling into each Financial Year will then be taxed separately using the applicable rates for each of the two relevant Financial Years, as shown in the above table.

What matters as far as any tax planning is concerned, of course, is the impact that this has on marginal Corporation Tax rates. This becomes quite a complex issue, but we will begin by looking at a simple example.

Example

St Etienne Limited draws up accounts to 30th June each year. For the year ending 30th June 2012, the company's taxable profits are £480,000.

The first part of this accounting period, from 1st July 2011 to 31st March 2012, falls into the 2011 Financial Year (i.e. the year ending 31st March 2012). This part of the accounting period is 275 days in duration, so the portion of St Etienne Limited's 2012 taxable profits falling into the 2011 Financial Year is therefore 275/366 x £480,000 = £360,656.

As this is a period of just 275 days, only the first £225,410 (£300,000 x 275/366) of this profit is subject to Corporation Tax at the small profits rate of 20%. The remaining £135,246 is taxed at the marginal rate for the 2011 Financial Year, 28.75%.

The other £119,344 (£480,000 - £360,656) of St Etienne Limited's profits for the year ending 30th June 2012 fall into the 2012 Financial Year. This equates to the profit arising for the 91 day period from 1st April to 30th June 2012, i.e. 91/366 x £480,000 = £119,344.

The first £74,590 (£300,000 x 91/366) of the profit falling into the 2012 Financial Year is taxed at the small profits rate of 20%. The remaining £44,754 (£119,344 - £74,590) is taxed at the marginal rate applying for the 2012 Financial Year, 27.5%.

St Etienne Limited's Corporation Tax bill for the year ending 30th June 2012 is therefore as follows:

2011 Financial Year:	*£225,410 @ 20% =*	*£45,082*
	£135,246 @ 28.75% =	*£38,883*
2012 Financial Year:	*£74,590 @ 20% =*	*£14,918*
	£44,754 @ 27.5% =	*£12,307*
Total:		*£111,190*

This equates to an overall effective Corporation Tax rate of 23.165%.

More importantly, however, the Corporation Tax on the top £180,000 of the company's profits (i.e. the amount in excess of £300,000) is derived as follows:

2011 Financial Year:	*£135,246 @ 28.75% =*	*£38,883*
2012 Financial Year:	*£44,754 @ 27.5% =*	*£12,307*
Total:		*£51,190*

*This equates to an effective **marginal** rate of 28.439% (£51,190/£180,000).*

The rate of 28.439% is therefore the effective marginal Corporation Tax rate applying to companies with profits between £300,000 and £1,500,000 for the year ending 30th June 2012.

Using similar principles, we can derive the effective marginal Corporation Tax rates for any company with any accounting period and any level of profit. These work out as detailed in Appendix C.

As we can see, every different accounting period over a four year period is subject to a different set of marginal Corporation Tax rates. At present, no further changes are proposed after 31st March 2015. However, if there is another thing that I can predict with any certainty, it is the fact that further changes *will* occur.

Nevertheless, the Corporation Tax rates currently proposed for the year ending 31st March 2015 remain our best forecast for the long term and we will therefore be basing our calculations on these rates when we come to make our long-term predictions regarding the benefits of a property company later in the guide.

Look Before You 'Leap'

I must confess that I cheated slightly in order to keep the table in Appendix C as 'simple' as possible.

An added complication is created by the fact that 2012 is a leap year. In effect, this makes the 2011 Financial Year a 'Leap Financial Year' of 366 days' duration.

This creates some slight distortions to the Corporation Tax rates applying to some companies for an accounting period that falls partly, but not wholly, into the 2011 Financial Year.

However, since the maximum overall effect on any company's Corporation Tax bill is just £60, I do not propose to dwell on this point any longer!

2.6 PAYING CORPORATION TAX

For most companies, payment of Corporation Tax is due in one single lump sum payable within nine months and one day after the end of the accounting period.

For example, the Corporation Tax for the year ending 31st December 2011 will be due by 1st October 2012.

34

As usual, interest is charged on late payments. Unlike Income Tax, however, interest on overdue Corporation Tax is a deductible expense.

Large companies paying Corporation Tax wholly at the main rate (with no marginal relief) must pay their tax in quarterly instalments.

Corporation Tax due in respect of periods ending after 31st March 2010 must be paid online.

2.7   CASHFLOW BENEFITS OF USING A COMPANY

It is worth noting that the timing of a company's Corporation Tax payment is totally dependent on its accounting year-end date. This is quite different to individuals and partnerships, where tax is always due on the same dates under the Self Assessment system (i.e. instalments on 31st January during the tax year and 31st July following the tax year, with a balancing payment, or repayment, the following 31st January).

For stable and profitable property businesses, there is a huge cashflow advantage to using a company. This is quite independent of any tax savings that might be involved. Let's look at an example by way of explanation:

Example

Gordon has a thriving property letting business. His Income Tax liability has remained at the same level for a number of years (pretty rare in practice, but this is just an example, after all) and hence he has to pay half his tax on 31st January within the tax year and half on the following 31st July. If we 'averaged out' these two payments, this would be equivalent, for cashflow purposes, to a single payment on 1st May.

*Remember that, like any other individual with property letting income, Gordon MUST pay tax based on his profits for the year ending 5th April. Hence, on average, he effectively has to pay his tax just **26 days** after the end of his accounting period!*

If we contrast this 26-day 'average' payment period with the nine months and a day available to companies, we can see what a large cashflow advantage the companies have – over eight months!

Wouldn't you rather keep your money for an extra eight months? Think what you could do with it in that time, especially in the rapidly moving property investment sector!

What if Profit isn't Stable?

The example above is perhaps not entirely typical, as it is based on a stable annual profit. In practice, profits tend to fluctuate, which can sometimes mean that the company cashflow advantage is not quite so great. Nevertheless, in the vast majority of cases, the 'average' payment date for an individual investor (or a partnership) would still fall somewhere within three months of the end of the accounting period, meaning that a company would usually produce at least six months of cashflow advantage.

Wealth Warning

Note, however, that if the company is making large enough profits to be under the quarterly instalment system (see Section 2.6 above), its 'average' payment date is actually about a month **before** the end of its accounting period. In this case, the company actually produces a cashflow *disadvantage* (although, by the time profits have reached this kind of level, other considerations are likely to be far more important).

Tax Tip

As already explained, a company may choose any accounting year-end date that it wishes, whereas an individual property investor is effectively forced to stick with 5th April (accounts can be drawn up for any period but the tax liability will always be based on profits for the year to 5th April).

In the corporate regime this can sometimes provide scope to delay the tax on profits that do not arise regularly over the year. This is particularly relevant to those letting furnished holiday accommodation or student accommodation.

Example

Laura lets out a number of student flats through a company, Laura's Lettings Limited. Generally, they are let from October to June, but are often vacant during the summer months. Hence, all of Laura's profit arises during the nine months to June.

If the company were to draw up its accounts to 30th June each year, its Corporation Tax liability would be due on 1st April the following year. Instead of this, however, Laura arranges for Laura's Lettings Limited's accounting year-end to be 30th September. The company's Corporation Tax is therefore not due until 1st July the following year.

This one simple step has given Laura an additional three-month cashflow saving every year!

2.8   COMPANY TAX RETURNS

Companies fall under a Self-Assessment system referred to as Corporation Tax Self Assessment or 'CTSA' for short.

Under Corporation Tax Self Assessment, the company is generally required to submit a Tax Return within twelve months of its accounting date.

The Corporation Tax Self Assessment Tax Return document is called a CT600. At four pages, the basic CT600 (Short) Return used by most companies is actually shorter than the Tax Return for individuals.

However, with its Corporation Tax Self Assessment Tax Return, the company is also required to submit:

- Its statutory accounts (small and medium-sized companies who are permitted to file abbreviated accounts with Companies House must nevertheless still submit a full set of accounts to HM Revenue and Customs with their Tax Return).

- A Corporation Tax computation (i.e. a calculation of the amount of profits and gains chargeable to Corporation Tax for the accounting period).

- A Corporation Tax Self-Assessment (i.e. a calculation of the amount of Corporation Tax due).

These last two items can generally be prepared as a single combined calculation and there is plenty of accountancy software available to produce this.

Both the Corporation Tax Return and the supporting computation will need to be prepared in the 'official' format, which we looked at in Section 2.3.

Compulsory Online Filing

Online filing of Corporation Tax Returns and supporting documentation is compulsory for accounting periods ending after 31st March 2010. Electronic versions of the supporting documents outlined above need to be submitted in 'iXBRL' format.

For further guidance visit: www.hmrc.gov.uk/ctsa

2.9   PENALTIES

In general terms, it is fair to make the point that the corporate regime has a few more 'teeth' and is a little stricter on those who do not quite meet its rigorous requirements. This, perhaps, is the price we must pay for more beneficial tax rates.

There is a progressive system of penalties for late Tax Returns under Corporation Tax Self Assessment, as follows:

i) Returns filed up to three months late incur a penalty of £100.

ii) Returns filed more than three months late incur a penalty of £200.

iii) The above amounts are generally increased to £500 and £1,000 respectively in the case of a third, or subsequent, late submission.

iv) The company is also liable for a 'tax-geared' penalty of 10% of unpaid tax if it files its return between 18 and 24 months after the end of the accounting period.

v) The 'Tax-Geared' penalty increases to 20% if the Tax Return is filed more than two years after the end of the relevant period.

Wealth Warning

It is important to note that the flat-rate penalties described under (i) to (iii) above are applied regardless of whether or not the company has any Corporation Tax liability for the period.

Property investors who begin to operate through a company should bear this point in mind, as it differs from the current position under Self Assessment for individuals. (Currently, there is no late filing penalty for individuals if no actual tax liability arises, although there are proposals to introduce such penalties in the near future.)

Chapter 3

Different Types of Property Company

3.1 INTRODUCTION

In Chapter 2 we looked at the basic mechanics of how a company is taxed in the UK. We will now begin looking in more detail at the UK taxation issues relating specifically to *property* companies.

Whilst it would be possible to come up with a very long list of different 'types' of property companies, I would tend to regard the following four categories as the definitive list as far as UK taxation treatment is concerned:

    a) Property investment (or letting) companies
    b) Property development companies
    c) Property trading (or dealing) companies
    d) Property management companies

Before we go on to look at the detailed tax treatment of these different types of property companies, it is perhaps worth spending a little time to explain exactly what these different terms mean in a taxation context.

I should probably also point out at this stage that there is nothing different about the way in which these different types of companies are formed, nor usually in their constitutions (see Section 14.2). No, it is the nature of the property business itself that determines what type of company we are looking at.

It is also important to understand that these different types of property business are not exclusive to companies and that these different categorisations may also be applied to an individual property investor, a partnership, or any other kind of property investment vehicle.

Over the course of the next five chapters, we will examine the Corporation Tax consequences of having a company which falls into each of the four categories that I have outlined above, as well as the implications for the owner of the company.

Stamp Duty Land Tax and VAT will then be considered in Chapters 8 and 9 respectively. National Insurance payable by companies was covered in Section 2.1 and will be unaffected by the type of property business involved.

A company can, of course, carry on more than one type of property business, which would result in a mixture of tax treatments. I will spend a little time on the possible consequences of this in Section 3.6.

Why Does It Matter?

As we will discover over the next few chapters, the type of property business carried on by the company has only a relatively minor effect on the way in which the company itself is taxed.

The impact on the owner of the company is more significant, however, as there are several important Capital Gains Tax and Inheritance Tax reliefs which are dependent on the type of property company which you have.

Even more important is the fact that individuals who are not using a company are taxed very differently on different types of property businesses.

This means that the contrast between an individual investor's tax position and a company investor's tax position is significantly affected by the type of property business involved.

Hence, it is absolutely crucial to understand what type of property business you have in order to be able to determine whether a company is appropriate for you.

We will return to take a detailed look at the contrast between individual and company investors with different types of property business in Chapters 11 to 13 when we have finished looking at how the various types of property companies and their owners are taxed.

3.2 PROPERTY INVESTMENT COMPANIES (AKA PROPERTY LETTING COMPANIES)

These are companies that predominantly hold properties as long-term investments. The properties are the company's fixed assets, which are held to produce income in the form of rental profit.

Whilst capital growth will be anticipated and will form part of the company's business plan, property disposals should usually only take place where there is a strong commercial reason, such as an anticipated decline in value in that particular geographical location or a need to realise funds for other investments.

Example

All Blacks Limited purchases three properties 'off-plan'. On completion of the properties, the company sells one of them in order to provide funds for continued expansion. The other two properties are then rented out for a number of years.

Although All Blacks Limited sold one of the properties very quickly, there was a good commercial reason for doing so. Hence, the company may still be regarded as a property investment company.

In general, therefore, most properties will usually be held for a long period and rapid sales for short-term gain will be exceptional.

Having said that, however, where exceptional opportunities for short-term gains do arise, it would be unreasonable to suggest that the company, like any other investor, should not take advantage of those opportunities.

In some cases, the investors themselves will have a minimal level of involvement in the day-to-day running of the business, but there are also many other property letting businesses which are much more 'hands on'.

As long as the company meets the overall long-term investment criterion outlined above, it remains a property investment company for all tax purposes, regardless of the level of the investor's own personal involvement on a day-to-day basis.

Managing your company's own properties would not, in itself, mean that you had a property management company.

Tax Treatment

A property investment company is <u>not</u> regarded as a trading company for tax purposes. This has some unfortunate consequences for the owner of the company, including:

- The shares in the company are not eligible for entrepreneurs' relief or holdover relief for Capital Gains Tax purposes (see further in Chapter 7).

- The shares in the company are not eligible for business property relief for Inheritance Tax purposes, meaning that the full value of the company would be included in the investor's estate on his or her death when calculating the Inheritance Tax due.

Tax Tip

Furnished holiday lettings (see Section 4.6) enjoy a special status for tax purposes.

While companies whose income is derived mainly from these lettings continue to be regarded as property investment companies for a number of purposes, shares in such companies will remain eligible for entrepreneurs' relief and holdover relief. Shares in such companies will sometimes also be eligible for business property relief for Inheritance Tax purposes.

So how are property investment companies taxed?

A property investment company must account for its rental profits under the specific rules applying to property income (see Chapter 4).

Interest and other finance costs are not treated as part of the company's rental business but are regarded as a general overhead of the company with some very generous rules applying to the way in which these costs are relieved for Corporation Tax purposes. We will cover those rules in Section 4.7.

Property disposals are dealt with as capital gains (see Chapter 6).

Is there any advantage to having a property investment company rather than any other type of property company?

Very little!

For a company, the only advantage in having a property investment business rather than any other type of property business is the availability of indexation relief against capital gains arising on the company's investment properties.

Individuals (as well as partnerships, trusts, etc.), however, **do** enjoy a number of advantages if regarded as having a property investment business, rather than one of the other types of property business.

It is therefore essential to understand what type of property business you have, or will have, before deciding whether you want to operate it within a company.

Wealth Warning

Although there is little advantage to this type of tax treatment for a company, it is nevertheless important to appreciate that it is the way in which you carry on your business that determines the tax treatment: you are not allowed to choose how your company is taxed!

44

The vast majority of landlords and 'buy-to-let' investors are carrying on a property investment business and hence, if they form a company, they will therefore have a property investment company.

This is, perhaps, unfortunate, since it is in the case of property investment businesses that we see the most uncertainty over whether the use of a company is beneficial or not. The subject therefore warrants a great deal of further detailed examination and we will return to this issue in Chapters 11 and 12.

For other types of property business, it is often far more clear-cut that a company would be beneficial.

3.3 PROPERTY DEVELOPMENT COMPANIES

These are companies that predominantly acquire properties or land and carry out building or renovation work with a view to selling developed properties for profit.

The term covers quite a broad spectrum of activities, from major building companies that acquire vacant land and construct vast new property developments, to small owner-managed companies that acquire the occasional 'run-down' property to 'do up' for onward sale at a profit. No one would doubt that the former are correctly categorised as property development companies, but not everyone realises that the latter type of activity may also lead to the company being regarded as a property development company.

Generally speaking, a property will be disposed of as soon as possible after building or renovation work has been completed. It is the profit derived from this work which produces the company's income and it does not usually look to rent properties out other than as a matter of short-term expediency.

Example

All Whites Limited purchases three old barns in February 2011 and converts them into residential property. The work is completed in August 2011 and the company sells two of the former barns immediately.

The third property, unfortunately, proves difficult to sell. In order to generate some income from the property, All Whites Limited lets it out on a short six-month lease. The property is never taken off the market during the period of the lease and a buyer is found in January 2012, with completion taking place in March.

Although All Whites Limited let one of the properties out for a short period, its main business activity remained property development. This was reinforced by the fact that the property remained on the market throughout the lease. All Whites Limited is therefore a property development company.

Tax Treatment

A property development company is regarded as a *trading company*. Shares in the company are eligible for both entrepreneurs' relief and holdover relief for Capital Gains Tax purposes (see Chapter 7).

It is important to stress that we are talking here about the <u>shares</u> in the company rather than the <u>properties</u> owned by the company. Companies cannot qualify for entrepreneurs' relief or holdover relief on the properties that they own (nor, indeed, on any other assets).

Shares in a property development company are also eligible for business property relief for Inheritance Tax purposes.

The company's profits from its property development activities, i.e. the profits arising from development property sales, are taxed as trading profits. We will look at the taxation of trading profits in more detail in Chapter 5.

Interest and other finance costs relating to the company's property development activities are simply treated as part of its normal trading expenses and do not require the special treatment set out in Section 4.7.

Capital gains treatment will continue to apply to any disposals of the company's long-term fixed assets, such as its own offices, for example.

Where, as in the example above, there is some incidental short-term rental income it should, strictly speaking, still be dealt with under the specific rules applying to property income. In practice, however, it has sometimes been known for this to be accepted as incidental trading income. This is very important, since this treatment ensures that the company's trading status is not affected.

Property developers who utilise the services of subcontractors for any building work, including plumbing, decorating and electrical work, are required to operate the Construction Industry Scheme for tax purposes. This may involve having to deduct tax, at a special rate particular to the Construction Industry Scheme, from payments made to subcontractors and then account for it to HM Revenue and Customs, rather like PAYE.

The current rate for the mandatory deductions under the Construction Industry Scheme is either 20% or 30%, depending on whether the subcontractor is registered under the scheme.

3.4   PROPERTY TRADING COMPANIES

This type of company used to be fairly rare, but has become more common in recent years.

Property trading companies are companies that generally only hold properties for short-term gain. Properties are bought and sold frequently and are held as trading stock. Properties will not usually be rented out, except in the interests of short-term financial expediency.

Such companies may sometimes also be known as property dealing companies.

The company's income is derived from making a profit on the properties it sells. These companies differ from property development companies in that no actual development takes place on the properties. Profits are made simply by ensuring a good margin between buying and selling price.

Example

All Greys Limited has bought 20 different properties 'off-plan' over the last few years. In each case, it has sold the properties immediately on completion of the development.

Since All Greys Limited has neither developed the properties, nor held on to them as investments for any length of time, it is clearly a property trading company.

Tax Treatment

A property trading company's profits should be taxed as trading income (see Chapter 5). Interest and other finance costs relating to the company's property trading activities will represent trading expenses.

Any incidental letting income that does arise should be dealt with under the specific rules applying to property income.

Shares in such a company are specifically not eligible for business property relief for Inheritance Tax purposes.

As for Capital Gains Tax, the theory is that a property trading company is still a 'trading company' and hence the shares in such a company should be eligible for both entrepreneurs' relief and holdover relief (see Chapter 7).

In practice, however, I feel that there is a strong danger that some resistance will be encountered, with HM Revenue and Customs contending that the company is, in fact, a property investment company, so that its shares do not qualify for these reliefs.

Wealth Warning

The major difference between property investment and property trading lies in the treatment of the profit arising on property disposals. In essence, the question is whether such 'profits' are capital gains or trading profits.

This is very much a 'grey area' and hence HM Revenue and Customs can be expected to examine borderline cases very carefully and to argue for the treatment that produces the most tax.

As explained above, HM Revenue and Customs may be inclined to deny the existence of a trading activity where entrepreneurs' relief or holdover relief is at stake.

Conversely, where an investor is potentially exempt from Capital Gains Tax (e.g. a non-resident individual), HM Revenue and Customs may argue that there is a trading activity in order to be able to levy Income Tax on that investor instead. We will take a closer look at the use of a company in this situation in Section 16.6.

3.5   PROPERTY MANAGEMENT COMPANIES

These companies do not generally own properties at all. Instead, they provide management services to property owners. If you have a property letting agent taking care of the day-to-day running of your properties, the chances are that your agent is probably a property management company.

A property management company's income is derived from the management or service charges that it charges to the actual owners of the property.

Tax Treatment

A property management company is a trading company for all tax purposes. Hence, shares in such a company are usually eligible for entrepreneurs' relief and holdover relief for Capital Gains Tax purposes (see Chapter 7) and business property relief for Inheritance Tax purposes.

The company's profits from its property management activities will be treated as trading profits. Interest and other finance costs incurred in relation to property management activities will be treated as trading expenses.

Capital gains treatment will apply to any disposals of the company's long-term fixed assets, such as its own offices, for example.

Any incidental letting income should, as usual, be dealt with under the specific rules applying to property income.

The interesting point is that, under the right circumstances, you may be able to set up your own property management company. The possible use of such a company for tax-planning purposes is considered in Section 17.1.

3.6   COMPANIES WITH A 'MIXED' PROPERTY BUSINESS

"What if my company doesn't happen to fit neatly into one of these four categories?" you may be asking.

If the company has a 'mixed' property business, involving more than one of the four types of property business described above, then, for Corporation Tax purposes, each of the business types will need to be dealt with separately. It may even be necessary to draw up separate accounts for the different elements of the business.

The impact on the owner of the company will depend on which types of property business are involved in the mixed business and in what proportions.

Capital Gains Tax

For Capital Gains Tax purposes, the company will only be

considered to be a trading company, with its shares eligible for both entrepreneurs' relief and holdover relief (see Chapter 7), if its activities do not include any 'substantial' element of non-trading activities. For this purpose, property investment and property letting are deemed to be non-trading activities (but not furnished holiday lettings).

HM Revenue and Customs have very helpfully told us that they will regard 'substantial' as meaning 'more than 20%'. "More than 20% of what?" you ask. Here, they have attempted to retain a little more control over the situation since, depending on the facts of the case, they may apply this '20% rule' to any of the following:

- Turnover (i.e. gross income)
- Profit
- Expenditure
- Time spent by directors and employees
- Asset values

HM Revenue and Customs' view of the meaning of 'substantial' is not, however, the law; it is merely their interpretation of the law.

Whether their interpretation of this point will be held up in court remains to be seen. In particular, some experts suggest that it should only be necessary to keep non-trading activities under the 20% level according to a majority of the various measures set out above.

Nevertheless, until a suitable test case on this subject does come before the courts, HM Revenue and Customs' interpretation is all that we have to go on. Until that time, therefore, the only absolutely certain way to ensure that both entrepreneurs' relief and holdover relief are available on the shares of a company carrying on a mixed property business is to keep the company's non-trading activities down to a level which does not exceed 20% of any of the measures set out above.

Tax Tip

As we shall see in Chapter 7, whether your company qualifies as a trading company for Capital Gains Tax purposes can make an enormous difference to the amount of tax you will eventually pay on a sale of your shares or a winding up of your company.

For a couple owning a company together, the potential tax saving generated by preserving the company's trading status could be up to £1.8m!

To preserve the trading status of the company, it will often be worth keeping any 'non-trading' activities, such as property letting, separate from those activities that are accepted by HM Revenue and Customs as having trading status. This can be done either by keeping the 'non-trading' activities out of the company, or by putting them into a different company. The possible benefits of multiple companies are examined further in Section 16.4.

Impact on Business Property Relief for Inheritance Tax

The test for whether shares in a company with a 'mixed' property business qualify for business property relief is considerably less stringent than the Capital Gains Tax test set out above.

It is only necessary to ensure that the company's business does not consist wholly or mainly of property investment, property letting or dealing in property.

'Mainly' is defined as over 50%, meaning that a property company's shares will be eligible for business property relief as long as over half of its business comes from property development or property management.

Chapter 4

Property Rental Income and Expenses

4.1 CORPORATION TAX ON RENTAL PROFITS

In this chapter, we will look at how rental income and other property investment income received by a company are taxed. In the next chapter, we will move on to the tax treatment of companies with property businesses that are classed as trades.

The first point to note is that interest and other finance costs incurred by the company in connection with investment or letting properties are not treated as expenses of the letting business, but as general overheads instead. We will look at the treatment of these costs, and how the company obtains Corporation Tax relief for them, in Section 4.7.

Subject to this rather peculiar quirk, property letting is treated like any other business from a purely accounting point of view. The company has to draw up accounts, usually once a year, which detail all of its rental income, as well as all relevant expenses.

If the company is letting a number of UK properties on a commercial basis, these will be treated as a single UK property business. Landlords operating through companies may, of course, draw up separate sets of management accounts for any individual property, or group of properties, if they wish.

Some types of letting must, however, be accounted for separately for Corporation Tax purposes, as they are subject to different tax rules. In these cases, a separate set of accounts will be required in support of the company's Corporation Tax calculations.

Separate letting accounts are required in the following cases:

- Overseas lettings.
- Non-commercial lettings.

Separate accounts may also be advisable in the case of any 'furnished holiday lettings' (see Section 4.6) in order to safeguard the additional taxation benefits attaching to such lettings.

'Non-commercial lettings' refers to cases where less than full market rent is charged for a property due to some special relationship between the landlord and the tenant. Generally, as we will see later in the guide, I would advise strongly against holding such properties through a company.

In tax jargon, UK letting income, as well as most other non-trading income from UK land and property received by a company, is referred to as 'Schedule A income'. Income from overseas property falls under 'Schedule D Case V', which is tax jargon for foreign income.

Company accounts must be drawn up in accordance with UK 'Generally Accepted Accounting Principles' (GAAP). The most important aspect of GAAP is that accounts must be drawn up on an 'accruals' basis. This means that income and expenditure is recognised when it arises, or is incurred, rather than when it is received or paid (the latter being the 'cash basis', which is not permitted for Corporation Tax purposes).

Example

Jake, Sandy and Tilly own a small property company, Braun Properties Limited, which draws up accounts to 30th November each year. Braun Properties Limited acquires a new property on Kirkcaldy High Street in October 2011 and rents it out for the first time on 29th November at a monthly rent of £1,000 payable in advance.

At 30th November 2011, Braun Properties Limited will have received one monthly rental of £1,000. However, under the 'accruals' concept, Braun Properties Limited is only required to account for two days' rent. This amounts to just £66, calculated as follows: £1,000 x 12 x 2/365 = £66.

This simple (and correct) adjustment will reduce Braun Properties Limited's Corporation Tax bill on 1st September 2012 by up to £272.

Tax Tip

Expenses should similarly be recognised as they are incurred. The timing of allowable expenditure is therefore critical in planning your Corporation Tax affairs and it is the date that expenses are *incurred* (i.e. when work takes place, or goods are purchased) that is important, not when they are invoiced or paid for.

Example

Aileen has a company with an accounting date of 31ˢᵗ March, and has some roof repairs carried out on one of the company's rented properties in March 2011. The roofer does not get around to invoicing Aileen's company until May and she pays him in July.

Despite the fact that Aileen does not pay for the repairs until July, she may nevertheless still deduct the cost in her company accounts for the year ending 31ˢᵗ March 2011.

4.2 CALCULATING RENT RECEIVABLE

A company is subject to Corporation Tax on its rental **profits**, rather than its gross rental **income**.

It is tempting to think, therefore, that it does not matter whether rental expenses are shown separately in the accounts, or just deducted from rental income, as long as the net rental profit is correct.

This is not the case, however, as the correct calculation of gross rental income is important for a number of reasons, including:

- The wear and tear allowance (see Section 4.5)
- Accounting disclosure requirements (see Section 14.6)
- The VAT registration threshold (see Section 9.2)
- The audit threshold (see Section 14.7)

Gross rental income is derived from rent receivable and therefore includes any amounts of rent due but unpaid (i.e. bad debts). Any agent's commission deducted from rents received must also be added back for these purposes and shown separately as an expense.

Rent receivable also includes tenant's deposits retained at the end of a lease. The law requiring deposits from new tenants after March 2007 to be held in escrow doesn't alter this position (although it may have reduced the number of deposits retained).

4.3   EXPENSES YOU CAN CLAIM

The rules on what types of expenditure may be claimed by the company as deductions are generally much the same as for property-letting businesses run by individuals or partnerships.

Some of the main deductions include:

- Property maintenance and repair costs
- Heating and lighting costs, if borne by the landlord company
- Insurance costs
- Letting agent's fees
- Advertising for tenants
- Accountancy fees
- Legal and professional fees (see further below)
- The cost of cleaners, gardeners, etc, where relevant
- Ground rent, service charges, etc.
- Bad debts
- Pre-trading expenditure (see further below)
- Administrative expenditure (see further below)
- Salaries paid to staff or directors (the latter is covered in more detail in Section 10.2)

All expenses must be incurred wholly and exclusively for the purposes of the company's business and, naturally, must actually be borne by the company itself (i.e. the company cannot claim any expenses if the tenant is paying them directly).

Interest and other finance costs are not deducted from letting income received by a company, but are treated as general company overheads instead. We will look at how Corporation Tax relief is obtained for these costs in Section 4.7.

Legal and Professional Fees

Most legal fees and other professional costs incurred for the purposes of the business may be claimed as a deduction against rental income. Typically, this will include items such as the costs of preparing tenants' leases and, perhaps, debt collection expenses.

Legal fees and other costs incurred on the purchase or sale of properties, however, may not be claimed against rental income. All is not lost though, as these items may usually be claimed as allowable deductions for capital gains purposes (see Chapter 6).

Wealth Warning

There remains the problem of abortive expenditure, such as the cost of building surveys on properties that you do not, in fact, actually purchase. HM Revenue and Customs tend to regard these as capital items, which therefore cannot be claimed against rental income. But, since the property is never actually purchased, they cannot be claimed against any capital gain either.

In my view, there is an argument that such expenses are part of the general administrative cost of running a property investment company and should therefore still be claimed against rental income. Some resistance to this approach may, however, be encountered from HM Revenue and Customs.

Tax Tip

A more persuasive argument is that expenditure of this type only becomes capital if it is incurred after the decision to acquire the property has been taken. The best approach, therefore, is to ensure that, wherever possible, you record the fact that such expenditure is being incurred 'with a view to deciding whether or not the property should be purchased by the company' – i.e. that no such decision has yet been made.

This can be done by way of directors' board minutes or within a letter instructing the surveyor (or other professional, as the case may be) to carry out the work.

Another Tax Tip

Part of the professional fees arising on the purchase of a property will often relate to the raising of finance.

It may therefore be worth arranging to have this element of the fees invoiced separately, so that they can be claimed as a finance cost within general overheads, as detailed in Section 4.7.

This will provide Corporation Tax relief for these costs without having to wait until the property is sold.

Pre-trading Expenditure

You may incur some expenses for the purposes of your property business before you form your company or start to let out any properties.

In general, deductible expenses incurred within seven years before the commencement of a business may still be allowable if they would otherwise qualify under normal principles. In such cases, the expenses can be claimed as if they were incurred on the first day of the business.

Tax Tip

In the case of a new company, a number of 'pre-trading' expenses will often have been paid for by the investor personally before the company has been formed.

The best thing to do in these circumstances is to:

i) Keep track of the relevant expenditure, retaining receipts, etc, as usual.

ii) Once the company has been formed, 'recharge' the expenses to the company. What this means in practice is that a 'director's loan account' is set up in the company recording the expenditure previously incurred by the director.

iii) The expenses recharged by the director may (subject to the normal principles of deductibility) be claimed in the company's first accounting period.

iv) The director may be repaid the 'loan account' as soon as the company has available funds.

Administrative Expenditure

This heading is perhaps the broadest, and can extend to the cost of running an office, motor and travel costs.

In the case of a company, it will also cover costs associated with running the company itself (as opposed to running its business). This would include filing fees payable to Companies House and audit fees, if applicable. Costs of the company formation (see Section 14.1) are not allowable as these are deemed to be a capital item.

As usual, the general rule is that any expenditure must be incurred wholly and exclusively for the purposes of the business. Unfortunately, however, business entertaining expenditure is specifically excluded. (Staff entertaining is allowed though – and will not even give rise to Income Tax charges for the staff unless HM Revenue and Customs' prescribed limits are exceeded.)

4.4 CAPITAL EXPENDITURE YOU CAN CLAIM

The main type of disallowable expenditure in a property-letting or property-investment business is capital expenditure on property improvements and on furniture, fixtures and fittings.

Some relief is, however, given for certain types of capital expenditure in the form of capital allowances.

Apart from the fact that any rule changes generally apply from 1ˢᵗ April for companies, instead of 6ᵗʰ April for individuals or partnerships, the rules explained in this section are pretty much the same as for individuals or partnerships with rental property.

Plant and Machinery Allowances

The main type of capital allowances currently available is 'plant and machinery allowances'. These allowances are available on qualifying plant, machinery, furniture, fixtures, fittings, computers and other equipment used in a business.

Since 1ˢᵗ April 2008, 'plant and machinery allowances' have also been available on 'integral features' within qualifying property. This term is explained further below.

More details on the type of expenditure qualifying for 'plant and machinery allowances' are given in the Taxcafe.co.uk guide 'How to Avoid Property Tax'.

Capital Allowances on Rental Properties

Capital allowances are available on qualifying expenditure within rented commercial property (shops, offices, etc) and furnished holiday lettings (see Section 4.6).

Wealth Warning

Under certain circumstances, landlords providing fixtures and fittings within commercial property need to make a joint election with their tenants that the landlords will retain the right to capital allowances on that expenditure.

So-called 'industrial property' also currently attracts allowances on the cost of the building itself. These allowances generally only apply to large structures, such as factories and warehouses, although they sometimes also extend to garage workshops, for example. Similar allowances also apply to qualifying agricultural property.

This type of allowance is being phased out. The current rate available for expenditure during the year ending 31st March 2011 is just 1%. Thereafter, these allowances will be abolished altogether.

Residential Property

Sadly, any expenditure on assets for use within a rented 'dwelling-house' is ineligible for capital allowances.

Hence, capital allowances cannot generally be claimed on expenditure within a residential rental property. There are some important exceptions to be aware of, however, including:

- Furnished holiday lets (see Section 4.6)
- Expenditure within communal areas (e.g. lift machinery or a utility room in a block of flats)

A company which rents out residential property may also claim 'plant and machinery allowances' on equipment purchased for its own business use outside its rental properties, such as computers and office furniture.

Like other landlords, companies may claim a 'wear and tear allowance' on furnished lettings. This is not part of the capital allowances regime but does still provide a form of tax relief for the cost of furnishing the property. See Section 4.5 for further details.

The Amount of Allowances Available

We will now look at how 'plant and machinery allowances' are calculated. As these are the only type of capital allowances which we will be concerned with for the rest of this section, I will simply refer to them as 'capital allowances' from now on.

The precise amount of capital allowances available depends on the date on which the qualifying expenditure is incurred. At present, the most important allowance for the majority of businesses is the annual investment allowance.

The Annual Investment Allowance

Qualifying companies are currently entitled to an annual investment allowance of up to £100,000. (The allowance is also available to sole traders and most partnerships. Note, however, that where a company is a member of a partnership, the allowance will not be available to that partnership.)

The annual investment allowance provides 100% tax relief for qualifying expenditure on plant and machinery up to a specified limit in each accounting period.

The specified limits are as follows:

1st April 2008 to 31st March 2010:	£50,000
1st April 2010 to 31st March 2012:	£100,000
From 1st April 2012:	£25,000

Transitional rules apply where a company's accounting period spans a change in the specified limit.

For example, a property company with a twelve month accounting period ending 31st December 2010 will be entitled to a maximum annual investment allowance for that period of:

£50,000 x 90/365 =   £12,329
£100,000 x 275/365 =£75,342
Total: £87,671

The company's claim in respect of expenditure incurred during the first part of its accounting period, prior to 1st April 2010, will also be restricted to a maximum of £50,000.

A company with a twelve month accounting period ending 31st December 2012 will be entitled to a maximum annual investment allowance for that period of:

£100,000 x 91/366 = £24,863
£25,000 x 275/366 = £18,784
Total: £43,647

In this case, the company's claim in respect of expenditure incurred during the latter part of its accounting period, after 31st March 2012, will be restricted to a maximum of £18,784.

Tax Tip

In order to maximise the benefit of the annual investment allowance, it may make sense to ensure that as much qualifying expenditure as possible takes place before 1st April 2012, or possibly before the end of the company's last accounting period ending before that date.

Restrictions on the Annual Investment Allowance

The annual investment allowance is restricted where a company has an accounting period of less than twelve months' duration. This will often apply to a new company's first accounting period.

For example, a company drawing up accounts for the nine month period ending 30th June 2011 will be entitled to a maximum annual investment allowance of:

£100,000 x 273/365 = £74,795

The annual investment allowance is also restricted where the company is a member of a group or is closely related to another company.

The annual investment allowance is not available for expenditure on cars.

First Year Allowances

Qualifying expenditure in excess of the annual investment allowance incurred by a company during the period between 1st April 2009 and 31st March 2010 is eligible for a first year allowance of 40%.

This allowance is of limited use to property investment companies, however, as it is not available on any expenditure falling into the 'special rate pool' (see below).

Furthermore, under HM Revenue and Customs' interpretation of the capital allowances legislation, *any* expenditure within *any* rental property would be ineligible for this allowance. This view may be debatable but the issue can generally be avoided by claiming the annual investment allowance on any such expenditure instead.

Expenditure on cars is again also excluded from this allowance.

The balance of any qualifying expenditure which is left after claiming the first year allowance is carried forward to the company's next accounting period.

Various qualifying energy-saving or environmentally beneficial equipment is eligible for a 100% first year allowance. This allowance is available in addition to the annual investment allowance. Further details can be found at www.eca.gov.uk

Writing Down Allowances

Qualifying expenditure in excess of the annual investment allowance incurred after 31st March 2010 (or between 1st April 2008 and 31st March 2009) is eligible for 'writing down allowances'.

The writing down allowance also applies to any expenditure on qualifying plant and machinery incurred by a company between 1st April 2009 and 31st March 2010 which is not eligible for either the annual investment allowance or first year allowances.

The rate of writing down allowances on most plant and machinery is currently 20% but will reduce to just 18% with effect from 1st April 2012.

Transitional rules will apply to accounting periods which straddle 1st April 2012 with the result that such periods will benefit from a writing down allowance somewhere between 18% and 20%. *(E.g. the writing down allowance for a property company with a twelve month accounting period ending 31st December 2012 will be 18.5%)*

Qualifying expenditure in excess of the annual investment allowance is pooled together with the unrelieved balance of qualifying expenditure brought forward from the previous accounting period. This pool of expenditure is known as the 'general pool'.

The writing down allowance is then calculated at the appropriate rate on the total balance in the general pool.

The remaining balance of expenditure is then carried forward and the appropriate percentage of that balance may be claimed in the next accounting period. And so on.

However, where the balance in the general pool reduces to £1,000 or less, the full balance may then be claimed immediately.

The Special Rate Pool

Certain expenditure must be allocated to a 'special rate pool' instead of the general pool. This includes:

- Expenditure of £100,000 or more on plant and machinery with an anticipated working life of 25 years or more.

- Certain defined categories of 'integral features' within commercial property or qualifying furnished holiday accommodation (see below).

- Expenditure on thermal insulation of an existing building used in a qualifying trade.

Expenditure in the special rate pool is currently eligible for a writing down allowance of just 10% instead of the usual 20%. This rate will also be reduced with effect from 1st April 2012, to just 8%.

It is worth noting, however, that the annual investment allowance may be allocated to any such expenditure in preference to expenditure qualifying for the normal rate of writing down allowance.

Where the balance on the special rate pool reduces to £1,000 or less, the full balance may then be claimed immediately in the same way as for the general pool.

Integral Features

Expenditure on assets included in a defined list of 'integral features' within commercial property, qualifying furnished holiday accommodation, or communal areas within rented residential property, falls into the special rate pool.

However, as explained above, these assets remain eligible for the annual investment allowance, so up to £100,000 per year of qualifying expenditure on assets in this category could currently attract immediate 100% relief.

The following items are classed as integral features:

- Electrical lighting and power systems
- Cold water systems
- Space or water heating systems, air conditioning, ventilation and air purification systems and floors or ceilings comprised in such systems
- Lifts, escalators and moving walkways
- External solar shading

The integral features regime applies to expenditure incurred by companies after 31st March 2008, including fixtures within second-hand buildings purchased after that date.

It is worth noting that some of the items within the list of 'integral features' were not previously eligible for plant and machinery allowances, particularly cold water systems (i.e. basic plumbing) and most electrical lighting and power systems.

In other words, for expenditure incurred by companies from 1st April 2008 onwards, these items represent significant additions to the categories of expenditure within commercial property, qualifying furnished holiday accommodation, and communal areas within rented residential property which attract capital allowances.

Combining this with the annual investment allowance, many property investment companies are able to benefit quite significantly.

Example

Hook Limited draws up its accounts to 31ˢᵗ March each year. In June 2011, the company buys an old property and then converts it into office units to rent out.

Although the office units are really just basic 'shells' with the absolute minimum of fixtures and fittings, Hook Limited's surveyors nevertheless calculate that the company has spent £80,000 on 'integral features' and other fixtures qualifying as plant and machinery.

Hook Limited can therefore claim an annual investment allowance of £80,000 for the year ending 31ˢᵗ March 2012.

Thermal Insulation of Commercial Property

Expenditure on thermal insulation of an existing commercial building used in a qualifying business also falls into the special rate pool. The annual investment allowance is again available on this expenditure, providing immediate tax relief on up to £100,000 each year.

Planning with the Annual Investment Allowance

The annual investment allowance is available to each qualifying business entity. Any individual or company with a property rental business is a qualifying business entity.

Individuals or companies who own joint shares in rental properties, but who are not operating as a partnership, are each deemed to have their own separate property business.

A couple buying property jointly (but not as a partnership) could therefore currently claim annual investment allowances of up to £100,000 each. Such a couple paying 'super tax' at 50% could therefore potentially benefit from a total tax saving of up to £100,000, simply by buying the right property!

A company can only claim one single annual investment allowance, regardless of how many shareholders it has. Even this is subject to the 'related company' rules.

Unincorporated businesses (i.e. not companies) under the control of the same person, or persons, are also subject to restrictions in the amount of annual investment allowance which they can claim.

However, for the purposes of the annual investment allowance, a company cannot be treated as being related to an unincorporated business.

Hence, an individual could buy property jointly with his or her own company (but not as a partnership) and both the individual and the company would be eligible for an annual investment allowance of up to £100,000 each.

Furthermore, a couple could even form a company together, buy property jointly with that company (but not as a partnership) and claim three separate annual investment allowances (one for each of the couple and one for the company), thus providing immediate 100% tax relief on up to £300,000 of qualifying expenditure.

Taking this idea one step further, each member of the couple could form their own company and all four entities (two individuals and two companies) could buy property jointly (but not as a partnership), thus providing scope to claim immediate 100% tax relief on up to £400,000 of qualifying expenditure in total!

(In the last scenario, the two companies would be associated companies for Corporation Tax purposes if the couple were married. See Section 16.4 for further details.)

Balancing Charges

When a property is sold, a sum equal to the lower of

i)   The proportion of sales proceeds relating to qualifying fixtures and fittings within the property, or
ii)   The original cost of those qualifying fixtures and fittings claimed for capital allowances purposes,

must be deducted from the company's general and special rate pools. (The deduction applying to each pool is calculated independently.)

Items of expenditure on which no capital allowances have been claimed do not need to be included.

Tax Tip

The sums at (i) and (ii) may be considered on an item by item basis and the lower amount can be taken in each case.

If the sum to be deducted exceeds the balance on the relevant pool, the excess is added to the company's income for Corporation Tax purposes. This is known as a 'balancing charge'.

Example

In March 2011, Williams Limited buys Shane House, a commercial property. The company is able to claim £40,000 in respect of 'integral features' and £30,000 in respect of other qualifying fixtures and fittings.

Two years later, Williams Limited sells Shane House. The proportion of the sale proceeds allocated to 'integral features' is £45,000 and the proportion allocated to other qualifying fixtures and fittings is £25,000.

Williams Limited will therefore need to deduct £40,000 from the special rate pool and £25,000 from the general pool (i.e. the lower of (i) and (ii) above in each case; ignoring the 'Tax Tip' given above for the sake of illustration).

Let's say that the balance on Williams Limited's special rate pool at this time is £60,000 and the balance on its general pool is £10,000.

After deducting the £40,000 relating to Shane House, Williams Limited will be left with a balance of £20,000 on its special rate pool and can therefore still claim a writing down allowance of £1,600 (8%) on this pool.

When we turn to the company's general pool, however, the £25,000 deduction relating to Shane House exceeds the balance by £15,000. Williams Limited will therefore be subject to a balancing charge of £15,000, will not be able to claim any writing down allowance on the general pool and will be left with a nil balance carried forward on this pool.

Note that a remaining balance on one pool (e.g. the special rate pool in the example above) cannot be used to reduce the balancing charge arising on the other pool. This makes it especially important to ensure that sales proceeds are allocated carefully.

Before 2008, balancing charges were fairly rare since they could generally only arise if the business ceased or the relevant assets were sold for a sum in excess of the balance on the general pool.

The impact of balancing charges on small property investment companies is now likely to be far more pronounced, however, due to the fact that most qualifying expenditure will already have been claimed in full by way of the annual investment allowance.

Other Equipment Used in the Business

See Section 5.5 for more details on the practical aspects of claiming capital allowances on the company's own plant and equipment, including motor cars.

4.5   FURNISHED LETTINGS

Income from furnished residential lettings (other than furnished holiday lettings, as defined in Section 4.6) is treated in much the same way as other rental income. The only differences, quite naturally, arise from the treatment of the furnishings.

It is important to stress that: **No allowance is given for the initial expenditure in furnishing the property.**

Thereafter, the landlord company may claim either:

a)   Renewal and replacement expenditure, or
b)   The 'wear and tear allowance'

Repair costs continue to be allowable under both methods and this extends to replacements of fixtures which are effectively part of the property itself, such as sinks or toilets, for example.

The two alternative methods described above are therefore intended to cover the cost of replacing furniture and furnishings. Whichever method is used, there will be no allowance for the original cost of furnishing the property or buying additional or improved items but the cost of any repairs to furniture and furnishings (including 'white goods' and any other electrical items) will continue to be allowable.

The Wear and Tear Allowance

A 'Wear and Tear Allowance' of 10% of net rents receivable may be claimed against the rental income from furnished residential lettings. This allowance is given as an alternative to the 'Renewals and Replacements Basis'.

In calculating the allowance, we first need to establish the amount of 'net rents receivable' for the property in question.

As explained in Section 4.2, it is important to remember that rent receivable includes any amounts of rent due but unpaid (i.e. bad debts) and any deposits retained at the end of a lease. Any agent's commission deducted from rents received should also be added back for the purposes of this calculation.

To arrive at 'net rents receivable' we must then deduct any amounts borne by the landlord which would normally be a tenant's own responsibility (e.g. council tax, water rates or electricity charges).

Additionally, if the rental includes any material amount representing a payment for additional services which would normally be borne by the occupier, rather than the owner, of the property, then these amounts must also be deducted before calculating the 10% allowance.

Example

Carling Limited owns a large flat in Twickenham, which is let out for £2,500 per month (£30,000 per annum). This includes a charge of £250 per month for the provision of a cleaner. Carling Limited also pays the water rates for the property, which amount to £1,000 per year, but the tenants pay their own council tax.

Carling Limited is therefore able to claim a wear and tear allowance as follows:

Total rent receivable:	£30,000
Less:	
Cleaning charges:	£3,000 (12 x £250)
Water rates	£1,000
Net rent receivable:	£26,000
Wear and tear allowance:	£2,600 (10%)

Note that whilst we only have to deduct the COST of the water rates, it is the amount that Carling Limited CHARGES for the provision of cleaning services which must be deducted in this calculation. (Although only the cost of the cleaning services can be deducted when arriving at the company's overall total rental profits.)

The Alternative: The 'Replacements Basis'

The wear and tear allowance is not mandatory. Landlords may, instead, claim the cost of replacing or renewing furniture and other furnishings. They may not, however, claim the costs of the *original* furniture and furnishings when the property is first let out, or the cost of improvements or additional items.

For example, replacing one bed with another would normally be allowed under the replacements basis, but replacing an old single bed with a king-size four-poster would not, as it would represent an improvement.

The 'Catch'

The wear and tear allowance and the replacements basis are alternatives. You may claim one OR the other, but NOT both.

The 'BIG Catch'

Once you have chosen one method, you must stick with it on ALL of your company's furnished lets of all properties!

Hence, once the wear and tear allowance has been claimed, no deductions can ever be claimed for any renewals or replacements of furniture and other furnishings.

So, Which Method Is Best?

Conventional wisdom states that the wear and tear allowance is usually best. This is generally because this method provides some relief immediately, from the first year onwards. Generally, it will take longer before replacement expenditure starts to come through, with the original capital cost of furnishings being unallowable.

In short, wear and tear generally provides faster relief. However, it is worth bearing in mind that this will not always be the case.

Example

Beaumont Limited rents out a number of small flats to students at the local Polytechnic (sorry, it's called a UNIVERSITY now).

Bill (who owns Beaumont Limited) is constantly frustrated by the fact that the company's student tenants frequently wreck the furniture. However, he combats this by buying cheap furniture and keeping their security deposits. (Watch out for the law requiring deposits to be held in escrow Bill!)

As a result, Beaumont Limited's total annual rental income is £20,000. Out of this, the company has paid Council Tax and Water Rates totalling £2,000 and spent £3,000 on replacement furniture.

If Beaumont Limited were to claim the wear and tear allowance, it would only be able to deduct £1,800 from its rental income. Hence, in this case, the company is much better off claiming £3,000 under the replacement basis.

(With apologies to all those students who treat their landlord's property with the utmost respect and to any student landlords who do not buy cheap furniture or look for any excuse to hang on to their security deposits.)

So How Do You Choose?

Despite the example of Beaumont Limited, most property investment companies will be better off with the wear and tear allowance. However, before you submit your first claim, I would suggest you do a few quick calculations to see which method is likely to be better for you on average in the long run (and not just in the first year).

4.6   FURNISHED HOLIDAY LETTINGS

Properties qualifying as 'furnished holiday lettings' enjoy a special tax regime, with many of the tax advantages usually only accorded to a trade.

The benefits for a shareholder owning a company that is mainly engaged in furnished holiday lettings were considered in Section 3.2.

It is now worth us taking a brief look at the qualification requirements for a 'furnished holiday letting':

    i)   The property must be situated in the European Economic Area

ii) The property must be furnished. As with other furnished lettings, however, there is no stipulation regarding the standard to which it must be furnished. HM Revenue and Customs' view is that the property must be 'fully furnished' which, in practice, would generally have to be interpreted to mean at least the minimum level of furnishing which an occupier would usually expect in order to regard the property as 'furnished'

iii) It must be let out on a commercial basis with a view to the realisation of profits

iv) It must be available for commercial letting to the public generally for at least 140 days in a twelve-month period (under current proposals, this requirement will be increased to 210 days for company accounting periods beginning after 31st March 2012)

v) It must be so let for at least 70 such days (under current proposals, this requirement will be increased to 105 days for company accounting periods beginning after 31st March 2012 – but see further below)

vi) The property must not normally be in the same occupation for more than 31 consecutive days at any time during a period of at least seven months out of the same twelve-month period as that referred to in (iv) above

There is some debate as to whether, strictly speaking, the tenants actually have to be using the property for the purposes of a 'holiday', or whether they could, in fact, actually be businessmen, for example (as long as the tests at (i) to (vi) above are still met). HM Revenue and Customs' view is that, whilst the property need not be in a recognised holiday area, the lettings should strictly be to holidaymakers and tourists in order to qualify. On this occasion, I am inclined to agree with them.

For accounting periods commencing after 31st March 2012, companies can elect for properties within the furnished holiday letting regime to stay within that regime for up to two further accounting periods despite failing to meet the test under (v) above.

In effect, this means that properties will generally only need to meet this test once every three years. The property will still need to meet all of the other tests, however, and the company must make genuine efforts to meet the test under (v) every year.

4.7 INTEREST AND FINANCE COSTS

As explained previously, interest and other finance costs incurred in connection with a company's property investment or property letting business are treated as general overheads of the company rather than expenses of the letting business itself.

This provides a tremendous advantage for property investment businesses run through a company when compared with the same type of business run by an individual or a partnership.

The interest and finance costs incurred in connection with the company's property investment business may be set off against any income or capital gains received by the company during the same accounting period.

If we contrast this with the position for an individual or a partnership where these same costs can only be set against rental income, we can readily see what an enormous advantage this provides.

Furthermore, as an alternative, the company may instead:

a) Carry the costs back for set off against any interest, and certain other limited categories of income, received in the previous year,

b) Carry the costs forward for set off against any non-trading income, including rental profits, **and** capital gains in future periods, or

c) Surrender the costs as 'group relief' (where the company is a member of a group of companies).

Tax Tip

Option (b) above enables a property investment company to effectively 'roll up' its accumulated interest costs and set them off against the capital gains arising on the sale of its investment properties.

This presents a massive advantage over individual investors who cannot set rental losses, which are usually predominantly made up of interest costs, against capital gains.

We will look at the effect of this in practice in Chapter 13.

What do we mean by 'Other Finance Costs'?

In addition to interest, other costs falling within this category include:
- Guarantee fees
- Loan arrangement fees
- Early redemption fees
- Reimbursement of lender's expenses
- Professional costs relating to the raising of finance

Loans and other Facilities Provided by the Company's Owner

In general terms, interest and other finance costs (as described above) may continue to be claimed for Corporation Tax purposes even when paid to one of the company's directors, shareholders, or another connected person. There are two important provisos here, however:

i)   The amount paid must not exceed a normal commercial rate.

ii)   Payment must actually be made within twelve months of the end of the company's accounting period.

We will consider the issue of loans from the owner to the company in more detail in Chapter 13.

Non-Commercial Lettings

Corporation Tax relief for interest and other finance costs incurred in connection with any 'non-commercial' lettings (see Section 4.1) will be restricted so that, broadly speaking, relief is only given against any income from those lettings.

4.8   TAX TREATMENT OF RENTAL LOSSES

Given the fact that interest and finance costs incurred in connection with a company's property rental business are not treated as an expense of that business (see Section 4.7 above), rental losses within a company should be a fairly rare occurrence. In this section, however, we will look at what happens when such losses do arise.

UK Property Lettings

Subject to the exception for non-commercial lettings set out below, for Corporation Tax purposes, all of a company's UK property lettings are treated as a single UK property business. Hence, the loss on any one such property is automatically set off against profits on other commercially let UK properties for the same period.

Any overall net losses arising from a company's UK property-letting business will be set off against the company's other income and capital gains for the same period (if any). This again represents a major advantage over individual property investors, or partnerships, who can only carry forward any net rental loss (other than losses from furnished holiday lettings prior to 6th April 2011).

Any remaining surplus rental loss incurred by the company is carried forward and set off against the company's **total** profits (including capital gains) for the next accounting period, then the next, and so on. Rental losses may be carried forward for as long as is necessary in this way, provided that the company is still carrying on a UK property-letting business in the accounting period for which the claim to offset the losses is made.

If the company's UK property-letting business ceases, but the company still has an 'investment business', then any unused UK rental losses are converted to 'management expenses'. 'Management expenses' may also be carried forward and set off against the company's total profits, including capital gains, for as long as the company continues to have an 'investment business'.

An 'investment business' is any business that consists of making investments. For example, the company may have an 'investment business' if:

- It owns subsidiary companies
- It has foreign investment property
- It holds a portfolio of stock market investments

It is questionable, however, whether simply holding cash on deposit constitutes an 'investment business'.

Nevertheless, it is clear that there are many ways for a company to preserve the value of its UK rental losses and ensure that Corporation Tax relief is ultimately obtained. This contrasts with individual investors who effectively lose the value of any UK rental losses if they cease to carry on a UK rental business.

A company will only lose the value of its unused rental losses if it ceases to carry on both its UK letting business and any other type of 'investment business'.

Example

Reivers RIP Limited has a UK property-letting business, as well as a steady income of £10,000 each year in interest. Unfortunately, in the year ending 31ˢᵗ December 2011, the company incurs a loss of £50,000 in its letting business.

£10,000 of the loss is therefore set off against the company's interest income for the year and the remaining £40,000 is carried forward.

In the year ending 31ˢᵗ December 2012, Reivers RIP Limited makes a profit of £8,000 on its property letting business.

The brought forward loss of £40,000 is treated as a letting loss for the year, resulting in an overall net loss on the letting business for Corporation Tax purposes this year of £32,000. As before, £10,000 of this is set off against the interest income of the period, leaving a loss of £22,000 to carry forward.

In the year ending 31ˢᵗ December 2013, the company makes a final profit of £3,000 from UK property letting before deciding to give this business up.

The brought forward loss of £22,000 is again treated as a letting loss for the year, resulting in an overall net loss on the letting business for Corporation Tax purposes in 2013 of £19,000. Once again, £10,000 of this is set off against the interest income for the period.

Whether the remaining unrelieved loss of £9,000 may be carried forward in the form of management expenses will depend on whether Reivers RIP Limited has an 'investment business'. If the company does not have a continuing 'investment business' after giving up its UK property letting business then the remaining loss of £9,000 will, unfortunately, effectively be 'wasted'.

For the sake of illustration, I have ignored the impact of any capital gains made by Reivers RIP Limited at the time of cessation of its UK letting business in this example. In practice, with careful timing, it should generally be possible to set any remaining unrelieved UK rental losses against the capital gains arising on the disposal of the company's investment properties.

Tax Tip

As long as the company continues to have a UK letting business or an 'investment business', it may effectively continue to set brought forward rental losses off against other income and capital gains. Hence, a company with UK rental losses may often be used as a vehicle to generate what will effectively be tax-free income or capital gains.

Either a UK letting business or an 'investment business' must be continued, but this could be on a much smaller scale than previously, if desired. Renting out just one lock-up garage anywhere in the world would be sufficient for this purpose, for example. (As long as it is let to an unconnected third party on arm's length commercial terms)

Wealth Warning

It should be noted that rental losses incurred in a company can only be set off against the company's income of the same or future periods.

There is no scope for setting such losses off against any rental profits that the owner of the company may have as an individual.

Overseas Lettings

All of a company's commercial overseas lettings are treated as a single business for Corporation Tax purposes. This is treated as a separate business to the company's UK property letting business (if any).

Any loss on this business may be carried forward and set off against future profits from the same business – i.e. against future overseas rental profits received by the company.

Furnished Holiday Lettings

Any losses arising from furnished holiday lettings (see Section 4.6) in company accounting periods beginning before 1st April 2011 are also eligible for the same forms of relief as trading losses (as detailed in Section 5.6).

Non-Commercial Lettings

Losses arising on any non-commercial lettings (i.e. lettings made on terms which are not normal, commercial, 'arm's length' terms) may only be set against future profits from the same letting.

4.9   OTHER PROPERTY INVESTMENT INCOME

Any form of income, profit or gains derived from property that the company receives will generally be subject to Corporation Tax. We will look at property trading profits in the next chapter and capital gains in Chapter 6, but in this section, it is worth considering some other items that may arise.

In Section 4.2, we saw that the company's rental income will include any tenant's deposits retained at the end of a lease.

HM Revenue and Customs also takes the view that any dilapidation payments received should also usually be treated as rental income unless the payment is put towards the cost of repairs, when they consider that it should be netted off those costs.

This view is questionable and some experts argue that dilapidation payments are a capital receipt – i.e. effectively a part disposal of the property, meaning that the sum received represents a capital gain and that part of the property's original cost is therefore properly deductible.

HM Revenue and Customs do agree with this view if the property is not rented out again after receipt of the payment and is subsequently sold or adopted for some other purpose (e.g. as the company's own office premises).

Some items are specifically excluded from treatment as property income, including:

- Any amounts taxable as trading income or capital gains.
- Profits from farming and market gardening.
- Income from mineral extraction rights.

Wayleave payments received in respect of access rights (e.g. for the electric company to have access to an electricity pylon on the company's land) are, however, sometimes included as property income.

Another important source of property income is lease premiums, which we will examine in the next section.

4.10 LEASE PREMIUMS

Lease premiums have a particularly complex treatment for Corporation Tax purposes.

Granting A Short Lease

Premiums received for the granting of short leases of no more than 50 years' duration are treated as being partly property income and partly capital disposal proceeds, potentially giving rise to a capital gain.

The proportion of the premium treated as capital disposal proceeds is equal to 2% of the total premium received for each full year of the lease's duration in excess of one year. The capital gain arising is calculated on the basis of a part disposal of the relevant property.

The remainder of the premium is treated as rental income.

Example

Telstra Limited owns the freehold to a property. The company grants a twelve-year lease to Fiji Limited for a premium of £50,000.

The lease exceeds one year by eleven years and hence 22% of this sum (£11,000) falls within the capital gains regime. This will be treated as a part disposal of the property and may or may not give rise to a taxable capital gain for Telstra Limited.

What is certain, however, is that Telstra Limited will be subject to Corporation Tax on deemed rental income of £39,000 (i.e. £50,000 less 22%).

A tenant paying a premium for the grant of a short lease of less than 50 years' duration may claim a deduction in respect of the proportion of the premium treated as rental income in the grantor's hands (i.e. £39,000 in the above example).

This claim must be spread over the length of the lease (e.g. £3,250 per annum for twelve years in Fiji Limited's case) and is only available if the tenant has a taxable business of their own.

If the tenant subsequently assigns the lease, they must restrict their base cost for capital gains purposes (see Section 6.3) to the element of the original lease premium treated as capital disposal proceeds in the grantor's hands (e.g. £11,000 in our example above). This base cost will then be subject to further restriction as explained below.

Granting A Long Lease

The grant of a lease of more than 50 years' duration is treated purely as a capital disposal. The base cost (see Section 6.3) to be used has to be restricted under the 'part disposal' rules. In essence, what this means is that the base cost is divided between the part disposed of (i.e. the lease) and the part retained (the 'reversionary interest') in proportion to their relative values at the time that the lease is granted.

Example

JPR Limited owns the freehold of a commercial property in Llanelli. The company grants a 60-year lease to Brian, a businessman from Belfast moving into the area. Brian pays a premium of £90,000 for the lease. The value of JPR Limited's reversionary interest is established as £10,000.

The base cost to be used in calculating JPR Limited's capital gain on the grant of the lease is therefore 90% of its base cost for the property as a whole.

Assigning a long lease with no less than 50 years' duration remaining

This is simply a straightforward capital disposal. The capital gain arising is calculated in more or less the same way as for a freehold property sale (see Chapter 6). Any applicable capital gains reliefs may be claimed in the usual way.

Assigning a short lease with less than 50 years' duration remaining

This is treated entirely as a capital disposal. However, leases with less than 50 years remaining are treated as 'wasting assets'. The company is therefore required to reduce its base cost in accordance with the schedule set out in Appendix F.

For example, for a lease with 20 years remaining, and which had more than 50 years remaining when first acquired, the base cost must be reduced to 72.77% of the original premium paid for the lease (plus other applicable purchase costs).

Where the lease had less than 50 years remaining when originally acquired, the necessary reduction in base cost is achieved by multiplying the original cost by the factor applying at the time of sale and dividing by the factor applying at the time of purchase.

Example

Calcutta Cup Limited pays a premium of £10,000 for the assignment of a lease with ten years remaining. Five years later, the company assigns the lease to Murrayfield Limited at a premium of £6,000.

When calculating the capital gain, the amount that Calcutta Cup Limited may claim as its base cost is:

£10,000 x 26.722/46.695 = £5,723

Chapter 5

Property Trading Income and Expenses

5.1   HOW PROPERTY TRADING PROFITS ARE TAXED

Some property companies are not taxed under the rules for rental profits, as set out in Chapter 4, but are, instead, taxed on the basis that the income from their property business represents trading profit. In tax jargon, trading profits in a company are referred to as 'Schedule D Case I' income.

The most important differences in being a 'trading company' are probably the implications for the owner which we looked at in Chapter 3. As far as the computation of profits is concerned, the differences are not huge and there is therefore little point in repeating all of the rules from scratch once more.

What I will do in this chapter, however, is consider the differences for a company between the taxation of trading profits and the taxation of rental profits.

Trading losses are also subject to a different set of rules to rental losses and we will look at these in Section 5.6.

5.2   TRADING PROFITS VERSUS RENTAL PROFITS

The major differences between the taxation of rental profits and trading profits in a company may be summarised as follows:

- In the case of property development or property trading, the disposal proceeds received on the sale of a property represent trading income. Likewise, the cost of properties acquired represents 'cost of sales' and may be deducted from sale proceeds at the time of the property's sale.

- Legal and professional fees and other costs incurred on the purchase or sale of properties may also be included within 'cost of sales'.

- Any abortive costs relating to property purchases or sales may be claimed as company overheads.

- The costs related to any unsold properties are included in the company's accounts as 'trading stock'. We will look at the implications of this in more detail in the next section.

- Interest and other finance costs relating to a company's trading activities are treated as a trading expense. They are deducted from trading profits and will also form part of any trading loss, to be dealt with as explained in Section 5.6 below.

- The wear and tear allowance (see Section 4.5) is not applicable in a trading profits computation.

- Capital allowances may only be claimed in respect of assets acquired as long-term fixed assets of the business. We will look at this further in Section 5.5.

- The cost of any furnishings purchased and sold with a property may be deducted as 'cost of sales' against the disposal proceeds from that property.

- All of the company's business will usually be treated as a single business, regardless of where its properties are located. This will all be treated as UK trading income if the business is all <u>run</u> from the UK.

Notwithstanding any of the above, any costs related to a property acquired as a long-term fixed asset of the business (such as its own offices, for example) remain capital in nature and do not form part of the company's trading stock or 'cost of sales'. A disposal of the company's own trading premises would continue to be dealt with under the rules for capital gains.

5.3 PROPERTIES AS TRADING STOCK

Properties held for development or sale in a property development or property dealing company are not regarded as long-term capital assets. They are, instead, regarded as the company's *trading stock*.

For tax purposes, all of the company's expenditure in acquiring, improving, repairing or converting the properties becomes part of the cost of that trading stock. Many of the issues that we need to deal with in a property investment company regarding the question of whether expenditure is revenue or capital in nature therefore become completely academic. Most professional fees and repairs or improvement expenditure are treated as part of the cost of the company's trading stock.

(The term 'revenue expenditure' means expenditure deductible from income, whereas capital expenditure is subject to different rules.)

When properties are sold, the related costs become 'cost of sales' and may be deducted from the company's sale proceeds. Sometimes, however, it may be some considerable time before this occurs. In the meantime, the property will have to be dealt with as 'trading stock'. In this section, we will take a detailed look at what this means in practice.

The way in which trading stock works for tax purposes can best be illustrated by way of an example.

Example

In November 2011, Grand Slam Limited buys a property in Swansea for £260,000. The company also pays Stamp Duty Land Tax of £7,800 and legal fees of £1,450. Previously, in October, it had also paid a survey fee of £750.

Grand Slam Limited is a property development company and draws up its accounts to 31st December each year.

In the company's accounts to 31st December 2011, the Swansea property will be included as trading stock with a value of £270,000, made up as follows:

	£
Property purchase	260,000
Stamp Duty Land Tax	7,800
Legal fees	1,450
Survey fee	750

	270,000
	=======

Points To Note

The important point to note here is that, whilst all of Grand Slam Limited's expenditure is regarded as revenue expenditure (because it's a property development company), the company cannot yet claim any deduction for any of it, because it still holds the property.

Example Continued

Early in 2012, Grand Slam Limited incurs further professional fees of £10,000 obtaining planning permission to divide the property into two separate residences. Permission is granted in July and by the end of the year, Grand Slam Limited has spent a further £40,000 on conversion work.

In the company's accounts to 31st December 2012 the property will still be shown in trading stock, as follows:

	£
Costs brought forward	270,000
Additional professional fees	10,000
Building work	40,000

	320,000
	=======

Grand Slam Limited still doesn't get any tax relief for any of this expenditure.

By March 2013, Grand Slam Limited has spent another £5,000 on the property and is ready to sell the two new houses. One of them sells quickly for £185,000. Grand Slam Limited incurs a further £3,500 in estate agent and legal fees in the process.

Grand Slam Limited's taxable profit on this sale is thus calculated as follows:

	£	£
Sale proceeds		*185,000*
Less cost:		
Total cost brought forward:	*320,000*	
Additional building costs:	*5,000*	

Trading stock prior to sale of first property	*325,000*	
Allocated to property sold (50%):	*162,500*	
Add additional costs:	*3,500*	

		166,000

Profit on sale		*19,000*
		======

This profit will form part of Grand Slam Limited's trading profit for the year ending 31st December 2013.

Points to Note

The additional building spend of £5,000 was allocated to trading stock as this still related to the whole property.

The legal and estate agent's fees incurred on the sale, however, were specific to the part that was sold and may thus be deducted in full against those sale proceeds.

In the example, I have split the cost of trading stock equally between the two new houses. If the two new houses are identical then this will be correct. Otherwise, the costs should be split between the two properties on a reasonable basis – e.g. total floor area, or in proportion to the market value of the finished properties.

The latter approach would be the required statutory basis if these were capital disposals. Although it is not mandatory here, it might still be a useful yardstick.

The most important point, however, is that even if Grand Slam Limited fails to sell the second new house before 31st December 2013, its profit on the first new house will still be taxable in full.

There is one exception to this, as we shall now examine.

Net Realisable Value

Trading stock is generally shown in the accounts at its cumulative cost to date.

On this basis, Grand Slam Limited's second house, if still unsold at 31st December 2013, would have a carrying value of £162,500 in its accounts.

If, however, the market value of the property is less than its cumulative cost then its carrying value in the accounts may be reduced appropriately.

Furthermore, since the act of selling the property will itself give rise to further expenses, these may also be deducted from the property's reduced value in this situation. This gives us a value known in accounting terminology as the property's 'net realisable value'.

Practical Pointer

Trading stock should always be shown in the accounts at the lower of cost or net realisable value.

To see the effect of this in practice, let's return once more to our example.

Example

The second new house in Swansea doesn't sell so quickly. Grand Slam Limited therefore decides to take the house off the market and build an extension on the back to make it more attractive to potential buyers.

Unfortunately, however, there are some problems with the foundations for the extension and the costs turn out to be more than double what Grand Slam Limited had originally expected.

By 31st December 2013, the company has spent £27,500 on the extension work and it still isn't finished. The total costs to date on the second new house are now £190,000. Furthermore, the further expenditure required to complete the extension is estimated at £12,000.

The estate agent reckons that the completed property will sell for around £200,000. The agent's own fees will amount to £3,000 and there will also be legal costs of around £750.

The net realisable value of the property at 31st December 2013 is thus:

	£	£
Market value of completed property		*200,000*
Less:		
Costs to complete	*12,000*	
Professional costs to sell	*3,750*	

		15,750

Net Realisable Value at 31/12/2013		*184,250*
		========

Since this is less than the company's costs to date on the property, this is the value that should be shown as trading stock in the 2013 accounts.

The result of this is that Grand Slam Limited will show a loss of £5,750 (£190,000 less £184,250) on the second house in its 2013 accounts.

This loss will automatically be set off against the £19,000 profit on the first house.

By June 2014, the second house is ready for sale. Fortunately, there is an upturn in the market and Grand Slam Limited manages to sell the property for £215,000 in October 2014.

The actual additional expenditure on the extension work amounted to £11,800 and the professional fees incurred on the sale were actually £3,900.

Grand Slam Limited's taxable profit on this property in 2014 is thus:

	£	£
Sale proceeds		215,000
Less:		
Value of trading stock brought		
forward, as per accounts:	184,250	
Additional building cost	11,800	
Professional fees on sale	3,900	

		199,950

Taxable profit in year to 31/12/2014		15,050
		=======

Points To Note

When preparing the accounts, we use the most accurate estimates available at that time to calculate net realisable value. In the case of sale price, however, we use the completed property's market value at the accounting date (i.e. 31st December 2013 in this example).

When calculating Grand Slam Limited's profit for 2014, we use actual figures for everything which took place after 31st December 2013, the company's last accounting date (i.e. the sale price, the final part of the building work and the professional fees on the sale). The property's net realisable value in the accounts at 31st

December 2013 is, however, substituted for all of the costs incurred up until that date.

In this example, as often happens in practice, the selling price and actual costs incurred after the last accounting date turned out to be different to the estimates previously available. As a result, the apparent loss that the company was able to claim in 2013 effectively reversed and became part of its profits in 2014.

In the end, the net effect is that the true amount of profit that Grand Slam Limited actually made on the development has been taxed. The effect of the net realisable value calculation, however, was to provide some early Corporation Tax relief for a loss that was reasonably anticipated at that time. For this reason, it will always be worth considering whether properties held as trading stock have a net realisable value less than cost at each accounting date.

5.4   WORK-IN-PROGRESS & SALES CONTRACTS

Generally, for speculative property developers, their company's trading stock, as we have seen, is valued at the lower of its cumulative cost to date or its net realisable value.

However, if a contract for the sale of the property exists, the development company has to follow a different set of rules.

This is a complex area of accounting, but, broadly speaking, the company is required to value properties under development, for which a sale contract already exists, at an appropriate percentage of their contractual sale value. This is done by treating the completed proportion of the property as having already been sold.

The same proportion of the expected final costs of the development can be deducted from the sale. Any remaining balance of development costs is included in the accounts as 'Work-in-Progress', which is simply a term for trading stock that is only partly completed.

Example

Aayan Limited is building a new house on a plot of land and has already contracted to sell it for £500,000.

Aayan Limited draws up accounts to 31st March each year and, at 31st March 2011, the new house is 75% complete. Aayan Limited's total costs to date are £320,000, but further costs of £80,000 are anticipated before the house is completed.

Aayan Limited will need to show a sale of £375,000 (75% of £500,000) in its accounts to 31st March 2011.

The company will, however, be able to deduct costs of £300,000, which equates to 75% of its anticipated final total costs of £400,000 (£320,000 + £80,000).

In other words, Aayan Limited will show a profit of £75,000 in its accounts to 31st March 2011, which is equal to 75% of the expected final profit on the development of £100,000.

The remaining £20,000 of Aayan Limited's costs to date will be shown in its accounts at 31st March 2011 as Work-in-Progress.

During the following year, Aayan Limited completes the property at an actual cost of £77,000.

The company's accounts for the year ending 31st March 2012 will show a sale of £125,000, i.e. the remaining 25% of the total sale proceeds of £500,000.

From this, Aayan Limited can deduct total costs of £97,000, which is made up of £20,000 of Work-in-Progress brought forward and actual costs in the year of £77,000.

This gives Aayan Limited a development profit of £28,000 for the year ending 31st March 2012.

As we can see from the example, the effect of this accounting treatment is to accelerate part of the profit on the development.

As there is no specific rule to the contrary, the tax position will also follow the accounting treatment, so that the development company is taxed on part of its property sale in advance.

It follows that the whole profit on a property for which a sales contract exists will need to be included in the company's accounts once the property is fully completed.

Where this accounting treatment applies, the company may nevertheless claim deductions to reflect:

- Any doubt over the purchaser's ability, or willingness, to pay.
- Rectification work that is still to be carried out.
- Administration and other costs relating to completion of the sale.

Tax Tip

Whilst this accounting treatment leads to an acceleration in the taxation of company profits, it can also lead to a 'smoothing out' of the company's annual profits. This might sometimes be beneficial.

Example

Lomu Limited has a 31st March accounting date and is undertaking a large development which is expected to be completed in early 2013 and to yield total profits of £900,000. If all of this profit were taxed in the year ending 31st March 2013, the company's total Corporation Tax bill would be £225,000 (£300,000 at 20% and £600,000 at 27.5% - see Section 2.5).

However, Lomu Limited has contracted to sell the development and, under the accounting principles applying to contractual sales, must account for its profits on the development in line with the overall completion of the development.

One-third of the development is completed in each of the years ending 31st March 2011, 2012 and 2013. Hence, in each year, the company will have a taxable profit of £300,000.

From our table in Section 2.5, we can see that this will lead to Corporation Tax bills of £63,000 in 2011 (21%) and £60,000 in both 2012 and 2013 (20%). The company's total tax bill on the development will therefore amount to £183,000.

So, whilst the accounting principles for contractual sales mean that Lomu Limited pays much of its Corporation Tax in advance of its actual sale, they also mean that the company saves £42,000.

5.5   CAPITAL ALLOWANCES FOR TRADING COMPANIES

As explained in Section 5.2, a property trading company can generally only claim capital allowances on its *own* long-term fixed assets. Any furniture, furnishings or equipment within its trading properties will form part of its trading stock. (In certain circumstances, a developer constructing a new qualifying 'industrial' or 'agricultural' building (see Section 4.4) before 1st April 2011 may be able to claim allowances of 1%)

In general terms, property development companies are likely to have greater scope for claiming capital allowances than companies with residential property investment businesses but possibly less scope than those with commercial property investments.

Property dealing companies and property management companies, however, are unlikely to be able to claim very many allowances.

The principles outlined below will also apply equally to any assets that a property investment company purchases for use in its own business.

Plant and Equipment

Subject to the general comments above, plant and equipment purchased for use in the trade will be eligible for the 'plant and machinery' allowances described in Section 4.4.

'Plant and equipment' may include the following items used in the company's trade:

- Building equipment and tools
- Computers
- Office furniture, fixtures and fittings
- Vans

Example

During the year ending 31st March 2011, Triple Crown Limited spends £130,000 on plant and equipment for use in its trade.

The company is therefore entitled to an annual investment allowance of £100,000 plus writing down allowances of 20% on the remaining £30,000 of its expenditure, i.e. £6,000. The company's total capital allowances claim for the year is thus £106,000. (For the sake of illustration, I am assuming that the company has no balance brought forward on its general pool.)

The remaining £24,000 of expenditure is carried forward to the year ending 31st March 2012, when it is eligible for writing down allowances of 20%, or £4,800. This leaves £19,200 to be carried forward to the year ending 31st March 2013, when it will attract writing down allowances of 18% (see Section 4.4), or £3,456.

Thereafter, the unrelieved balance of expenditure will continue to be carried forward and attract writing down allowances of 18% each year until the remaining unrelieved balance on the company's general pool (see Section 4.4) reduces to £1,000 or less.

Motor Cars

The capital allowances regime for cars purchased by companies after 31st March 2009 may be summarised as follows:

- Cars are not eligible for the annual investment allowance

- Cars with CO2 emissions in excess of 160g/km fall into the special rate pool and attract writing down allowances at just 10% (8% from 1st April 2012)

- Cars with CO2 emissions in excess of 110g/km, but no more than 160g/km, fall into the general pool and attract writing down allowances at 20% (18% from 1st April 2012)

- Cars with CO2 emissions of no more than 110g/km attract enhanced capital allowances at 100%

See Section 4.4 for further details on the general and special rate pools.

A different system applies to cars purchased before 1st April 2009. For full details see the previous (eighth) edition of this guide: a complimentary PDF copy is available on request by contacting team@taxcafe.co.uk

Private Use

For cars owned by a company, there is no restriction in the amount of the capital allowances available to reflect any private use of the vehicle.

Instead, however, the person enjoying that private use is subject to Income Tax on a 'Benefit-in-Kind' charge. This charge will generally be somewhere between 15% and 35% of the original purchase cost of the car when new.

In addition to the Income Tax charge on the individual, the company itself will have to pay Class 1A National Insurance at 13.8% on the same 'Benefit-in-Kind' charge (12.8% prior to 6th April 2011).

In total, the annual Income Tax and National Insurance costs of running a company car could add up to as much as 26.5% of the cost of that car when it was brand new.

Company cars are a complex subject in their own right. Suffice to say, you should carefully review your own situation before deciding to buy a car through your company.

Capital Allowance Disclaimers

It is worth noting that capital allowances are not mandatory and any proportion of the available allowance may be claimed, from zero to 100%.

Allowances not claimed are generally referred to as 'capital allowance disclaimers'.

Where an allowance is disclaimed in one period, a greater balance of expenditure is carried forward to the next period, thus increasing later capital allowance claims.

For expenditure during the year ended 31st March 2010, or before 1st April 2008, a capital allowance disclaimer could be used as a means of preventing or reducing a balancing charge.

For expenditure incurred by companies after 31st March 2010, however, a capital allowance disclaimer will seldom be beneficial.

5.6 TRADING LOSSES

Trading losses may be set off against the company's other income *and capital gains* of the same accounting period. Unlike rental losses, however, the company is not forced to make this set-off and may choose not to claim it.

For example, where the company is anticipating a higher marginal rate of Corporation Tax in the following year, it may prefer to carry its loss forward (see below).

Loss Carry Back

If the claim for set-off of trading losses within the same accounting period *has* been made, the company may additionally claim to carry back any surplus loss against its total profits and capital gains in the twelve months preceding the accounting period which gave rise to the loss.

If, however, the loss-making trade was not being carried on by the company throughout the previous twelve months, the relevant period for loss set-off is the period beginning with the commencement of that trade.

The catch here, though, is that the current year set-off claim must have been made first, even if this is of less value than carrying the loss forward (see below).

Example

(See Section 2.3 regarding the Corporation Tax rates referred to in this example.)

Betsen Limited makes a trading loss of £100,000 in the year ending 31st March 2011. In the same year, the company has capital gains and investment income of £70,000.

In the previous year, ended 31st March 2010, Betsen Limited had total taxable profits of £400,000.

The company's marginal Corporation Tax rate in the previous year was therefore 29.75%, making a loss carry back very valuable. In order to claim a loss carry back, however, the company will also need to set £70,000 of its loss against its other income in the current year. This will only save tax at a rate of 21%.

In total, therefore, by claiming to set its trading loss off against total profits in the current and previous years, Betsen Limited will save Corporation Tax as follows:

£70,000 @ 21% =   £14,700
£30,000 @ 29.75% =   £8,925

Total   £23,625

An added benefit of setting a trading loss off against other income in the current and previous years is that the resultant tax saving is more or less immediate.

Nevertheless, whether a loss carry back claim is the company's best course of action under these circumstances will depend on the position for later accounting periods falling after the loss-making period.

Additional Loss Carry Back

Companies are generally permitted to carry trading losses back against profits arising in the previous twelve months only. For company accounting periods ending between 24th November 2008 and 23rd November 2010, however, up to £50,000 of any remaining loss can also be carried back to be set against the company's profits in the preceding two years.

Losses must be set against profits arising in later periods first and the £50,000 limit applies independently to all accounting periods ending between 24th November 2008 and 23rd November 2009 and all accounting periods ending between 24th November 2009 and 23rd November 2010.

Once a company makes a claim to carry losses back, the full amount of relief available under the above rules must be taken. It cannot be restricted in any way, such as to prevent losses from being set against profits under £300,000, for example.

Loss Carry Forward

Any trading losses which still remain unrelieved after any claim for set-off in the current year or carry back to the previous year (or previous three years), will be carried forward and will automatically be set off against future profits from the same trade.

In this case, there is no need to make any claim and there is no choice in the matter as this treatment is automatic.

Nevertheless, despite this lack of flexibility, the carry forward option may sometimes still prove to be the best way for a company to use its losses.

Example Revisited

After the poor year in 2011, Betsen Limited bounces back in the year ending 31st March 2012 and makes a trading profit of £450,000. This gives the company a marginal Corporation Tax rate of 28.75%.

Hence, by not making any claim to use its 2011 trading loss in either of the previous two years, Betsen Limited will be able to make a saving on its Corporation Tax bill for the year ending 31st March 2012 of:

£100,000 x 28.75% = £28,750

By carrying its trading loss forward, Betsen Limited can therefore make an additional saving of £5,125 (£28,750 - £23,625). However, it does have to wait a year longer to achieve this saving!

Whether it is worth waiting for this additional saving will depend on the company's circumstances. The £5,125 additional saving effectively provides a 'rate of return' of 21.7% on the smaller saving of £23,625 that could be made a year earlier.

I would suggest that this 'rate of return' is the most appropriate measure to use in judging whether the loss carry forward is preferable.

Maximising Your Company's Loss Relief

Where trading losses are available in a company, there are three alternative possible ways to claim relief for them:

i)   Set off against other income and capital gains of the same year, with any remainder carried forward for automatic set-off against future profits from the same trade.

ii) Set off against other income and capital gains of the same year **and** then against the company's total income and capital gains in the previous twelve months (or previous three years), with any remainder carried forward for automatic set-off against future profits from the same trade.

iii) Carry all losses forward for automatic set-off against future profits from the same trade.

Companies which are members of a group of companies may also surrender some or all of their trading losses as group relief.

As we have seen in our example, the question of which method is best for the company will depend on the pattern of its profits and other income over a number of years.

The choice of which loss relief method is to be used must be made within two years of the end of the loss-making accounting period. This is the time limit for making any claims to set off losses within the same accounting period, or against profits and capital gains within the previous twelve months (or three years), or to surrender losses as group relief.

In Betsen Limited's case, therefore, the directors would have until 31st March 2013 to decide on their best course of action and, on the basis of the figures in the example above, this would have enabled them to achieve their optimum result.

In practice, the carried forward loss may not always be relieved quite so quickly, and it is then often a case of 'a bird in the hand is worth two in the bush'.

Chapter 6

Corporation Tax on Capital Gains

6.1   WHEN DOES A CAPITAL GAIN ARISE?

In Chapter 3, we examined the various different types of property companies and we saw that some property disposals give rise to trading profits.

We also saw, however, that property disposals made by property investment companies (see Section 3.2) give rise to capital gains instead.

Furthermore, other property companies disposing of their long-term fixed assets, such as their own office premises, for example, will also be subject to capital gains treatment.

In each case, the calculation of the amount of capital gain chargeable to Corporation Tax is as follows:

Capital Gain = Proceeds Less Base Cost

6.2   HOW TO CALCULATE THE 'PROCEEDS'

In most cases, the amount of 'Proceeds' to be used in the calculation of a capital gain will be the actual sum received on the disposal of the asset.

However, from this, the company may deduct incidental costs in order to arrive at 'net proceeds', which is the relevant sum for the purposes of calculating the capital gain.

Example

Yachvilli Limited sells a house for £375,000. In order to make this sale, the company spends £1,500 advertising the property, pays £3,750 in estate agent's fees and pays £800 in legal fees.

Yachvilli Limited's net proceeds are therefore £368,950 (£375,000 less £1,500, £3,750 and £800).

There are, however, a number of cases where the proceeds we must use in the calculation of a capital gain are not simply the actual cash sum received. Three of the most common such exceptions are set out below.

Exception 1 – Connected Persons

Where the person disposing of the asset is 'connected' with the person acquiring it, the open market value of the asset at the time of transfer must be used in place of the actual price paid (if any).

A company will be deemed to be 'connected' with any person who controls that company, as well as close relatives of that person and other companies also controlled by that person and/or their relatives.

Example

Beckham Limited is a property investment company and is wholly owned by Victoria.

Beckham Limited sells a property to Victoria's son, Cruz, for £500,000. The market value of the property at the time of this sale is £800,000. The company pays legal fees of £475 on the sale.

Beckham Limited will be deemed to have received net sale proceeds of £800,000 (the market value). The legal fees the company has borne are irrelevant, as this was not an 'arm's-length' transaction.

The concept of 'connected persons' is important for a number of reasons, as we will see throughout this guide. A list of the persons deemed to be 'connected' with each other is therefore given in Appendix D.

Exception 2 – Transactions not at 'arm's-length'

Where a transaction takes place between 'connected persons', as above, there is an automatic assumption that the transaction is not at 'arm's-length' and hence market value must always be substituted for the actual proceeds.

There are, however, other instances where the transaction may not be at 'arm's-length', such as:

- A sale of an asset to an employee
- A transaction which is part of a larger transaction
- A transaction which is part of a series of transactions

The effect of these is much the same as before – the asset's market value must be used in place of the actual proceeds, if any.

The key difference from Exception 1 above is that the onus of proof that this is not an 'arm's-length' transaction is on HM Revenue and Customs, rather than there being an automatic assumption that this is the case.

Example

Brooklyn Limited owns an investment property with a market value of £200,000. If the company sold the property at this price, it would have a capital gain of £80,000.

Not wishing to incur a Corporation Tax liability, Brooklyn Limited decides instead to sell the house to Romeo Limited for £120,000. However, Brooklyn Limited only does this on condition that Romeo Limited gives it an interest-free loan of £80,000 for an indefinite period.

The condition imposed by Brooklyn Limited means that this transaction is not at 'arm's-length'. The correct position is therefore that Brooklyn Limited should be deemed to have sold the property for £200,000 and still have a capital gain of £80,000.

Exception 3 – Non-cash proceeds

Sometimes all or part of the sale consideration will take a form other than cash.

The sale proceeds to be taken into account in these cases will be the market value of the assets or rights received in exchange for the asset sold.

Example

Little Property Company Limited owns an office block in central London.

Big Properties plc (a quoted company) wants to buy the property from Little Property Company Limited but, as it is experiencing some short-term cashflow difficulties, it offers Little Property Company Limited 500,000 shares for the property rather than cash.

Little Property Company Limited accepts this offer and takes the shares, which are worth £1.25 per share at the date of sale.

Little Property Company Limited's sale proceeds for Corporation Tax purposes will therefore be £625,000 (500,000 x £1.25).

Wealth Warning

Note that if, as in the above example, you take non-cash consideration for a sale, you will be taxed on the value of that consideration at that date. If the value of the non-cash asset that you receive should subsequently fall, you will still be taxed on the original value!

This problem can sometimes possibly be alleviated by disposing of the asset that has fallen in value and thus generating a capital loss, but:

- This is not always desirable, and
- A capital loss cannot be carried back to an earlier accounting period.

6.3 HOW TO CALCULATE THE 'BASE COST'

The 'Base Cost' is the amount that may be deducted in the capital gains calculation in respect of an asset's cost.

The higher the base cost, the lower the chargeable gain and the less Corporation Tax payable!

As with proceeds, the basic starting point in most cases will be the actual amount paid to purchase the asset.

Added to the actual amount paid are:

- Incidental costs of acquisition (e.g. legal fees, Stamp Duty Land Tax, etc).
- Enhancement expenditure (e.g. the cost of building an extension to a property).
- Expenditure incurred in establishing, preserving or defending title to, or rights over, the asset (e.g. legal fees incurred as a result of a boundary dispute).

Base Cost – Special Situations

There are again a number of special situations where base cost is determined by reference to something other than the actual amount paid for the asset.

The major exceptions fall into three main categories:

- The asset was not acquired by way of a 'bargain at arm's length'.
- The asset was acquired for non-cash consideration.
- The asset was acquired before 1st April 1982.

Assets Not Acquired by Way of a 'Bargain at Arm's Length'

In the case of an acquisition which is not a 'bargain at arm's length', the acquiring company's base cost will generally be the asset's market value at the time of purchase, as this will be the deemed 'proceeds' on which the person selling the asset is taxed.

Example

Martin owns a property investment company called Johnson Limited. The company buys a warehouse from Martin for £100,000. The warehouse, which Martin held as an investment, has an open market value of £200,000.

Johnson Limited will therefore have a base cost for the warehouse of £200,000. (Note that Martin's personal Capital Gains Tax liability will be based on a sale for deemed 'proceeds' of £200,000.)

Gifts of Business Assets

In the case of a property that qualifies as a 'business asset' for Capital Gains Tax purposes, the usual rule for a 'bargain not at arm's length' may be over-ridden by a 'hold-over' relief claim (see Section 15.2).

This would alter the position and the acquiring company would then be treated as acquiring the property for the greater of:

i) The amount actually paid, or
ii) The property's open market value less the amount of 'held over' gain.

This treatment can generally only apply to furnished holiday letting property or property used as a long-term fixed asset in the transferor's own trading business.

We will return to this subject in more detail in Chapter 15.

Assets acquired for non-cash consideration

Where an asset was acquired for non-cash consideration, its base cost will be determined by reference to the market value of the consideration given.

Assets acquired before 1st April 1982

Generally speaking, the base cost will usually be the greater of the asset's actual cost or its open market value at 31st March 1982. A few exceptions arise when assets are being sold at a loss but these are not very likely in the context of property companies!

6.4   HOW TO CALCULATE THE INDEXATION RELIEF

Indexation relief was introduced in 1982 to eliminate the purely inflationary element of capital gains. Unlike individuals, for whom indexation relief was abolished in April 2008, companies continue to be entitled to indexation relief on their capital disposals.

The relief is based on the increase in the retail prices index over the period of the company's ownership of the asset (or from 31st March 1982 until the date of sale, if the asset was acquired before then).

Where the base cost of the asset is made up of original cost and later enhancement expenditure, each element of the base cost will attract indexation relief at its own appropriate rate.

Example

Wilkinson Limited bought a property for £100,000 in June 1987. In August 1991, the company spent £50,000 building an extension to the property. The property was sold for £600,000 in July 2011.

The retail prices index was 101.9 in June 1987, 134.1 in August 1991 and 232.0 in July 2011 (the last figure is my estimate).

The retail prices index increased by 127.7% between June 1987 and July 2011, so the indexation relief due on the company's original purchase cost is £127,700 (£100,000 x 127.7%).

The retail prices index increased by 73.0% between August 1991 and July 2011, so the indexation relief due on the company's enhancement expenditure (i.e. the cost of the extension) is £36,500 (£50,000 x 73%).

Wilkinson Limited's chargeable gain is therefore calculated as follows:

	£	£
Sale proceeds		*600,000*
Less:		
Original cost	*100,000*	
Enhancement expenditure	*50,000*	

		150,000
Indexation relief		
On original cost	*127,700*	
On enhancement expenditure	*36,500*	

Total:		*164,200*

Chargeable gain:		*£285,800*
		========

It should be noted that indexation relief may not be used to create or increase a capital loss. Hence, in some cases, the amount of relief has to be restricted. Where a capital loss already arises, no relief is given at all. Where there is a capital gain before indexation, the relief cannot exceed the amount of the gain before indexation.

The Retail Prices Index

A full table of retail prices index factors for use in calculating indexation relief on capital disposals by companies is reproduced in Appendix E.

The rate of indexation relief to be claimed is calculated as follows:

Indexation Relief Rate = (RD – RA)/RA

RA is the retail prices index for the month of acquisition, or other allowable expenditure. For expenditure prior to 1st April 1982 (or for March 1982 values used instead) use 79.44.

RD is the retail prices index for the month of disposal.

Example

To calculate the indexation relief rate applying to the cost of a property purchased by a company in May 2000 and sold by that company in November 2010, we find from Appendix E that RA is 170.7 and RD is 226.8.

The indexation relief rate is therefore (226.8 – 170.7)/170.7 or 56.1/170.7, which equates to 32.9%.

6.5   MAKING THE MOST OF CAPITAL LOSSES

Any capital losses that arise may be set off against capital gains (after indexation relief) arising in the same accounting period.

Surplus capital losses are then carried forward and set off against capital gains arising in later accounting periods.

Capital losses cannot be carried back to earlier accounting periods and nor can they be set against capital gains made by the company owner, even on shares in the company making the capital losses.

Tax Tip

It may be worth considering disposing of loss-making properties before the end of an accounting period in which the company has made capital gains.

Another Tax Tip

Unless there are strong commercial reasons for doing so, a company which has unused capital losses carried forward should not be wound up as there will always be a possibility of realising tax-free capital gains through it in the future.

Chapter 7

Capital Gains Tax on Company Shares

7.1 INTRODUCTION

Company owners are not subject to Capital Gains Tax on the capital gains which their company makes on the disposal of properties. As we have seen in previous chapters, the company pays Corporation Tax on those gains instead.

Company owners are, however, subject to Capital Gains Tax on the disposal of shares in their property company. A 'disposal' for this purpose includes:

- A sale of the company,
- A winding up of the company, or
- A transfer of shares to another person.

In the case of a transfer to a connected person (see Appendix D), or any other transfer which is 'not a bargain at arm's length' (see Section 6.2), the market value of the shares is substituted in place of the actual sale proceeds for Capital Gains Tax purposes.

Holdover relief may sometimes be available in these circumstances (see Section 7.6). Transfers to the owner's spouse are also generally exempt from Capital Gains Tax.

As we saw in Chapter 3, some property company shares will also be eligible for entrepreneurs' relief, which we shall be looking at in detail in Section 7.3.

7.2   CAPITAL GAINS TAX RATES

For disposals made by individuals after 22nd June 2010, Capital Gains Tax is charged at three rates:

- 10% where entrepreneurs' relief is available (Section 7.3)
- 18% on other gains made by basic rate taxpayers
- 28% on other gains made by higher rate taxpayers

The 18% rate applies to the extent that the individual has any remaining basic rate tax band available after accounting for their total income for the tax year.

Each individual is also entitled to an annual Capital Gains Tax exemption each tax year. The annual exemption for 2010/11 is £10,100; the estimated annual exemption for 2011/12 is £10,600.

Example

In May 2011, Andy sells some shares in his property investment company and makes a capital gain of £50,000. The shares do not qualify for entrepreneurs' relief.

Andy's total taxable income for 2011/12 is £30,000. After deducting his personal allowance of £7,475, his income uses up £22,525 of his basic rate band, leaving £12,475 available for Capital Gains Tax purposes (see Appendix A for details of Income Tax allowances, bands, etc for 2011/12).

After deducting his annual exemption of £10,600 (estimated), Andy is left with a taxable capital gain of £39,400. His Capital Gains Tax bill is therefore as follows:

£12,475 x 18% =	*£2,246*
£26,925 x 28% =	*£7,539*
Total	*£9,785*

Earlier Gains

Capital gains arising between 6th April 2008 and 22nd June 2010 were subject to Capital Gains Tax at a single flat rate of 18% (subject to the annual exemption and any available entrepreneurs' relief – as explained in Section 7.3).

Capital gains arising between 6th April and 22nd June 2010 do not need to be included in assessing whether an individual has utilised their basic rate band for 2010/11.

7.3   ENTREPRENEURS' RELIEF

For capital gains arising after 22nd June 2010, entrepreneurs' relief operates by substituting a Capital Gains Tax rate of 10% in place of the 18% or 28% rate.

Each individual may only claim entrepreneurs' relief on a maximum cumulative lifetime total of £5m of qualifying capital gains. Thereafter, the Capital Gains Tax rate on all further capital gains will revert to the 18% and 28% rates (see Section 7.2).

Whilst companies themselves do not qualify for entrepreneurs' relief, property company owners may benefit from this relief when they dispose of shares in a qualifying 'personal company'.

The definition of a 'personal company' for the purposes of entrepreneurs' relief is broadly as follows:

i)   The individual holds at least 5% of the ordinary share capital
ii) The holding under (i) provides at least 5% of the voting rights
iii) The company is a trading company (see below)
iv) The individual is an officer or employee of the company (an 'officer' includes a director or company secretary)

Each of these rules must be satisfied for the period of at least one year prior to the disposal in question or, where the company has ceased trading, for at least one year prior to the cessation. In the latter case, the disposal must take place within three years after cessation.

As we saw in Chapter 3, property development companies, property management companies and, in theory, property dealing companies, all qualify as trading companies for the purposes of entrepreneurs' relief.

As discussed in Section 3.2, qualifying furnished holiday lettings are also deemed to be a trade for the purposes of entrepreneurs' relief.

For the availability of entrepreneurs' relief on shares in a company with a 'mixed' property business, see Section 3.6.

To illustrate the impact of entrepreneurs' relief, let's look at an example.

Example

Redpath Limited and Delaglio Limited are both property development companies. Both companies were set up for an initial investment of just £1,000 each and started trading immediately afterwards.

Both companies also have some rental income, meaning that, in HM Revenue and Customs' view, they have some non-trading activity. Redpath Limited, however, manages to keep the non-trading activity below the level that HM Revenue and Customs regards as 'substantial' (see Section 3.6), meaning that it is accepted as a trading company.

The shares in Redpath Limited therefore qualify for entrepreneurs' relief.

Brian, who owns all of the shares in Redpath Limited, decides to wind the company up in 2011 and receives net proceeds of £5,001,000, giving him a capital gain of exactly £5m.

Assuming that Brian has already used up his annual exemption on other gains, his Capital Gains Tax liability on the sale of his Redpath Limited shares will be £500,000 (£5m x 10%).

Lawrence, the sole shareholder of Delaglio Limited, also winds his company up in 2011 and also makes a capital gain of £5m.

However, Delaglio Limited's non-trading activities have unfortunately exceeded the level that HM Revenue and Customs regards as 'substantial', meaning that the company is not regarded as a trading company for entrepreneurs' relief purposes.

Hence, assuming that Lawrence is a higher rate taxpayer and has used up his annual exemption on other gains, his Capital Gains Tax liability on the sale of his Delaglio Limited shares will be £1,400,000 (£5m x 28%).

*That's £900,000 more than, or **almost triple**, Brian's Capital Gains Tax liability on a sale of very similar shares!*

Note that entrepreneurs' relief is not mandatory and taxpayers may choose whether to claim it.

Where a basic rate taxpayer claims entrepreneurs' relief on a capital gain arising after 22nd June 2010, this gain uses up their remaining basic rate band in priority to any other gains. In effect, this pushes more (or perhaps all) of those other gains up into the 28% Capital Gains Tax bracket.

The cumulative lifetime maximum of £5m applies to all entrepreneurs' relief claims on capital gains arising on or after 6th April 2008.

A maximum of £1m applied to claims on capital gains arising between 6th April 2008 and 5th April 2010 and a maximum of £2m applied to claims on capital gains arising between 6th April 2008 and 22nd June 2010.

Earlier Gains

Where entrepreneurs' relief was claimed on a capital gain arising between 6th April 2008 and 22nd June 2010, the relief operated by exempting four ninths of the qualifying gain. The remaining five ninths was then taxed at 18%, producing an overall effective rate of 10%.

7.4 ENTREPRENEURS' RELIEF FOR PROPERTY INVESTMENT COMPANIES

Subject to the overall limit of £5m, entrepreneurs' relief is available on the whole of a capital gain arising on the disposal of shares in a company which meets the 'personal company' conditions set out in Section 7.3 for the relevant one year period, even if the company did not previously meet those conditions.

Hence, entrepreneurs' relief will be available in full as long as the company qualifies as a 'trading company' for the one year period prior to the disposal of the shares, or the year prior to cessation of its business (provided that the other necessary conditions are met).

Tax Tip

Entrepreneurs' relief would be available on shares in a former property investment, or other 'non-trading', company which changes its business and becomes a qualifying 'trading company' for the one year period prior to the disposal of the shares or cessation of the company's business.

As usual, qualifying furnished holiday lettings (see Section 4.6) count as 'trading' for this purpose and may therefore provide an easy way for a residential property investment company to undergo the necessary conversion.

7.5 ENTREPRENEURS' RELIEF AND COUPLES

It is worth noting that the £5m cumulative lifetime maximum for entrepreneurs' relief applies on a 'per person' basis.

Hence, if both members of a couple own at least 5% of the ordinary shares in a qualifying 'trading company' each, they will potentially be able to claim entrepreneurs' relief on total capital gains of up to £10m. This will provide total Capital Gains Tax savings of up to £1,800,000.

Alternatively, if 5% or more of the ordinary shares in a qualifying 'trading company' are transferred to the owner's spouse at least a year prior to cessation or sale then the spouse may again be entitled to entrepreneurs' relief, once more giving potential relief on total capital gains of up to £10m.

Wealth Warning

For a disposal of shares to qualify for entrepreneurs' relief, the company must have qualified as the 'personal company' of the individual making the disposal for at least a year prior to cessation or sale.

A pre-sale transfer of shares to a spouse might therefore result in the loss of entrepreneurs' relief if the spouse did not meet all of the necessary qualifying conditions (see Section 7.3) for at least a year prior to cessation or sale.

It is also important to remember that pre-sale transfers to a spouse are only effective if the transferee spouse genuinely obtains beneficial ownership of the transferred shares. In other words, the transferee must be free to do as they wish with the transferred shares and must be beneficially entitled to their share of the sale proceeds.

Another Wealth Warning

Couples owning companies together are at risk of attack under potential future 'income shifting' legislation. We will explore this subject further in Section 10.4.

7.6 HOLDOVER RELIEF

Holdover relief is available on the transfer of shares in an unquoted trading company (except a transfer of shares to or from another company).

Where the transfer is an outright gift, the transferor and transferee may jointly elect to 'hold over' the entire capital gain arising. The effect of this is that no Capital Gains Tax is payable by the transferor and the transferee is treated as having acquired the shares for the same base cost (see Section 6.3) as the transferor.

For sales made for a consideration less than market value, a partial hold over is available. Broadly speaking, the amount of gain held over is equal to the difference between the market value and the sales price. The effect of this is that the transferor pays Capital Gains Tax based on the actual sales price and the transferee's base cost is equal to that price.

The definition of a 'trading company' for holdover relief purposes is the same as for entrepreneurs' relief purposes (see Chapter 3 and Section 7.3 for further details).

It follows that most unquoted shares which qualify for entrepreneurs' relief will qualify for holdover relief (but not necessarily vice versa). However, it is important to note that holdover relief will be restricted if the company has not qualified as a 'trading company' throughout the transferor's entire period of ownership.

Holdover Relief and Entrepreneurs' Relief

A holdover relief claim could be used to make a transfer of shares in a qualifying 'trading company' to another individual other than the owner's spouse free from Capital Gains Tax (e.g. to transfer shares to an unmarried partner or an adult child).

If the transferee then held the transferred shares for at least one year, and met all of the other qualifying conditions set out in Section 7.3, they would then be entitled to entrepreneurs' relief on those shares.

Chapter 8

Stamp Duty for Property Companies

8.1   INTRODUCTION

Stamp Duty is the oldest tax on the statute books. It was several centuries old already when Pitt the Younger introduced Income Tax in 1799. Even today, we are still governed (to a limited extent) by the Stamp Act 1891.

Since 2003, however, for transfers of real property (i.e. land and buildings or any form of legal interest in them), Stamp Duty has been replaced by Stamp Duty Land Tax (see Section 8.3).

8.2   STAMP DUTY ON SHARES

Despite talk of its abolition a few years ago, this ancient tax continues to apply to transfers of shares. The rate of Stamp Duty on purchases of shares and securities is still unchanged at a single uniform rate of only 0.5%. This has led to many tax-avoidance strategies, designed to avoid the excessive rates applied to property transactions by making use of this more palatable rate. Anti-avoidance legislation introduced by the previous Government has effectively blocked most of the more popular methods, however.

Nevertheless, for those investing in property through a company, there remains the possibility of selling shares in that company at a much lower rate of Duty than would apply to the sale of individual properties within the company.

Sales of shares for no more than £1,000 are now exempt from Stamp Duty.

8.3   STAMP DUTY LAND TAX

Stamp Duty Land Tax applies to transfers of real property (i.e. land and buildings or any form of legal interest in them). The tax is payable on all transfers of real property located in the UK regardless of where the vendor or purchaser are resident and regardless of where the transfer documentation is drawn up.

The rates of Stamp Duty Land Tax applying to transfers of property are the same for companies as they are for individuals.

Likewise, the type of property company which you have has no impact on the rate of Stamp Duty Land Tax.

The main rates of Stamp Duty Land Tax are currently as follows:

- Residential property up to £125,000 – Zero.
- Non-residential property up to £150,000 – Zero.
- Property over the above limits but not over £250,000 – 1%.
- Property over £250,000 but not over £500,000 – 3%.
- Property over £500,000 – 4%.

Under current proposals, a new, even higher, Stamp Duty Land Tax rate of 5% on purchases of residential property with a consideration of more than £1m is to be introduced with effect from 6th April 2011.

Like Stamp Duty, the Stamp Duty Land Tax payable should always be rounded up to the nearest £5.

Different rates apply to residential property in 'disadvantaged areas' (see Section 8.5) and to 'zero-carbon housing' (see Section 8.6).

There is also currently an additional exemption for 'first-time buyers' purchasing residential property for no more than £250,000. A number of qualifying conditions apply and the exemption is unlikely to be available to any companies.

Generally speaking, all of the amounts indicated above refer to the consideration paid for the purchase – whether in cash or by any other means.

However, in the case of a transfer of property to a 'connected' company (see Section 6.2), the deemed consideration for Stamp Duty Land Tax purposes will be the greater of the actual amount of consideration paid and the property's market value. We will explore some of the implications of this in Section 15.12.

Whenever any rate less than the maximum 4% is to be applied, the purchaser is required to certify that the lower rate is properly applicable.

Furthermore, it should also be noted that the rate of Stamp Duty Land Tax to be applied must be determined after taking account of any 'linked transactions'. Amongst other things, this means that, where two or more properties are purchased together, the rate of Stamp Duty Land Tax is based on the total purchase price.

It can readily be seen from the above table that a small alteration in the purchase price of a property can sometimes make an enormous difference to the amount of Stamp Duty Land Tax payable.

Example

McGeehan Limited is just about to make an offer of £250,001 for a house in Edinburgh when Ian, the company's managing director, realises that the Stamp Duty Land Tax payable on this purchase, at 3%, would be £7,505. Horrified at this prospect, he amends the offer to £249,999, thus reducing the potential Stamp Duty Land Tax payable to £2,500 (1%).

This sort of change is, of course, perfectly acceptable, because the whole situation is taking place at 'arm's-length'.

Where connected parties are involved, however, HM Revenue and Customs' Stamp Office is likely to scrutinise very closely any transactions where the consideration is equal to, or only just under, one of the limits set out above.

8.4 STAMP DUTY LAND TAX ON LEASES

Stamp Duty Land Tax is also payable on the granting of a lease. The amount of tax payable is based on the 'Net Present Value' of all of the rent payable under the lease over its entire term. Where the net present value does not exceed £125,000 (for residential property), or £150,000 (for non-residential property), no Stamp Duty Land Tax will be payable. For new leases with a net present value exceeding these limits, Stamp Duty Land Tax is payable at a single rate of 1% on the excess.

VAT is excluded from the rent payable under the lease for the purposes of Stamp Duty Land Tax calculations <u>unless</u> the landlord has already exercised the option to tax (this applies to commercial property only).

Example

Woodward Limited is about to take on a ten-year lease over a house in Kent at an annual rent of £18,000.

The Stamp Duty Land Tax legislation provides that the net present value of a sum of money due in twelve months' time is equal to the sum due divided by a 'discount factor'. The applicable discount factor is currently 103.5%.

For Stamp Duty Land Tax purposes, all of the first year's rent is treated as if it were one single lump sum due in twelve months' time.

The 'Net Present Value' of the first year's rent is therefore £17,391 (i.e. £18,000 divided by 103.5%).

Similarly, the second year's rent, which is due a further twelve months later, must be 'discounted' again by the same amount, i.e. £17,391/103.5% = £16,803.

This process is continued for the entire ten-year life of the lease and the net present values of all of the rental payments are then added together to give the total net present value for the whole lease. In this case, this works out at £149,699.

The Stamp Duty Land Tax payable by Woodward Limited is therefore £250 (1% of £149,699 LESS £125,000, rounded up to the nearest £5).

The current 'discount factor' (103.5%) may be changed in the future, depending on a number of factors, including the prevailing rates of inflation and interest.

8.5   DISADVANTAGED AREAS

There are over 2,000 areas in the UK that have been specifically designated as 'Disadvantaged Areas'. These areas are sometimes also known as 'Enterprise Neighbourhoods' or 'Enterprise Areas' and, in fact, very often are not really all that 'disadvantaged' at all – so don't be fooled by the name.

Residential properties within these areas are subject to the zero rate of Stamp Duty Land Tax on purchases where the consideration does not exceed £150,000.

8.6   ZERO-CARBON HOUSING

For a five year period ending 30th September 2012, new homes costing no more than £500,000 and meeting the 'zero carbon' standard are exempt from Stamp Duty Land Tax. For more expensive 'zero carbon' houses, there is a £15,000 reduction in the tax.

This relief also applies to new flats. The flats must be new builds and not conversions, however.

Chapter 9

VAT And Property Companies

9.1   VAT ON PROPERTY

VAT, or 'Value Added Tax', to give it its proper name, is the 'new kid on the block' in UK taxation terms, having arrived on our shores from Europe in 1973.

Despite its youth, VAT is, quite possibly, the UK's most hated tax and there are some nasty pitfalls awaiting the unwary property investor at the hands of this indirect form of taxation.

VAT on property is a very complicated area, and your company's position will depend on its own particular situation and the type (and history) of the properties involved.

VAT is currently charged at three different rates in the UK: a standard rate of 20%, a reduced rate of 5% and a zero rate. All of these rates may be encountered by property companies.

The standard rate was increased from 17.5% to 20% with effect from 4th January 2011. For the rest of this chapter, I will refer only to the current standard rate of 20% which will apply to all relevant transactions in the foreseeable future.

9.2   RESIDENTIAL PROPERTY LETTING

Generally speaking, a property investment company engaged primarily in residential property letting does not need to register for VAT. (Nor, indeed, very often would it be able to.)

The letting of residential property is an exempt supply for VAT purposes. VAT is therefore not chargeable on rent, although, of course, VAT cannot be recovered on expenses and the company should therefore claim VAT-inclusive costs for Corporation Tax purposes.

Beware, however, that the provision of ancillary services (e.g. cleaning or gardening) may sometimes be Standard-Rated, and hence subject to VAT at 20%, if the value of annual supplies of these services exceeds the registration threshold (£70,000 from 1st April 2010). Some companies making ancillary supplies of this nature prefer to register for VAT, even if they have not reached the registration threshold, as this means that they are able to recover some of the VAT on their expenses.

9.3   HOLIDAY ACCOMMODATION

The supply of holiday accommodation is a standard-rated supply for VAT purposes. This will certainly apply to any qualifying furnished holiday lets and may also apply to other holiday lettings.

The landlord will therefore need to register for, and charge, VAT if the total income received from holiday accommodation exceeds £70,000 per annum. For this purpose, 'income' will include both rentals and any charges for ancillary services.

9.4   COMMERCIAL PROPERTY LETTING

For commercial property, there is an 'option to tax'. In other words, the landlord company may choose, for each property (on a property-by-property basis), whether or not the rent should be an exempt supply for VAT purposes.

If the 'option to tax' is exercised, the rent on the property becomes Standard Rated (at 20%) for VAT purposes.

The landlord company may then recover VAT on all of the expenses relating to that property.

Ancillary services are again likely to be Standard Rated if the total taxable supplies made by the company exceed the £70,000 per annum registration threshold ('taxable supplies' will include all of the ancillary services provided by the company plus any rentals which it has opted to tax).

Charging VAT on your commercial property rent is usually known as 'exercising the option to tax', although, technically, the proper term, as sometimes used by HM Revenue and Customs, is 'exercising the option to waive exemption from the requirement to charge tax'. Either way, it means the same thing.

Tax Tip

> If the potential tenants of a commercial property are all, or mostly, likely to be VAT-registered businesses themselves, it will generally make sense to exercise the 'option to tax' on the property in order to recover the VAT on expenses incurred.

If your tenants themselves have a VAT registered and fully taxable business for VAT purposes, then everyone's happy. The problem comes when your tenants cannot recover the VAT that you are charging them. Furthermore, you cannot usually change your option on a property once it has been exercised (well, not for at least 20 years anyway). Hence, if you opt to charge VAT to a fully taxable tenant, you will still need to charge VAT to the next tenant in the same property, even if they cannot recover it.

Sometimes though, with non-taxable (for VAT) tenants, where you have not yet exercised your option to tax, you can refrain from doing so and negotiate a higher rent to compensate you for your loss of VAT recovery on your own costs.

Example

Benazzi Limited owns an office building and hasn't yet opted to tax the rents. The company incurs monthly costs of £2,000 plus VAT (i.e. £2,400 gross) and expects a monthly rent of £10,000. If Benazzi Limited opts to tax it will recover £400 a month from HM Revenue and Customs and make a monthly profit of £8,000.

However, Abdelatif Limited, the prospective tenant, is not registered for VAT. If Benazzi Limited opts to tax the property, Abdelatif Limited's rent will effectively be 20% higher, i.e. £12,000 per month.

So, as a better alternative, Benazzi Limited and Abdelatif Limited agree that Benazzi Limited will not opt to tax the building but will, instead, charge Abdelatif Limited rent of £11,000 per month. Now Benazzi Limited is making a monthly profit of £8,600 (£11,000 minus £2,400) and Abdelatif Limited's rent is effectively £1,000 less than it would have been. Benazzi Limited and Abdelatif Limited both win and HM Revenue and Customs loses.

9.5 RESIDENTIAL PROPERTY SALES

Sales of newly constructed residential property are zero-rated for VAT purposes. This means that the developer can recover all of the VAT on their construction costs without having to charge VAT on the sale of the property. (In theory, VAT is charged, but at a rate of zero.)

Furthermore, if your property development company contracts with a builder/contractor for the construction of a residential dwelling house, such services supplied should also be zero-rated, meaning that you will not even need to pay any VAT on these costs in the first place.

Zero-rating is generally also extended to the sale of a property that has just been converted from a non-residential property into a residential property (*e.g. converting a barn into a house*).

It is also extended to 'substantially reconstructed protected buildings'. In essence, this means the sale of a listed building following the carrying out of major alterations. Such alterations do, of course, require approval from the authorities.

Property development companies carrying out construction work under any of these headings are therefore able to register for VAT and then recover the VAT on the vast majority of their business expenses.

Other Residential Property Sales

Other sales of residential property are generally an exempt supply meaning, once again, that the company making the sale is unable to recover any of the VAT on its expenses.

This means that VAT cannot be recovered by most residential property investment companies.

Furthermore, property development companies that merely renovate or alter existing residential property prior to onward sale are also generally unable to recover VAT on their costs. Where, however, the work qualifies as a 'conversion', as described in Section 9.8, they may at least be able to reduce the amount of VAT payable.

9.6   COMMERCIAL PROPERTY SALES & PURCHASES

Where the 'option to tax' has previously been exercised on a commercial property, the sale of that property will again be Standard Rated and this has major implications for such transactions.

Sales of new or uncompleted commercial property are always Standard Rated for VAT purposes.

Wealth Warning

Where VAT must be charged on a commercial property sale, the Stamp Duty Land Tax arising must be calculated on the basis of the gross, VAT-inclusive price.

This can lead to an effective combined VAT and Stamp Duty Land Tax rate of up to 24.8%!

This represents a pretty hefty cost if the purchaser is not VAT registered, probably enough to prevent the sale from taking place in some cases.

Imagine a large insurance company buying a new office block in central London – the combined VAT and Stamp Duty Land Tax cost would be astronomical!

Where a property investment company incurs VAT on the purchase of a commercial property, the only way to recover that VAT will be for the company to exercise the 'option to tax' on the property. In this way, the Government generally forces everyone to maintain the taxable status of the building for VAT purposes.

If a VAT registered property development company incurs VAT on the purchase of a commercial property, it can recover the VAT in the same way as on any other purchase of goods or services for use in the business. This initial recovery is not dependent on exercising the 'option to tax', as the company has a taxable business for VAT purposes, but ...

Wealth Warning

If VAT has been recovered on the purchase of a commercial property, a sale of that property without first exercising the option to tax would be an exempt supply.

If that property were trading stock, this would result in the loss of all the VAT initially reclaimed on its purchase and on any development, renovation or conversion work carried out on it. Some of the VAT recovered on general overhead costs would probably also become repayable.

Furthermore, when more than £250,000 has been spent on the purchase or improvement of a property for use as the company's own trading premises, a sale of that property within ten years without first exercising the option to tax would also trigger a VAT liability.

9.7   VAT ON 'BUILD TO LET'

The 'VAT Refund Scheme' enables a 'DIY Housebuilder' to reclaim any VAT paid on the construction of a new dwelling house. Unfortunately, however, this scheme cannot apply to any person who is constructing the property for business purposes.

We looked at the position for a property development company selling newly constructed residential property in Section 9.5 and, clearly, such companies remain able to recover all of the VAT incurred on construction costs under general principles.

Sadly, however, property investment companies which are building their own properties to hold as long-term investments will not be able to recover any VAT incurred. Nevertheless, if a property investment company contracts with a builder/contractor for the construction of a new residential dwelling house, such services supplied should, again, be zero-rated, thus avoiding the most significant potential VAT cost.

Any work that is closely connected to the construction of a zero-rated building should also be zero-rated. This will include levelling and drainage of land. There must not, however, be any significant time delay between these services being carried out and the physical construction of the building.

Architects, surveyors, consultants and supervisors' fees are normally standard rated at 20%. These fees could be rated differently, however, depending on which type of agreement the company has with the builder/main contractor.

Chapter 3 of VAT Notice 708 gives further information on the usual types of building contracts used.

9.8   VAT ON CONVERSIONS

As explained in Section 9.5, the sale of previously non-residential property that has been newly converted for residential use is generally zero-rated. This does, however, depend on the history of the property and, broadly speaking, if it has had *any* residential use in the previous ten years, the sale will, instead, be exempt for VAT purposes.

In the case of both 'exempt' sales and conversions carried out by property investment companies planning to hold on to the converted properties for letting purposes, the company will not be able to reclaim any VAT costs incurred.

However, many forms of conversion work are eligible for a reduced VAT rate of 5%, as opposed to the standard rate of 20%.

The reduced VAT rate of 5% is available in respect of any building work carried out on a residential property where the work results in a change to the number of dwellings in the property.

For example, this would apply to the conversion of:

- One house into several flats.
- Two or more flats into a single house.
- Two semi-detached houses into a single detached house.

The reduced rate also applies to work carried out to convert a commercial property into residential use and to renovation work on residential property which had been vacant for two years or more before the work commenced. The minimum vacant period was three years where work commenced before 1st January 2008.

Approved alterations to listed properties are eligible for zero-rating.

Property companies carrying out projects of this nature should ensure that they only pay the appropriate lower VAT rate from the outset, as it is difficult to recover any excess paid in error.

9.9   VAT FOR PROPERTY MANAGEMENT COMPANIES

Property management services are Standard Rated for VAT and hence a property management company will need to register for VAT if its annual supplies (i.e. sales) exceed the £70,000 registration threshold. It may still register voluntarily even if the level of its sales is below the threshold.

Whether the properties under the company's management are residential or commercial makes no difference for this purpose. Naturally, a property management company that is registered for VAT can recover the VAT on most of its business expenses. There are, however, a few exceptions where VAT cannot be recovered (*e.g. on the purchase of motor cars*).

9.10 INTERACTION WITH CORPORATION TAX

Any company that is registered for VAT should generally include only the net (i.e. excluding VAT) amounts of income and expenditure in its accounts. Where VAT recovery is barred or restricted (*e.g. on the provision of private fuel for directors or staff*), however, the additional cost arising may generally be claimed as an expense for Corporation Tax purposes.

A non-registered company should include the VAT in its business expenditure for Corporation Tax purposes.

Chapter 10

Saving Tax When You Extract Profits

10.1 PROFIT EXTRACTION PRINCIPLES

As I explained at the beginning of the guide, the need to extract profits from your property company (or, indeed, any company) poses a major drawback. This is why property companies generally work better if the owners do not continually draw out all or most of the profits.

Clearly, if you are able to retain all of the profits within the company, profit extraction is not a problem.

However, sooner or later, almost everyone will want to take something out of the company, or else there wouldn't be much point in having a property business in the first place!

There are two main methods for extracting profits from your own company:

- Paying yourself a salary or a bonus (i.e. employment income), or
- Paying yourself dividends

Where the owner has loaned funds to the company, there is also the option of charging interest on those funds. In many cases, interest charges now provide the most tax efficient method for extracting funds from the company where this option is available. We will look at this subject in more detail in Chapter 13.

The relative merits of salaries, bonuses, dividends and interest depend on the company's accounting date and profit level, as well as the recipient's own tax position. This complex issue is examined in detail in the Taxcafe.co.uk guide *'Salary versus Dividends'*.

10.2 SALARIES, ETC

Employment income is subject to Income Tax and to both employer's and employee's National Insurance.

Payments of wages, salaries or bonuses are deductible against the company's taxable profits for Corporation Tax purposes, as long as they are incurred for the benefit of the company's business. Some care needs to be taken, therefore, if you do decide to pay yourself, your spouse, your partner or any other members of your family, any wages or salaries, as no deduction will be available if there is no business justification for the payment.

In other words, yes, the recipient does have to actually work in the business!

Tax Tip

Subject to my comments above, payment of a salary equal to the primary National Insurance threshold (£7,225 for the 2011/12 tax year) to yourself, your spouse, your partner or another adult family member, can be a useful tax-planning measure, where justified.

10.3 DIVIDENDS

Dividends are subject to Income Tax at the following rates:

Basic rate taxpayers (total income up to £42,475):   10%
Higher rate taxpayers (total income £42,475 to £150,000): 32.5%
'Super tax' payers (total income over £150,000):   42.5%

(Using the tax bands for 2011/12 – see Appendix A)

However, before being taxed, most dividends must be grossed up for a non-refundable tax credit equal to one-ninth of the dividend paid. This tax credit can be set off against the Income Tax arising.

The net result of this rather complex system is that the **_effective_** rates of tax suffered on the net dividend **_received_** are as follows:

Basic rate taxpayers:	Nil
Higher rate taxpayers:	25%
'Super tax' payers:	36.1%

These effective rates apply to most dividends received from both UK and foreign companies. There is one exception, however. Where the recipient owns 10% or more of the share capital in a company which is resident in a 'tax haven', the tax credit does not apply. Such dividends are therefore simply taxed at the rates of 10%, 32.5% or 42.5%, as described above.

Dividends represent a distribution of a company's after-tax profits and no deduction is therefore allowed for Corporation Tax purposes.

No business justification is required for dividends, although company law does require distributable profits to be available.

Hence, subject to the comments that follow in the next section, having your spouse, partner or another adult family member as a shareholder in your company may be a useful tax-planning measure. (Note that dividends paid to minor children from their parent's own company will be treated as the parent's own income for tax purposes.)

Jointly Held Shares

Where shares are held jointly by husband and wife, it is no longer possible for the dividend income arising to be automatically split 50/50 for Income Tax purposes. The income must now be split according to the couple's actual beneficial entitlement to it. (See also Section 10.4 below for further possible dangers affecting 'husband and wife' companies.)

10.4 INCOME SHIFTING: THE GATHERING STORM?

A severe problem may lie ahead in the near future for many shareholders attempting to extract funds from their property company tax efficiently.

In yet another attack on the UK's small and medium-sized business sector, the previous Labour Government proposed to introduce 'income shifting' legislation designed to prevent families and couples from planning how to divide up their business income tax efficiently.

Thankfully, that proposed legislation did not make it onto the statute books before the May 2010 General Election. Furthermore, the new Coalition Government does not appear to have any immediate plans to introduce any similar measures.

Nevertheless, it is important to be aware of the potential dangers that may lie ahead. The issue at stake is not a political one and our change of Government does not mean that the problem has gone away for good. HM Revenue and Customs remains very eager to bring in some form of 'income shifting' legislation and it is still possible that it could be brought into force within the life of this Parliament.

Furthermore, despite the deferral of the legislation, some shareholders still face a risk of attack under current law, as we shall see later in this section, so this is no time for complacency on this issue.

Family businesses and couples in business together are the most likely targets of any future 'income shifting' legislation, although no-one may be safe from attack except for sole traders and other 'one man bands'.

In this guide we are, of course, concerned only with property companies, but it is possible that almost any company or partnership could be affected by future legislation on this issue.

The previous Government's proposed 'income-shifting' legislation was their attempt to write the final instalment in a long-running saga called 'Arctic Systems', which all sprang from an attack on some basic tax planning for a 'husband and wife' company.

Before we look at the wider implications of any possible future legislation, therefore, let's take a look at that original attack which sparked it all off.

Dividends to Spouses or Partners

Many companies are owned by couples. Since the introduction of 'separate taxation' in 1990, these 'husband and wife' companies have often provided a useful mechanism for doubling the amount of tax-free income that could be paid out as dividends. Each spouse or partner is entitled to their own personal allowance and basic rate tax band which, when combined, are available to shelter up to a total of £76,455 in dividends from Income Tax (at 2011/12 tax rates).

For many couples, be they married, unmarried, or in a civil partnership, owning and managing their own company, this strategy has worked well for many years and continues to work well today.

A few years ago, however, HM Revenue & Customs started attacking small 'husband and wife' companies.

In essence, they took a dislike to any tax planning which utilised the payment of dividends to a non-working spouse.

At first, HM Revenue & Customs' attack seemed to focus on any arrangements involving complex share structures which effectively enabled the spouse of the main controlling shareholder to receive dividend income without having any real involvement in the company or its business.

At one stage, it had therefore been thought that keeping the share structure to a single class of ordinary shares would avoid these problems.

Since the emergence of the 'Arctic Systems' case in 2004, however, this strategy has been under the threat of attack by HM Revenue & Customs whenever the company is owned by a couple and one spouse or partner does not carry out a fully active role in the company's business.

In this infamous case, HM Revenue & Customs argued that, by not taking a full commercial rate of salary out of the company, a taxpayer was making a settlement in favour of his partner who held shares in the company. Where a person makes a settlement in favour of another person, the income received by that other person can, under certain circumstances, be treated for tax purposes as belonging to the person who made the settlement.

The case involved a married couple, Mr and Mrs Jones, who held perfectly normal ordinary shares in their own company. However, because Mr Jones performed all the work that gave the company its profits, but did not receive a commercial rate of salary for that work, HM Revenue & Customs attempted to deem all of the dividend income to belong to him.

HM Revenue & Customs originally won the 'Arctic Systems' case in the High Court. Thankfully, however, the High Court decision was later overturned by both the Court of Appeal and the House of Lords.

Why then, is there still a risk?

Firstly, whilst the decision which was finally handed down in the House of Lords in 2007 was a well deserved victory for the taxpayers (and all our thanks must go to Mr & Mrs Jones for 'sticking it out' all the way to the Lords), sadly it was not quite a complete victory.

The Lords actually decided that the structure used in the Arctic Systems case *did* represent a settlement. The taxpayers only won due to a technical argument based on an exemption available to married couples and civil partners.

So, here's the quandary: so far, HM Revenue & Customs has been attacking married couples. Ultimately, they have lost, but, in doing so, part of their argument has been vindicated; they only lost because their intended victims were a married couple. What then, is there to stop them from now attacking unmarried couples, families and other people in business together?

Secondly, it was at this point that the previous Labour Government announced, almost before the ink was dry at the House of Lords, that new legislation would be introduced to reverse this decision.

142

One has to ask what on Earth the point was of a long, protracted and expensive legal case if the Government's intention all along was to change the law anyway. It's rather like a World Cup final going all the way to a penalty shoot-out only for FIFA to announce they were changing the rules so that the losers could win anyway. Talk about 'moving the goalposts'!

So, despite the House of Lords' decision, the 'Arctic Systems' saga may not be over yet. HM Revenue & Customs clearly has a strong objection to couples using companies to mitigate their tax bills through dividend payments to a non-working spouse and they intend to have their way at whatever price.

I just wonder how many poor couples HM Revenue & Customs will need to persecute before they've paid the legal fees for the 'Arctic Systems' case?

Potential Future Income Shifting Legislation

It still remains possible that HM Revenue & Customs will ultimately get their way, with future legislation enabling them to deem all of the dividends paid by a company owned by a couple to belong, for Income Tax purposes, to the person who is the main contributor to the day-to-day running of the business.

In fact, the draft legislation published in 2007 went much further than the Arctic Systems case and, if enacted, would have enabled HM Revenue and Customs to attack dividends received by **any person**.

That draft legislation would have empowered HM Revenue and Customs to deem dividends received by one person to belong, for Income Tax purposes, to another person whenever they perceived that dividends were being allocated in a 'non-commercial' way in order to reduce the total tax burden of the company owners.

The greatest problem with the draft legislation was that HM Revenue and Customs would have had the right to decide what a commercial payment was. This was truly preposterous since, as anyone in business knows, measuring the value of each person's input into the business is an extremely complex matter depending on a whole host of different factors, many of which are impossible to measure objectively.

143

In short, the proposed legislation was truly unworkable and in danger of creating some ludicrously unfair and unreasonable results.

On top of all this, the very suggestion that dividends need to be 'earned' was ridiculous in itself.

It seems that, in the previous Government's eyes, an investor in a company should only receive dividends if they actually work in the business!

In my view, this stance ran contrary to basic principles of UK law which have stood for well over a century. What the old Government was effectively saying was that a dividend is not, as it should be, a reward for investment but, instead, a reward for effort, like a salary.

For some reason, however, this peculiar attitude only seemed to apply to private companies. There did not appear to be any suggestion that all of the dividends paid by quoted companies needed to be allocated to their executive directors. There seemed to be one rule for 'The City' and another rule for poor hard-working small and medium-sized business owners!

Thankfully, as we know, that particular draft legislation was eventually shelved and it remains to be seen what form any future 'income-shifting' rules may take. If and when any such rules do come into force, however, they could cost some property company owners over £14,000 per year in extra Income Tax for **each** so-called non-working shareholder.

Example

Gavin is the managing director of Henson Developments Limited, a successful property development company making profits of over £200,000 per annum after paying Gavin's salary of £120,000.

Gavin owns 20% of the shares in the company. His wife Charlotte and his three sons John, Peter and Rhys also own 20% of the shares each and each of them has no other income of their own.

In 2012/13, the company pays a total dividend of £200,000, i.e. £40,000 to each shareholder.

Gavin will have an Income Tax bill of £11,444 on his dividend but each of the other shareholders will have a bill of just £443 (using forecast 2012/13 tax rates, as detailed in Appendix B).

Let us suppose, however, that HM Revenue and Customs deem the dividends paid to Charlotte, John, Peter and Rhys to belong to Gavin for Income Tax purposes under new income-shifting legislation coming into force with effect from 6th April 2012.

Gavin will now have to pay Income Tax at an effective rate of 36.1% on additional dividends of £160,000, increasing his tax bill by £57,778.

The additional cost to the family will therefore be a total of £56,006 (£57,778 – 4 x £443).

Implications for Property Companies

Given that the previous Government's attempt at this legislation was eventually abandoned, we cannot be sure what form any final version might take. However, it does appear that HM Revenue and Customs is out to cast its net pretty wide and will be hoping to catch married and unmarried couples alike, as well as many family companies and anyone else who catches their eye too!

Personally, I would tend to argue that property trading businesses, which carry a far higher degree of commercial risk than the sort of personal service company used by Mr & Mrs Jones in the Arctic Systems case, should not be subject to any income-shifting rules.

As far as property investment companies are concerned, these are, after all, investment companies and here one has to come back to the fact that a dividend is properly regarded as a return on investment and not a reward for effort. The imposition of any income-shifting legislation on a property investment company is therefore a truly ludicrous proposition.

Sadly, this is all just my opinion and time will tell just how widely any new rules will be drawn and, more importantly, how they will be applied in practice.

In the meantime, at least we have a bit of 'breathing space' before any future new rules can potentially come into force.

What Should We Do In the Meantime?

For the time being, married couples and civil partnerships might wish to 'make hay while the sun shines' and ensure that they make the most of the current position, safe in the knowledge that HM Revenue and Customs' attack in the Arctic Systems case has failed.

A little more caution is warranted for unmarried couples, family companies and others with their own property company, as there remain significant doubts over whether they are safe from attack under the current law.

Nevertheless, in all cases, it is possible that property company owners may not be free to plan their affairs as tax efficiently as possible without interference from HM Revenue and Customs for much longer. Hence, even those who are not protected by the Arctic Systems decision may well be better to make the most of things before any future new legislation can come into force.

Planning for the New Legislation

In the longer-term, property company owners may need to take precautions to avoid problems under whatever 'income shifting' rules we might end up with. Couples and families are likely to be exposed to the greatest risks.

The position is likely to depend on how much each shareholder is involved in the company's business.

Looking forward, therefore, the main tax-planning point for everyone with their own property company is to make sure that each shareholder is actively involved in the company's business.

Bear in mind here that Mrs Jones, the wife in the 'Arctic Systems' case, did work in the company's business in an administrative capacity and HM Revenue & Customs still chose to attack Mr Jones.

To be as safe as possible from attack, therefore, each shareholder really needs to be working 'at the coal face' in the actual operation of the company's business. For some property investment companies, however, there may not actually be very much 'coal face' type work to do. Nevertheless, each shareholder should still play as active a role as possible and should participate in key investment decisions.

It is also worth considering that we already have other legislation which deems a business partner to be 'non-active' when they work an average of less than ten hours per week in the partnership's business.

It is quite possible that the final version of any income-shifting legislation coming into force in the future may also deem shareholders to be 'non-active' when they work less than ten hours per week in the company's business.

Another potential safeguard from attack may therefore be to ensure that each shareholder is working an average of at least ten hours per week in the company's business. Again, however, this may not be practical in the case of many property investment companies.

Chapter 11

Personal vs Company Ownership

11.1 INTRODUCTION

In the previous chapters, we have worked through the principles of how a property company and its owners are taxed.

In the next two chapters, we will be looking in detail at the decision itself: "Should I run my property business through a company?"

Before we do that, however, we are going to take a look in this chapter at the comparative level of tax on a personal property investor or a company investing in property.

There are a great many different criteria which we could choose for our comparison; almost an infinite number, in fact.

However, in order to keep things down to a manageable size, we are just going to look at a few different scenarios that, I believe, should be sufficient to amply demonstrate the principles involved.

In this chapter, we will mostly be looking at income, starting with rental profits and then moving on to income that is classed as a trading profit. Once we get into capital gains, the situation becomes even more complicated and can only really be assessed through the use of detailed examples. This will form a major part of the next chapter.

It is important to remember, as you consider the tables shown in this chapter, that these only represent one-off annual 'snapshots' of the position. Whilst they do provide useful illustrations of the potential tax savings involved, I must urge you to also consider the more detailed and longer-term issues that we will be looking at in the next two chapters.

As explained in Section 2.5, Corporation Tax rates are currently undergoing a series of changes, which will continue until 2015 (although the rates applying to companies with profits not exceeding £300,000 are not currently expected to change after March 2012).

For any investor considering whether to invest in property through a company, it makes sense to consider the long-term position and, as explained in Section 2.5, our best estimate of the long-term position at present is to use the rates proposed for the year ending 31st March 2015 onwards.

Most of the tax calculations given in this chapter are therefore based on the Corporation Tax rates currently proposed for the year ending 31st March 2015 onwards (see Section 2.5) and on estimated 2014/15 tax rates for individuals (see Section 11.2 and Appendix B). These are the rates being used throughout this chapter unless specifically stated to the contrary.

In each of Sections 11.4 to 11.18 we will look at a different scenario and produce a set of conclusions for that scenario. The changes in tax rates that we are now expecting over the next few years mean that our conclusions will differ from one scenario to another. To get an overall picture of what is happening we will therefore also summarise those conclusions in Section 11.19 near the end of the chapter.

11.2   PERSONAL TAX CHANGES

We have already examined the Corporation Tax changes that are expected over the next few years in Section 2.5. However, before we can go on to look at our detailed calculations of the comparative levels of tax paid by individuals or property companies, we also need to take a look at how the personal tax regime is expected to change over the next few years.

As explained in the previous section, when comparing the position of a company investing in property with the position for a personal property investor, it makes sense for us to consider the long-term.

For the company's position this means using the Corporation Tax rates currently proposed for the year ending 31st March 2015 onwards.

To produce an appropriate comparative position for the personal property investor, we therefore need to produce a set of forecast personal tax rates for the tax year 2014/15.

As explained in the Foreword, most of the personal tax rates and allowances for 2011/12 have already been announced.

A number of proposed changes (or, in some cases, freezes) to the personal tax system for subsequent years have also been announced, including:

- The higher rate Income Tax threshold will be frozen at its 2011/12 level of £42,475 for both 2012/13 and 2013/14
- The Income Tax personal allowance will be increased to £10,000 by 2015/16

In producing our forecast future tax rates for individuals we have taken the above proposed changes into account and combined them with estimated inflationary increases using the principles explained in the Foreword.

The resultant forecast future tax rates are set out in Appendix B, where you will find our estimate of 2014/15 tax rates for individuals as used in the calculations set out in this chapter.

Too Theoretical For You?

For a long-term property investor, comparisons based on long-term forecast tax rates must be the most appropriate measure to use and this is why we take this approach in this guide.

For anyone concerned that this is all a bit too theoretical, however, a comparison of our forecast personal tax rates for 2014/15 in Appendix B with the actual rates for 2011/12 in Appendix A will reveal that the differences are not too significant.

In fact, if we were to use 2011/12 tax rates in this chapter instead, the impact on the savings arising by using a company would vary between an increase of £378 and a reduction of £73, in the case of rental income, and between an increase of £435 and a reduction of £123, in the case of trading profits, provided that the total income within the company does not exceed £300,000.

Hence, in general terms, all of the conclusions reached in this chapter remain equally valid in the short-term.

11.3 BALANCING ACT

One thing which is immediately obvious is that, from 1st April 2011, the rate of Corporation Tax paid by companies with profits not exceeding £300,000 will be the same as basic rate Income Tax: 20%.

Does this mean that there is never any advantage for basic rate taxpayers to invest in property via a company?

No, it doesn't!

For a start, as explained in Section 1.3, there are many non-tax reasons for using a company.

Furthermore, the different treatment of interest and finance costs (see Section 4.7) and rental losses (see Section 4.8) in a company provide many further benefits.

For property businesses classed as trades, the situation is also very different due to the additional impact of National Insurance. We will be looking at this in detail in Sections 11.11 to 11.17.

On top of all this, there is also the question of whether the property income might itself push the investor's total income over the higher rate threshold. We will look at this situation in Section 11.6.

So, the only thing we can say for certain about this 'balancing act' is that investors with a profitable property business that is not classed as a trade, and who are unlikely to ever pay higher rate Income Tax, will not gain any advantage from using a company.

11.4 RENTAL PROFITS KEPT IN THE COMPANY

In this section, we will start out with the simplest situation. Here, we look at the tax burden on an individual who is already a higher rate taxpayer receiving additional rental income on top of their existing income. We then compare the individual's tax burden on their additional rental income with the tax that would have been paid by a company set up to run their property portfolio.

For the time being, in this section, we are also assuming that all profits are retained within the company.

Annual Rental Profits	Tax Paid Personally	Tax Paid By Company	Tax Saving
£5,000	£2,000	£1,000	£1,000
£10,000	£4,000	£2,000	£2,000
£25,000	£10,000	£5,000	£5,000
£50,000	£20,000	£10,000	£10,000
£100,000	£43,746	£20,000	£23,746
£200,000	£93,746	£40,000	£53,746

Assumptions

In this scenario, it is assumed that:

i)   The company does not have any associated companies (see Section 16.4).
ii) The company's accounting period is of twelve months' duration.
iii) Company profits are retained in the company (i.e. nothing is paid out to the individual investor).
iv) The individual has £50,000 of other taxable income for the same tax year. Most of the results given above would be the same for many other higher rate taxpayers: differences only arise when the individual's total taxable income (including the rental profits set out above) lies between £100,000 and £118,730 or exceeds £150,000.

152

The individual's 'other income', as per point (iv) above, could consist of employment income, partnership or self-employment trading income, interest, pensions or private rental income from an existing personal property portfolio. Where the 'other income' includes interest income, additional savings of up to £285 (at estimated 2014/15 rates) could arise in a few rare instances.

If part of the individual's 'other income' consists of dividend income, however, we would get slightly different results, producing an even greater saving when the company is used in some cases.

Conclusions

As we can see from the table, the company pays a much lower rate of tax on its rental profits, producing significant savings for the higher rate taxpayer investor. From 2011/12 onwards, the Corporation Tax rate applying to a company's first £300,000 of annual profits will be 20%. This produces a saving of 20% when compared with rental income received directly by a higher rate taxpayer individual, rising to a saving of 30% when the individual's total income would otherwise exceed £150,000.

An additional saving of up to £3,746 is also achieved whenever the individual's total income would have exceeded £100,000 were it not for the company. This is because, by using a company, the individual can keep their personal taxable income below £100,000 and thus retain their personal allowance (estimated at £9,365 for 2014/15).

If the company's profits exceed £300,000, the saving on any excess profits will reduce to 25% (25% versus 50%) until profits reach £1.5m, at which point the saving amounts to 26% (24% versus 50%) on all further profits. (At 2014/15 rates - refer to Section 2.5 for a reminder of all the Corporation Tax rates applying.)

To the extent that the individual has dividend income within their first £44,000 of 'other income' in 2014/15, the savings are increased by 2.5%. The principles behind these additional savings are explored in the Taxcafe.co.uk guide 'How to Save Tax 2010/2011'.

All of these conclusions, however, are based on the fact that no part of the company's profits are being extracted; neither as salary, dividend, nor by any other means. For an investor whose existing income in 2014/15 is already at least £44,000, this is not entirely unreasonable, although the day must surely come when they will wish to extract some profits. This is something that we will be exploring in the next chapter.

In the next section, however, we will look at the position for those who cannot wait so long.

11.5 RENTAL PROFITS EXTRACTED FROM THE COMPANY

Here we are looking at the position for a higher rate taxpayer who extracts all of the company's profits as dividends. This time, the 'Tax Paid via Company' column summarises the total tax burden using the company route, including both the Corporation Tax payable by the company and the individual's Income Tax on the dividends received.

Assumptions (i), (ii) and (iv), as detailed in the previous section, remain the same.

You will see that extracting all of the profits will generally eliminate the savings that we saw in the previous section.

Annual Rental Profits	Tax Paid Personally	Tax Paid via Company	Tax Saving
£5,000	£2,000	£2,000	£0
£10,000	£4,000	£4,000	£0
£25,000	£10,000	£10,000	£0
£50,000	£20,000	£20,000	£0
£100,000	£43,746	£43,746	£0
£200,000	£93,746	£91,524	£2,222

Conclusions

The above table demonstrates the fact that using a property investment company is generally of no value, as far as tax is concerned, where all profits are simply being extracted as

154

dividends each year. Only those whose total income would otherwise exceed £150,000 would still achieve any saving.

Once rental profits exceed £300,000 per annum, the use of a company would actually start to produce an overall cost if profits were still being wholly extracted as dividends each year.

Hopefully, however, most people would not need to extract this level of dividend from their company.

Wealth Warning

If dividends are paid without there being supporting accounts available to show that the company had sufficient distributable profits (**after tax**) at that time, they are illegal under company law. 'Illegal' dividends may then be treated as salary, resulting in Income Tax and National Insurance at a combined total rate of at least 42% (from 6th April 2011) for a higher rate taxpayer, plus a further 13.8% in National Insurance for the company.

In reality, therefore, it is usually best not to extract all of the company's after-tax profits as dividends every year.

It is also important to ensure that the company quite clearly has sufficient distributable profits before any dividend is paid and has the necessary supporting accounts to demonstrate this fact. Supporting accounts would generally consist of either the previous year's statutory accounts or up to date management accounts (e.g. to the end of the previous calendar month).

Documentation minuting the payment of a dividend is also advisable.

11.6   BASIC RATE TAXPAYERS WITH RENTAL PROFITS

In this section, we will look at the position for basic rate taxpayers who already have other annual income in 2014/15 of £15,000, £25,000 or £35,000.

In each case, we will look at the tax arising on additional rental profits received by those taxpayers and compare it with the Corporation Tax payable in a property investment company.

We assume all of the company's profits are being retained. Assumptions (i) and (ii) and the points made regarding the different types of 'other income' in Section 11.4 also apply here.

Annual Rental Profits	Tax Paid Personally with Other Income of:			Tax Paid By Company
	£15,000	£25,000	£35,000	
£5,000	£1,000	£1,000	£1,000	£1,000
£10,000	£2,000	£2,000	£2,200	£2,000
£15,000	£3,000	£3,000	£4,200	£3,000
£20,000	£4,000	£4,200	£6,200	£4,000
£25,000	£5,000	£6,200	£8,200	£5,000
£30,000	£6,200	£8,200	£10,200	£6,000
£40,000	£10,200	£12,200	£14,200	£8,000
£50,000	£14,200	£16,200	£18,200	£10,000
£100,000	£37,200	£39,946	£41,946	£20,000
£200,000	£84,446	£87,446	£90,446	£40,000

Annual Rental Profits	Tax Saving with Other Income of:		
	£15,000	£25,000	£35,000
£5,000	£0	£0	£0
£10,000	£0	£0	£200
£15,000	£0	£0	£1,200
£20,000	£0	£200	£2,200
£25,000	£0	£1,200	£3,200
£30,000	£200	£2,200	£4,200
£40,000	£2,200	£4,200	£6,200
£50,000	£4,200	£6,200	£8,200
£100,000	£17,200	£19,946	£21,946
£200,000	£44,446	£47,446	£50,446

Conclusions

The tables above clearly show that a profitable property investment company is of no benefit to a basic rate taxpayer even when they are willing to keep profits in the company.

However, once the individual's total income reaches the higher rate tax threshold, the company becomes beneficial due to the 20% tax saving explained in Section 11.4.

Hence, whilst the company is of no benefit to basic rate taxpayers, it begins to prove its worth once the combined total annual income of company and individual exceeds the critical higher rate tax threshold (which we estimate at £44,000 for 2014/15).

Tax Tip

The obvious conclusion is that a basic rate taxpayer investor should not start using a property investment company until their own personal income reaches the higher rate tax threshold.

In an ideal world, therefore, an investor should begin by investing in property personally until the additional rental profits bring their own personal income up to the level of the higher rate tax threshold.

Thereafter, any further investments should be made via a company – but only if the profits do not need to be withdrawn from the company every year.

In practice, of course, it will be difficult to follow this strategy precisely, since the investor's rental profits and other income are likely to vary from year to year and the higher rate tax threshold will also continue to change. In Section 11.8, we will be looking at a good compromise solution to use when it has not been possible to follow the above advice exactly.

The advice per the above 'Tax Tip' is also based on the assumption that the property business will yield rental profits. Where losses are arising, the situation is very different and a review of Sections 4.7 and 4.8 will quickly reveal the advantages that a company will provide in these circumstances.

11.7 BASIC RATE TAXPAYERS EXTRACTING PROFITS

We will now look at the position where our three basic rate taxpayers, as outlined in the previous section, extract all of their property investment company's profits as dividends each year. All other assumptions, as set out in Section 11.4, remain the same. As in Section 11.5, the term 'Tax Paid Via Company' now includes both Corporation Tax and the Income Tax payable on dividends received. For the comparative 'Tax Paid Personally' figures, just refer back to the previous section, as these are unaltered.

Annual Rental Profits	Tax Paid Via Company When Investor Has Other Income of:		
	£15,000	£25,000	£35,000
£5,000	£1,000	£1,000	£1,000
£10,000	£2,000	£2,000	£2,000
£15,000	£3,000	£3,000	£3,975
£20,000	£4,000	£4,000	£5,975
£25,000	£5,000	£5,725	£7,975
£30,000	£6,000	£7,725	£9,975
£40,000	£9,475	£11,725	£13,975
£50,000	£13,475	£15,725	£17,975
£100,000	£34,301	£38,676	£41,955
£200,000	£81,733	£84,983	£88,233

Annual Rental Profits	Overall Tax Saving When Investor Has Other Income of:		
	£15,000	£25,000	£35,000
£5,000	£0	£0	£0
£10,000	£0	£0	£200
£15,000	£0	£0	£225
£20,000	£0	£200	£225
£25,000	£0	£475	£225
£30,000	£200	£475	£225
£40,000	£725	£475	£225
£50,000	£725	£475	£225
£100,000	£2,899	£1,270	-£9
£200,000	£2,713	£2,463	£2,213

Conclusions

As before, the company produces no savings where the individual would have remained a basic rate taxpayer if they had received all of their rental profits personally.

There are some small savings in most of the cases where the individual would have been a higher rate taxpayer if they had received all of their rental profits personally but the amounts involved are generally too small to be worth any serious consideration (bearing in mind that there are additional costs involved in setting up and running a company, as we shall explore in later chapters).

The one-ninth tax credit on dividends (see Section 10.3) and the withdrawal of personal allowances for those with income over £100,000 combine together to produce a few quirks for those with total income around the £100,000 to £120,000 level and, as we can see from the table, can actually result in a small overall tax cost in some cases.

It is only once the total income (including the rental profits in the company) starts to exceed £150,000 that there is any significant benefit in using a company under these circumstances. Even then, the extraction of all of the company's after-tax profits as dividends still wipes out most of the advantage which we saw in Section 11.6.

In summary therefore, and subject to the points made in Section 11.3, basic rate taxpayers wishing to extract all of the profits from their property investment or letting business should **not** generally invest in property via a company unless they expect total annual income well in excess of £150,000.

11.8 MAKING THE MOST OF THE BASIC RATE TAX BAND

Previous sections have effectively told us that it is not generally worth using a property investment company when the owner wishes to extract *all* of the company's profits each year.

However, a basic rate taxpayer can extract *some* dividends from a company tax free. This is achieved by restricting the dividends paid to a maximum of 9/10ths of the taxpayer's remaining basic rate tax band after accounting for their other income.

The restriction to 9/10ths of the available basic rate tax band must be made to cater for the 'tax credit' of one-ninth, which is attached to a dividend received. As a result of this 'tax credit', every £9 of dividend income that you actually receive is treated as £10 of taxable income.

The maximum amount of tax-free dividends receivable by our three basic rate taxpayers are set out below. On this occasion, we are using the tax rates prevailing for the tax years 2011/12 to 2013/14.

Other Income	Basic Rate Tax Band Remaining		Maximum Tax-Free Dividend
£15,000	£27,475	x 9/10 =	£24,727
£25,000	£17,475	x 9/10 =	£15,727
£35,000	£7,475	x 9/10 =	£6,727

Where a basic rate taxpayer restricts the level of dividends withdrawn to these levels, they will avoid any Income Tax on the profits withdrawn from the company.

Barring any further major changes to the UK tax regime, taxpayers following a similar strategy in the future should continue to enjoy the overall tax savings shown in Section 11.6.

Hence, where the level of profit in the company is considerably greater than the amount that the investor wishes to extract from the company each year, the company does remain fairly beneficial overall. It won't be as good as following the ideal scenario suggested in the 'Tax Tip' given at the end of Section 11.6 but, in practice, with fluctuating levels of rental profit and other income, it does represent a good compromise.

11.9   INVESTORS WITH NO OTHER INCOME

The tax burden for 2014/15 on an individual or a company receiving rental income only (and having no other taxable income or gains) may be compared as follows:

Annual Rental Profits	Tax Paid Personally	Tax Paid By Company	Tax Saving
£5,000	£0	£1,000	-£1,000
£10,000	£127	£2,000	-£1,873
£15,000	£1,127	£3,000	-£1,873
£20,000	£2,127	£4,000	-£1,873
£25,000	£3,127	£5,000	-£1,873
£30,000	£4,127	£6,000	-£1,873
£40,000	£6,127	£8,000	-£1,873
£50,000	£9,327	£10,000	-£673
£100,000	£29,327	£20,000	£9,327
£200,000	£78,073	£40,000	£38,073

Assumptions

In this scenario, it is assumed that:

i)   The company does not have any associated companies (see Section 16.4).
ii) The company's accounting period is of twelve months' duration.
iii) The individual is not entitled to any additional allowances, other than the normal personal allowance.
iv) Company profits are retained.

Conclusions

This table suggests that, where the taxpayer has no other income, a property investment company will actually be detrimental to their overall tax position until total annual rental profits reach more than £50,000. (In fact, our current estimate of the required profit level before the company becomes beneficial for 2014/15 is £53,400.)

11.10 THE 'OPTIMUM SCENARIO'

This scenario is what one might call the 'best of both worlds', where we use the lessons from the previous sections in this chapter to produce an optimum position for a taxpayer with no other income using a property investment company.

Here I am assuming that the investor follows the 'Tax Tip' at the end of Section 11.6 and begins by building a property portfolio which yields an annual rental profit exactly equal to the higher rate tax threshold.

Thereafter, any further investments are made through a property investment company and the profits arising are retained within the company.

For 2014/15, we estimate that such an investor will already have net income after tax of £37,073 from their personal property portfolio.

Naturally, this strategy is only relevant once total annual rental profits begin to exceed the higher rate tax threshold (which we estimate at £44,000 for 2014/15).

Annual Rental Profits	Tax Paid Personally	Tax Paid using Company	Tax Saving
£50,000	£9,327	£8,127	£1,200
£75,000	£19,327	£13,127	£6,200
£100,000	£29,327	£18,127	£11,200
£200,000	£78,073	£38,127	£39,946

'Annual Rental Profits' refers to the total profits received by both the individual and the company. 'Tax Paid using Company' means the total tax burden, i.e. the total of the Income Tax paid by the investor and the Corporation Tax paid by the company.

The assumptions set out in the previous section also apply here.

Conclusion

The above table reflects the same savings for higher rate taxpayers which we discussed in Section 11.4. The company produces a saving of 20% where total profits are between £44,000 and £150,000 and 30% thereafter.

As before, an additional saving of up to £3,746 also arises whenever the total income exceeds £100,000 since, by using a company, the individual is able to retain their personal allowance (estimated at £9,365 for 2014/15).

11.11 TRADING PROFITS

Having covered rental profits, we will now look at the same comparison where the income from the property business is treated as trading income.

This makes no difference to the rates of Corporation Tax applying. The individual's tax position is significantly altered, however, due to the fact that National Insurance (both Class 2 and Class 4) is payable where this income is received personally (unless the individual is over state retirement age – see Section 11.20).

For our first trading scenario, we will consider the position where the taxpayer is already a higher rate taxpayer in 2014/15.

Annual Trading Profits	Tax Paid Personally	Tax Paid by Company	Tax Saving
£5,000	£2,000	£1,000	£1,000
£10,000	£4,325	£2,000	£2,325
£25,000	£10,648	£5,000	£5,648
£50,000	£21,148	£10,000	£11,148
£100,000	£45,894	£20,000	£25,894
£200,000	£97,894	£40,000	£57,894

Assumptions

In this scenario, it is assumed that:

i) The company does not have any associated companies (see Section 16.4).
ii) The company's accounting period is of twelve months' duration.
iii) Company profits are retained in the company (i.e. nothing is paid out to the individual investor).
iv) The individual has £50,000 of other taxable income, of which at least £44,000 is employment income.
v) The individual is under state retirement age on 5th April 2015.

As far as point (iv) is concerned, most of the results given above would be the same for most other higher rate taxpayers with employment income of at least £44,000: differences would only arise where the individual's total taxable income (including the trading profits set out above) lay between £100,000 and £118,730 or exceeded £150,000.

The results would also be broadly the same for an individual with existing partnership or self-employed trading income of at least £44,000 instead of employment income. (Where the additional trading profit, as above, is £5,000, the 'Tax Paid Personally' would be £100 more, at £10,000 it would be £125 less and in all other cases it would be £148 less)

The results given above are also based on restrictions to the total amount of National Insurance due which apply where an individual has both employment income and self-employment trading income. In practice, a claim will usually be necessary to ensure that these restrictions are applied.

Conclusions

The table above clearly indicates that using a company will be beneficial where the individual investor already has sufficient other income to make them a higher rate taxpayer.

From 2011/12 onwards, a higher rate taxpayer will save tax at 22% by using a company to run their property trading business (give or take a little bit of National Insurance).

This saving increases to 32% when the total income received by both the individual and the company reaches £150,000 and, as usual, there is an additional saving of up to £3,746 (at our estimated rates for 2014/15) whenever the total income exceeds £100,000.

In all, this means that **a company has the potential to provide a greater advantage where the underlying business is classed as a trade.**

Once annual profits begin to exceed £300,000, the saving (from 2014/15 onwards) will drop to 27% on the excess until profits of £1.5m per annum are reached. Thereafter, the saving on all further profits will amount to 28%.

It is important to remember, however, that these results are based on the assumption that no part of the company's profits is paid out to the company's owner.

11.12 TRADERS WITH RENTAL INCOME

In the previous section, we looked at individuals with sufficient employment income or partnership or self-employed trading income to make them a higher rate taxpayer.

In this section, we will consider the position where the individual's 'other income', which already makes them a higher rate taxpayer, is rental income.

The table below compares the position where that same individual also receives property trading income with the position where a company is used to receive the trading income.

All other assumptions, as set out in the previous section, remain the same.

Annual Trading Profits	Tax Paid Personally	Tax Paid by Company	Tax Saving
£5,000	£2,000	£1,000	£1,000
£10,000	£4,325	£2,000	£2,325
£25,000	£11,675	£5,000	£6,675
£50,000	£23,505	£10,000	£13,505
£100,000	£48,251	£20,000	£28,251
£200,000	£100,251	£40,000	£60,251

Conclusions

The savings demonstrated in the previous section generally become even greater when the trading income would be fully liable for National Insurance in the individual taxpayer's own hands.

Furthermore, a comparison of this table with the one in Section 11.4 shows that a taxpayer with both rental income and trading profits will save more tax by placing the trading activities into a company (if it should happen to be a question of one or the other). This is also easier to achieve in the case of an existing business, as we shall see in Chapter 15.

The results in this section would remain the same if the taxpayer's other income which already makes them a higher rate taxpayer, was pension income. They would also generally be the same where the other income is interest income, although additional savings of up to £285 (at estimated 2014/15 rates) may arise in a few instances.

Additional savings of 2.5% would also arise to the extent that the other income was dividend income in some cases.

11.13 TRADING PROFITS EXTRACTED FROM THE COMPANY

In Section 11.5 we saw that the extraction of profits from the company by way of dividend was highly detrimental in the case of a property investment company with rental income.

The table below sets out the position for a property trading company. As before, 'Tax Paid Via Company' includes both Corporation Tax and the Income Tax payable by the individual receiving the dividends. Apart from the extraction of profit by way of dividend, this scenario is based on the same set of assumptions as used in the previous section.

Annual Trading Profits	Tax Paid Personally	Tax Paid Via Company	Tax Saving
£5,000	£2,000	£2,000	£0
£10,000	£4,325	£4,000	£325
£25,000	£11,675	£10,000	£1,675
£50,000	£23,505	£20,000	£3,505
£100,000	£48,251	£43,746	£4,505
£200,000	£100,251	£91,524	£8,727

Conclusions

Again, the payment of all profits to the individual by way of dividend has drastically reduced the benefit of the property company. Nevertheless, as soon as the trading profits exceed the National Insurance primary threshold (estimated at £8,035 for 2014/15), a higher rate taxpayer whose other income consists of rental income, pension income, interest or dividends, does continue to benefit from the use of a company to run his or her property trade.

This benefit arises because such an individual's total effective tax rate on trading profits between £8,035 and £44,000 earned as a sole trader would be 49% (40% Income Tax plus 9% National Insurance), plus an extra £148 in Class 2 National Insurance.

From the year ending 31st March 2012 onwards, the total effective tax rate suffered when a higher rate taxpayer uses a company to run a property trade, but pays all the after-tax profits out as dividends, will be 40% (20% Corporation Tax plus Income Tax at an effective rate of 25% on the remaining 80%, i.e. a further 20%).

Hence, provided that the individual's total taxable income remains below £150,000, a saving of 9% arises (subject to a few quirks which arise where total taxable income is between £100,000 and £118,730, as we saw in Section 11.7).

Once trading profits exceed the higher rate tax threshold (estimated at £44,000 for 2014/15), the saving drops to 2% on any additional profits since the rate of National Insurance payable if the individual had run the trade personally would also have dropped to 2%. However, the rate of saving rallies again when the total combined income for the individual and the company exceeds £150,000. At this point the individual would have been paying 52% on any further trading profits received personally (50% Income Tax plus 2% National Insurance). By using a company but extracting the after-tax profits as dividends, the total effective tax rate is 48.9% (20% Corporation Tax plus Income Tax at an effective rate of 36.1% on the remaining 80%, i.e. 28.9%), thus leaving a saving of 3.1%.

Once the company's profits exceed £300,000, the saving disappears and this strategy would begin to yield a small overall tax cost. Hopefully, however, not many people with other income of at least £44,000 will also need to extract dividends of more than £240,000 as well.

For those whose other income consists of employment income or partnership or self-employment trading income, the savings under this scenario are generally the same as above, except that they will not enjoy the initial 9% saving described for trading profits between £8,035 and £44,000. Instead, they will generally start with a 2% saving, as described above, followed by the other saving rates set out above (give or take a few minor differences in the amount of National Insurance saved).

Readers should again refer back to the Wealth Warning given in Section 11.5 if considering trying to extract all annual profits by way of dividend.

11.14 BASIC RATE TRADERS

As with rental income, we will now examine the position for basic rate taxpayers receiving property trading income either directly or via a company. We will assume that their other income comprises rental profits and that they will restrict any dividends taken out of the company to the amounts set out in Section 11.8, so that no Income Tax is payable on them.

Annual Trading Profits	Tax Paid Personally with Other Income of:			Tax Paid Via Company
	£15,000	£25,000	£35,000	
£5,000	£1,000	£1,000	£1,000	£1,000
£10,000	£2,325	£2,325	£2,525	£2,000
£15,000	£3,775	£3,775	£4,975	£3,000
£20,000	£5,225	£5,425	£7,425	£4,000
£25,000	£6,675	£7,875	£9,875	£5,000
£30,000	£8,325	£10,325	£12,325	£6,000
£40,000	£13,225	£15,225	£17,225	£8,000
£50,000	£17,705	£19,705	£21,705	£10,000
£100,000	£41,705	£44,451	£46,451	£20,000
£200,000	£90,951	£93,951	£96,951	£40,000

Annual Trading Profits	Tax Saving with Other Income of:		
	£15,000	£25,000	£35,000
£5,000	£0	£0	£0
£10,000	£325	£325	£525
£15,000	£775	£775	£1,975
£20,000	£1,225	£1,425	£3,425
£25,000	£1,675	£2,875	£4,875
£30,000	£2,325	£4,325	£6,325
£40,000	£5,225	£7,225	£9,225
£50,000	£7,705	£9,705	£11,705
£100,000	£21,705	£24,451	£26,451
£200,000	£50,951	£53,951	£56,951

Conclusion

The property trading company continues to be beneficial for basic rate taxpayers.

This is because, from 2011/12 onwards, basic rate taxpayers will suffer a total effective tax rate of 29% (20% Income Tax plus 9% National Insurance) on trading profits in excess of the primary National Insurance threshold. This is 9% more than the Corporation Tax rate on the same income.

The benefit increases once the total of the trading profits taken together with the investor's other income exceeds the higher rate tax threshold. This benefit is preserved by restricting any dividends to the levels set out in Section 11.8.

11.15 TRADERS WITH ALTERNATIVE FORMS OF INCOME

As explained in Section 11.12, the savings shown in the previous section will be exactly the same when the taxpayer's other income comprises pension income, and possibly slightly greater when it includes interest or dividend income.

Where the taxpayer's other income is employment income or partnership or self-employed trading income, the savings achieved may be either a little more or a little less than those shown in the previous section, depending on the exact circumstances involved.

Where the taxpayer's other income is wholly made up of partnership or self-employed trading income, the position will be as set out in the table below. We will cover employment income in the next section.

As before, it is assumed here that any dividends are restricted to the amounts calculated in Section 11.8.

Annual Trading Profits	Tax Paid Personally with Other Income of:			Tax Paid Via Company
	£15,000	**£25,000**	**£35,000**	
£5,000	£1,450	£1,450	£1,450	£1,000
£10,000	£2,900	£2,900	£3,030	£2,000
£15,000	£4,350	£4,350	£5,130	£3,000
£20,000	£5,800	£5,930	£7,230	£4,000
£25,000	£7,250	£8,030	£9,330	£5,000
£30,000	£8,830	£10,130	£11,430	£6,000
£40,000	£13,030	£14,330	£15,630	£8,000
£50,000	£17,230	£18,530	£19,830	£10,000
£100,000	£41,230	£43,276	£44,576	£20,000
£200,000	£90,476	£92,776	£95,076	£40,000

Annual Trading Profits	Tax Saving with Other Income of:		
	£15,000	**£25,000**	**£35,000**
£5,000	£450	£450	£450
£10,000	£900	£900	£1,030
£15,000	£1,350	£1,350	£2,130
£20,000	£1,800	£1,930	£3,230
£25,000	£2,250	£3,030	£4,330
£30,000	£2,830	£4,130	£5,430
£40,000	£5,030	£6,330	£7,630
£50,000	£7,230	£8,530	£9,830
£100,000	£21,230	£23,276	£24,576
£200,000	£50,476	£52,776	£55,076

Conclusion

Under this new scenario a trading company produces significant savings for basic rate taxpayers with other trading income.

11.16 TRADERS WITH EMPLOYMENT INCOME

Where the basic rate taxpayer with a property trade also has employment income, the position will be as set out below.

Annual Trading Profits	Tax Paid Personally with Other Income of:			Tax Paid Via Company
	£15,000	£25,000	£35,000	
£5,000	£1,000	£1,000	£1,000	£1,000
£10,000	£2,325	£2,325	£2,525	£2,000
£15,000	£3,775	£3,775	£4,975	£3,000
£20,000	£5,225	£5,425	£7,425	£4,000
£25,000	£6,675	£7,875	£9,748	£5,000
£30,000	£8,325	£10,325	£11,848	£6,000
£40,000	£13,225	£15,048	£16,048	£8,000
£50,000	£17,705	£19,248	£20,248	£10,000
£100,000	£41,705	£43,994	£44,994	£20,000
£200,000	£90,951	£93,494	£95,494	£40,000

Annual Trading Profits	Tax Saving with Other Income of:		
	£15,000	£25,000	£35,000
£5,000	£0	£0	£0
£10,000	£325	£325	£525
£15,000	£775	£775	£1,975
£20,000	£1,225	£1,425	£3,425
£25,000	£1,675	£2,875	£4,748
£30,000	£2,325	£4,325	£5,848
£40,000	£5,225	£7,048	£8,048
£50,000	£7,705	£9,248	£10,248
£100,000	£21,705	£23,994	£24,994
£200,000	£50,951	£53,494	£55,494

The above table is based on the same assumptions as the previous two sections except for the fact that the individual's other income arises wholly from employment.

It is also assumed that the claim to restrict the total amount of National Insurance payable by the individual, as discussed in Section 11.11, would be made where appropriate.

Conclusion

A property trading company produces significant savings for basic rate taxpayers with employment income where the trading profits exceed the National Insurance primary threshold (£7,225 for 2011/12 and estimated at £8,035 for 2014/15).

11.17 TRADERS WITH NO OTHER INCOME

We will assume here that the individual has no other income and that company profits are distributed in the most beneficial way, as follows:

- An amount equal to the National Insurance primary threshold (estimated at £8,035 for 2014/15) is paid out as salary. This gives rise to a small amount of employer's National Insurance for the company (estimated at £25) but is otherwise received tax-free by the individual and provides Corporation Tax relief in the company (subject to the 'Wealth Warning' below).
- Dividends are restricted to the maximum level that can be paid out tax free. We estimate the maximum tax-free dividend that can be paid in 2014/15 under these circumstances to be £32,368. (This amount represents $9/10^{ths}$ of the amount by which the estimated higher rate tax threshold for 2014/15 exceeds the salary paid to the individual – see Section 11.8 for an explanation of the principles involved.)

These amounts of dividend and salary should ensure that the individual remains beneath the higher rate Income Tax threshold. The recipient shareholder would theoretically (but see the warning below) have no Income Tax or National Insurance to pay, while having total annual income of up to £40,403 (at estimated 2014/15 rates).

Where there are not actually sufficient profits available for the company to pay these optimum amounts of salary and dividend, we will assume that only the amount available is paid out (with salary being paid in preference to dividend).

As usual, 'Tax Paid Via Company' refers to the total tax burden using the company route. All other assumptions remain the same.

Annual Trading Profits	Tax Paid Personally	Tax Paid Via Company	Tax Saving
£5,000	£0	£0	£0
£10,000	£452	£413	£39
£15,000	£1,902	£1,413	£489
£20,000	£3,352	£2,413	£939
£25,000	£4,802	£3,413	£1,389
£30,000	£6,252	£4,413	£1,839
£40,000	£9,152	£6,413	£2,739
£50,000	£12,832	£8,413	£4,419
£100,000	£33,832	£18,413	£15,419
£200,000	£84,578	£38,413	£46,165

Conclusions

Where the taxpayer has no other income, a property trading company will start to produce an advantage once the trading profits exceed around £10,000.

Comparing the above results with those shown in Sections 11.9 and 11.10 also demonstrates that a property trading company produces better savings than a property investment company.

Wealth Warning

HM Revenue and Customs may try to argue that the salary was not paid for the benefit of the business and is thus not deductible for Corporation Tax purposes. This should not present a problem, however, where the taxpayer is able to demonstrate that they are actively involved in the company's business.

As explained in Section 11.5, HM Revenue and Customs may also look to see if the company had the necessary supporting accounts to prove that it had adequate distributable profits at the time of every dividend payment. Meeting these exacting requirements in practice may be difficult.

Detailed advice on the payment of salary or dividends is contained in the Taxcafe.co.uk guide *'Salary versus Dividends'*.

11.18 CAPITAL GAINS

For our final scenario in this chapter, we will take a quick look at the difference in the tax on a typical capital gain on a property held by an individual investor or by a property investment company. In this scenario, we will assume the following:

i)   The property is sold in March 2015, producing a total gain before exemptions and reliefs equal to the amount shown in the first column below.

ii) The gain arising is equal to 50% of the property's purchase price.

iii) The individual investor is a higher rate taxpayer.

iv) The gain does not qualify for entrepreneurs' relief.

v)   The indexation relief rate over the relevant period is 25%.

vi) Neither the company, nor the individual investor, have made any other capital gains during the same period.

vii) No other reliefs or exemptions are available to either the individual or the company.

viii) The company's total taxable income for the period, including this capital gain, will not exceed £300,000.

ix) The company does not have any associated companies (see Section 16.4).

x)   The company's accounting period is twelve months in duration.

xi) Company profits are retained.

Capital Gain Before Reliefs	Tax Paid Personally	Tax Paid By Company	Tax Saving
£10,000	£0	£1,000	-£1,000
£25,000	£3,696	£2,500	£1,196
£50,000	£10,696	£5,000	£5,696
£100,000	£24,696	£10,000	£14,696
£200,000	£52,696	£20,000	£32,696

Naturally, all of this is rather contrived, but it is perhaps the best that we can come up with by way of a simple illustration of the impact of the different tax regimes.

The company benefits in two ways:

i)   It pays Corporation Tax on capital gains at just 20% (provided its total income and gains for the accounting period do not exceed £300,000)
ii)   It is eligible for indexation relief

By contrast, the individual's only advantage is that they have an annual Capital Gains Tax exemption (estimated at £11,800 for 2014/15).

As a result, whilst the individual is better off with a small capital gain, the company is more advantageous for larger capital gains. In this scenario, based on the assumptions set out above, the company produces savings whenever the gain exceeds £18,355.

Basic rate taxpayer individuals pay Capital Gains Tax at a lower rate (see Section 7.2). Individual investors can also save Capital Gains Tax through joint ownership (so that two ACGTEXs are available).

These factors can mean that it takes a slightly greater capital gain before the company is beneficial. Keeping all of the other assumptions set out above the same, the amount of capital gain required before the company becomes beneficial is as follows:

- Individual owner with income not exceeding the personal allowance: £26,551
- Joint owners, both higher rate taxpayers: £36,712
- Joint owners, both with income not exceeding the personal allowance: £53,101

Although the company pays tax on capital gains at a higher rate than basic rate taxpayers, these figures prove that the impact of indexation relief means that, for large enough capital gains, the company is always likely to be beneficial.

It is important to remember, however, that no account has been taken here of the potential additional tax costs involved in extracting the sale proceeds from the company, nor the additional Corporation Tax arising when the company's total profits and capital gains for the accounting period exceed £300,000.

We will look at these factors in the next chapter, which includes a far more detailed analysis of the impact of the difference between the company and personal tax regimes for capital gains.

11.19 SUMMARY

I will attempt here to briefly summarise our findings in this chapter. Before I do so, however, I would like to make a few key points:

i) As explained in Section 11.1, these findings are based on our current best estimate of the long-term tax regime for both companies and individuals in the UK. To do this, we have used our estimated forecast of the tax rates applying for 2014/15.

ii) These findings are based on tax considerations only and are thus subject to the important non-tax considerations examined in Chapter 1.

iii) These findings are also based simply on a 'snapshot' of the position for a single year. In the next chapter we will look at the more detailed factors that should be considered in the long term.

iv) These findings take no account of the more beneficial regime for relieving interest and other finance costs when using a property investment company. We will look at the importance of interest relief in more detail in Chapter 13.

v) These findings are subject to any special circumstances that may apply. We will look at some of these in the next two sections.

Rental Income

Where the investor is already a higher rate taxpayer and does not need to extract profits from the company each year, a property investment company is beneficial.

However, where the investor extracts all of the company's profits each year, the company ceases to be beneficial unless the total income received by both the company and the individual exceeds £150,000. Even then, this strategy becomes disadvantageous if it is continued after the company's profits exceed £300,000.

The best position for a basic rate taxpayer is to first build a property portfolio personally until such time as the rental profits from that portfolio bring their total income up to the higher rate tax threshold. Thereafter, the investor will benefit from using a property investment company to make further investments provided that they do not withdraw the profits from the company each year.

Property Trades

A property trading company is beneficial in most circumstances and generally produces better savings than a property investment company.

The benefits are greatly reduced if all of the profits are extracted from the company as dividends each year, but some benefit generally remains, provided that this strategy is not continued after the company's profits exceed £300,000.

Capital Gains

Generally speaking, taking indexation relief into account, capital gains arising within a company enjoy a better overall effective tax rate once the investor's annual exemption has been exhausted.

This, however, is before considering the additional costs of extracting sale proceeds from the company.

11.20 OLDER PROPERTY INVESTORS

Investors over state retirement age are exempt from all classes of National Insurance.

As a result, anyone over state retirement age will suffer the same effective tax rates on trading income as they do on rental income. Hence, for these investors, a property trading company is only as beneficial as a property investment company and the results shown in Sections 11.4 to 11.10 apply to all types of property business.

Taxpayers aged 65 or over are also eligible for higher personal allowances, although these are progressively withdrawn once their total income exceeds £24,000 (at 2011/12 rates). This does not affect higher rate taxpayers, but will slightly alter some of the analyses given for basic rate taxpayers in Sections 11.6 to 11.9.

In some cases, the use of a company may enable a taxpayer aged 65 or over to avoid the withdrawal of their higher personal allowances, thus providing a benefit. If, however, the taxpayer intends to withdraw all of the company's profits each year, a company will be of no benefit. (But see Section 1.3 regarding the possible use of a property company in Inheritance Tax planning.)

11.21 TAX CREDIT CLAIMANTS

Where the investor is claiming Tax Credits, a company will provide a useful mechanism to avoid the withdrawal of Tax Credits when the property business yields profits.

From 6th April 2011, Tax Credits will be withdrawn at the rate of 41% for each £1 of income in excess of £6,420.

This gives rise to total effective tax rates of up to 73% for some basic rate taxpayers (Income Tax at 20%, National Insurance at 12% and Tax Credit withdrawal at 41%) and even 83% for a few higher rate taxpayers (Income Tax at 40%, National Insurance at 2% and Tax Credit withdrawal at 41%).

By using a company, however, the profits from the property business can be kept out of the equation as far as the owner's Tax Credits are concerned. It may even possible to withdraw up to £10,000 from the company every second year without losing any Tax Credits. This subject is covered in depth in the Taxcafe.co.uk guide *'Salary versus Dividends'*.

Chapter 12

Making the Big Decision

12.1 THE 'BIG PICTURE'

Before you can decide whether a company is for you or not, you will need to look at what I call the 'Big Picture'.

Many investors concentrate almost exclusively on the taxation treatment of their income. Others are mainly concerned with capital gains.

Neither approach is correct. The only way to carry out effective tax planning is to take every applicable tax into account. In the case of property companies, we are not concerned only with income, nor solely with capital gains, but with both. On top of that, we must also consider the costs of extracting profits and sale proceeds from the company.

VAT, Stamp Duty, Stamp Duty Land Tax and any other tax costs should also be considered and, if one is taking the really long view, it makes sense to give some thought to Inheritance Tax as well.

Fully effective tax planning is only possible once all potential tax costs have been taken into account, however and whenever they are likely to arise. But, even this is still not truly the 'Big Picture'.

Bayley's Law

'The truly wise investor does not seek merely to minimise the amount of tax paid, but rather to maximise the **wealth** remaining once all taxes have been taken into account.'

Taking the Long Term View

The more favourable regime for obtaining tax relief for interest and other finance costs may sometimes provide the greatest benefit when using a property company. Undoubtedly, this is an important factor and we will therefore be looking at this issue in detail in Chapter 13.

The most effective tax planning, however, is always based on a long-term view. This is seldom more true than it is when looking at the issue of whether or not to use a property company. My aim in this chapter is therefore to show you the likely outcome provided by using a property company in the long-term.

In the long-term, history shows that UK property tends to grow in value at an average annual rate of around 7.5%. Due to the compound effect of this growth, this roughly equates to properties doubling in value every ten years.

In order to take a long-term view, therefore, we will use this growth rate for the models which we will explore in this chapter.

Readers will, of course, be acutely aware that actual growth rates fluctuate significantly and we do not always see these sort of growth rates in the short term.

Nevertheless, our purpose in this chapter is to look at the 'Big Picture' and to plan for the long-term. This necessitates taking a hypothetical approach based on long-term trends. I make no apologies for this, because this is the right approach when considering effective long-term planning.

In reality, however, the short-term position will, of course, often be very different and it is imperative that readers form their own opinion on current and likely future market conditions. The models used in this chapter are entirely hypothetical and are in no way intended to be a true indication of the likely performance of the property market over the next few years.

12.2 TYPES OF PROPERTY BUSINESS REVISITED

Following on from our conclusions in Section 11.19, it is already reasonable to surmise that the current tax regime produces the potential to make significant tax savings by operating most property development, property trading or property management businesses through a company.

This arises mainly because of the preferential Corporation Tax rates when compared with the combined Income Tax and National Insurance cost of trading on a personal basis.

Add to this the fact that a trading company's shares will usually qualify for entrepreneurs' relief (see Section 7.3) and the position appears fairly clear-cut in the case of any property trade producing a substantial level of annual profits.

As discussed in Section 11.13, the only exceptions arise when the company's profits begin to exceed £300,000 and the investor still wishes to extract the whole amount as dividends each year. Otherwise, the only danger seems to lie in potential future changes to the tax regime or, perhaps, with the investor's inability to comply with the more stringent administrative necessities involved in operating a company.

We will return to take a more detailed look at the advantages of property trading companies in Section 12.11.

As far as property investment companies are concerned, our findings in Chapter 11 tell us that these are not generally beneficial for basic rate taxpayers.

The position for higher rate taxpayers, however, is rather less certain once we take account of the fact that, sooner or later, the investor is bound to want to extract their profits from the company!

This is therefore where we are going to concentrate for most of the remainder of this chapter.

12.3 THE RENTAL INCOME POSITION

In the preceding chapters, we have looked at the mechanics of how UK resident companies are taxed. We will now begin to look at how this all affects property investment businesses and whether a company therefore becomes beneficial or not.

The best way to illustrate this is by way of an example.

Example 'A', Part 1

Humphrey has decided to begin investing in property with the intention of building up a property portfolio over the next few years. He is already a higher rate taxpayer, even before taking any rental income into consideration.

Although his friend Charlie said "you'd be daft not to use a company, old boy", Humphrey goes ahead and buys six flats in his own name for £100,000 each and begins to rent them out.

During the following year, Humphrey receives rental income of £10,000 from each flat, but has deductible expenditure totalling £28,000 (including mortgage interest), leaving him with a profit of £32,000. Humphrey's accountant, Edmund, therefore advises him that he has an Income Tax liability of £12,800 (£32,000 at 40%).

Feeling somewhat frustrated by his inability to persuade Humphrey to invest through a limited company, Charlie decides to try it out for himself. He sets up a company, Murrayfield Limited, and, through this, he too buys six flats for £100,000 each. He incurs the same level of expenses as Humphrey and Murrayfield Limited therefore also has a taxable profit of £32,000.

Murrayfield Limited's profits are taxed at 20% (using the rate applying from 1st April 2011 - see Section 2.5) and the Corporation Tax payable by the company is thus £6,400.

At first glance, therefore, Charlie appears to be some £6,400 better off than Humphrey, indicating that a company seems to be highly beneficial.

Now feeling rather pleased with himself, Charlie shows what he has done to Edmund (who happens to be his accountant too). Unfortunately for Charlie, Edmund has two pieces of bad news for him.

Firstly, as using a company has a few extra complications, Edmund's fees to Charlie will be rather more than he charged Humphrey. However, the difference is not a huge sum compared with the tax he has saved, and is a tax-deductible expense in itself, so Charlie is not too concerned by this.

Secondly though, Edmund points out that if Charlie wants any of the money that Murrayfield Limited has made, he will have to pay himself a dividend. When he receives this dividend, Charlie, who is also a higher rate taxpayer, will have to pay Income Tax on it at an effective rate of 25%.

Ignoring Edmund's additional fees for the sake of illustration, the maximum dividend that Charlie can take out of Murrayfield Limited is £25,600. This sum is arrived at by deducting the company's Corporation Tax bill of £6,400 from its rental profits of £32,000.

*Charlie's dividend gives rise to an Income Tax liability of £6,400 (25% of £25,600). In total, Charlie's overall tax burden therefore amounts to £12,800 (Corporation Tax of £6,400 plus Income Tax of £6,400): exactly the **same** as Humphrey's!*

(Note that, in this example, I have assumed that both Humphrey and Charlie have less than £100,000 of taxable income in total after receiving the additional income from their property investments.)

Analysis of Example 'A' so Far

In tax terms alone, Charlie is no better off than Humphrey. Furthermore, after taking account of Edmund's higher fees and other costs associated with running a company, Charlie will actually be worse off. This is mainly because Charlie has withdrawn all of his rental profits from the company by way of dividend.

In this example, we have examined the position of two higher rate taxpayers who both want to spend all of the profits from their property business. The example confirms our findings in Chapter 11 that a company is of no benefit in this situation.

Humphrey and Charlie are typical of the type of property investor who already has a good level of income from other sources and wishes to supplement it through property investment.

Conclusion

Using a property investment company is of no benefit when all of the profits are needed to fund the investor's current lifestyle.

12.4   REINVESTING RENTAL PROFITS

In the previous section, we saw that a property investment company was of no benefit when all of its profits were being withdrawn by the proprietor. In other words, the company is of no use when the rental profits are merely being used to support the investor's own lifestyle (subject to the comments in Chapter 11 regarding those with income over £150,000).

However, where a property investment company can really produce significant financial benefits is when the property investor does not need their rental income immediately and reinvests their profits in order to build up a substantial investment portfolio over a number of years.

To see how a company may benefit these investors, let's return to our friends Humphrey and Charlie.

Example 'A', Part 2

For the next few years, Humphrey and Charlie both accumulate a property portfolio. After ten years, each has a total of 20 properties, which have cost a total of £2,500,000. Each of them now has total annual rental income of £300,000 and annual expenditure of £100,000, leaving rental profits of £200,000.

Let us also assume that Humphrey and Charlie each have existing annual income from other sources of £50,000 and that our forecast tax rates for 2014/15 (see Appendix B) still prevail at this time.

Humphrey will therefore face Income Tax on his rental income as follows:

£100,000 (£150,000 - £50,000) x 40% =	*£40,000*
£100,000 (£200,000 - £100,000) x 50% =	*£50,000*
£9,365 (lost personal allowance) x 40% =	*£3,746*
Total	*£93,746*

The Corporation Tax payable by Murrayfield Limited on the same level of profit is £40,000 (£200,000 at 20%).

If Charlie is still withdrawing all of his profits after tax (£160,000) as a dividend, he will also have further tax to pay. Adding on the one ninth tax credit (see Section 10.3), Charlie would have additional taxable income of £177,778, giving him the following Income Tax bill:

£100,000 (£150,000 - £50,000) x 32.5% =	*£32,500*
£77,778 (£177,778 - £100,000) x 42.5% =	*£33,056*
Less tax credit	*(£17,778)*
£9,365 (lost personal allowance) x 40% =	*£3,746*
Total	*£51,524*

Charlie's total tax burden for the year would then amount to £91,524 (£40,000 + £51,524) and he would therefore be only £2,222 better off than Humphrey, even before taking account of the inevitable extra costs that running a company brings.

Let us suppose instead, however, that Humphrey and Charlie each wish to reinvest £150,000 of their rental profits in a new property.

In Humphrey's case, this makes absolutely no difference to his Income Tax bill, which remains £93,746. Similarly, this reinvestment makes no difference to Murrayfield Limited's Corporation Tax bill of £40,000.

*However, what the reinvestment **does** mean is that, since Murrayfield Limited is reinvesting £150,000 of its rental profits in a new property, Charlie will only be taking out a dividend of £10,000, giving him an Income Tax bill of only £2,500. His total tax burden for the year will therefore be reduced to only £42,500, which is £51,246 less than Humphrey's!*

Analysis of Example 'A', Part 2

To begin with, the example reinforces the fact that there is little benefit in using a company, even at higher levels of profit, if all of the income continues to be withdrawn (some benefit begins to arise once total income exceeds £150,000, but the savings are not significant).

However, it can also be seen that using a company can save a considerable amount of tax on the investor's rental profits where these are **not** all withdrawn by way of dividend (or, indeed, by any other means).

Hence, a property investment company proves highly beneficial for income purposes when a substantial proportion of the profits are being reinvested.

12.5   CAPITAL GAINS

In Chapter 6, we looked at the basic mechanics of how a company is taxed on its capital gains.

Now, in order to illustrate the impact of the differences between how capital gains are taxed in a company and how individuals are taxed on capital gains, let's turn to another example.

Example 'B', Part 1

Michelle and Louise share a lottery win and each decide to invest £250,000 of their proceeds in property. Michelle buys her property personally; Louise forms a company, Dawson Limited, to buy her property. Both properties are rented out to provide income. Ten years later, Michelle and Louise both sell their properties for £500,000. They are both higher rate taxpayers by this time.

Over this ten-year period inflation has totalled 40% and the Capital Gains Tax annual exemption has been increased to £15,000.

Michelle has made a capital gain of £250,000. After deducting her annual exemption, her taxable gain therefore amounts to £235,000, giving her a Capital Gains Tax liability of £65,800 (£235,000 x 28%).

Dawson Limited also has a gain of £250,000, but may deduct indexation relief at 40% on cost (£250,000), i.e. £100,000. This leaves Dawson Limited with a chargeable gain of £150,000. The amount of tax arising depends on the level of the company's income, but, if there are no other investments in the company, it is likely to amount to £30,000 (at the small profits rate of 20%).

Again, at first glance, we see that the corporate investor appears to be better off. Even at the highest possible effective rate of Corporation Tax (25% in the long-term), the tax payable by Dawson Limited, £37,500, would still be considerably less than that for an individual.

However, once again, we must also consider how to extract the after-tax proceeds from the company.

If Louise removes the net proceeds of £470,000 from Dawson Limited as a dividend, as a higher rate taxpayer she would have to pay Income Tax of at least £162,868 (using forecast 2014/15 rates, as usual).

Analysis of Example 'B', Part 1

Clearly, Louise now appears to be much worse off than Michelle, but could she have done something better than simply paying herself this enormous dividend?

The answer is yes, but we will need to look at what happens to a property company which is no longer required (Section 12.6) before we can see how it works. The position also depends on how the company was financed in the first place (we will cover that topic in detail in Chapter 13).

Another alternative for Louise might be to leave the proceeds in the company for reinvestment in new property (or some other form of investment). Again, we can see from this example that a property company works best in a reinvestment environment.

In practice, however, it is highly unlikely that a property investor like Louise would have simply taken a dividend of this magnitude out of the company.

Firstly, Louise's case is unusual as she did not have any borrowings, thus meaning that the proceeds which she wished to remove from the company were somewhat inflated.

Secondly, company law would prevent her from taking a dividend out of Dawson Limited in excess of its distributable profits. (We will cover the extraction of the original capital invested in the company in Section 12.6.) For the sake of illustration, therefore, let's consider Louise's tax position if she only withdraws her after-tax profit on the property from Dawson Limited, rather than her entire proceeds.

Example 'B', Part 2

Louise takes a dividend of £220,000 out of Dawson Limited, representing her after-tax profit on the sale of the property. As a higher rate taxpayer, her Income Tax liability on this dividend will be at least £72,590 (using our forecast 2014/15 rates).

Combining this with the Corporation Tax already suffered in Dawson Limited (£30,000) gives a total tax cost on the property disposal of at least £102,590.

Analysis of Example 'B', Part 2

Now that we have altered the situation so that we are only looking at the profit element of the proceeds, we can clearly see that Louise, the corporate investor, is still considerably worse off than Michelle, the private investor.

As a higher rate taxpayer, Louise would, in fact, be at least £36,790 worse off (£102,590 - £65,800). If she were a basic rate taxpayer, the deficit would be slightly less (as part of her dividend would be tax free), but is still likely to be over £25,000.

This clearly demonstrates that a company is not a good investment vehicle if the investor wishes to realise capital gains and extract them from the company for private use, rather than reinvest them within it.

12.6 WINDING UP THE COMPANY TO REDUCE TAX

In Section 12.5 we encountered a situation where an investor was left with funds in a company that had perhaps outlived its usefulness. In such a case, the most tax-efficient procedure may be to wind the company up. Unfortunately, however, this can be a very expensive process if the company still has assets and liabilities or has recently been in active business.

For the sake of illustration, however, let us return to Example 'B' and ignore the impact of these costs.

Example 'B', Part 3

Rather than pay herself a huge dividend, Louise decides instead to wind Dawson Limited up.

First, however, she pays herself enough dividend to take her taxable income up to £100,000. She does this because the effective rate of tax on this dividend will be 25%, which is less than the rate of Capital Gains Tax suffered by a higher rate taxpayer (28%). She restricts it to this level in order to retain her personal allowance.

As she is already a higher rate taxpayer, the maximum dividend which fulfils her criteria will be £50,400 (at forecast 2014/15 rates), giving rise to an Income Tax liability of £12,600 (at 25%).

The remaining net proceeds left in Dawson Limited now amount to £419,600 (£470,000 - £50,400).

Ignoring costs, this sum can now be distributed to Louise on the winding up and will therefore be treated in her hands as a capital disposal subject to Capital Gains Tax and not Income Tax.

Louise originally invested £250,000 in Dawson Limited in order to enable it to purchase the property. Hence, her capital gain on her shares in Dawson Limited is £169,600. After deducting her annual exemption of £15,000, this leaves a taxable gain of £154,600.

Louise's Capital Gains Tax liability at 28% will therefore be £43,288. Combining this with the Corporation Tax paid by Dawson Limited (£30,000) and the Income Tax on her dividend (£12,600), gives Louise a total tax cost on this disposal of £85,888.

Analysis of Example 'B', Part 3

Firstly, it is worth noting that entrepreneurs' relief is not available on the disposal of Louise's property company shares. As explained in Section 3.2, this will generally be the case for property investment companies (but see Section 7.4 for a possible way to obtain this relief).

By winding up the company rather than merely paying herself a single huge dividend, Louise has improved her position from Part 2 (Section 12.5). In effect, changing the way that part of her sale proceeds are treated to a capital gain instead of a dividend has reduced the effective tax rate on part of her profits from 36.1% to 28%. This strategy has also allowed her to retain her personal allowance, saving her a further £3,746 (at forecast 2014/15 rates).

It's an improvement, but still not enough to match the private investor's position. In fact, as a higher rate taxpayer, Louise would still remain at least £20,088 worse off than Michelle (£85,888 - £65,800).

A basic rate taxpayer could extract more dividends from the company before the winding up and part of these would be tax free (see Section 11.8).

However, even an individual with no other taxable income whatsoever could only save just over £11,000 in this way (at forecast 2014/15 rates): still leaving them around £9,000 worse off than the private investor in our scenario.

Hence, it appears quite conclusive that a company is not beneficial when we are looking at fairly static levels of capital growth, without any serious reinvestment activity, which are ultimately being returned into the hands of the individual investor.

12.7 WHAT IF THE COMPANY STILL HOLDS PROPERTY WHEN WOUND UP?

Generally, this would not be a good idea:

- Firstly, the costs of the winding up would be considerably greater.
- Secondly, the company would be treated as having made a disposal of the property at its market value and taxed accordingly.
- Thirdly, the shareholder would be taxed on the 'disposal' of the company shares, again based on the market value of the property!

In Louise's case, for example, tax liabilities of £87,400 would be incurred without there being any actual sale proceeds from which to fund them. This demonstrates the fact that, once you have your investments in a company, it can be very difficult (or expensive) to get them out if you should want to!

12.8 LONG-TERM REINVESTMENT

In Section 12.4, we looked at the benefits of incorporation where some or all of the annual rental profit was being reinvested. Then, in Sections 12.5 and 12.6, we looked at the taxation position on the ultimate capital gains arising in a property business.

What we have not yet considered, however, is just how the incorporated property business's long-term capital growth might benefit from its ability to reinvest a greater share of its rental profits owing to the fact that its annual tax bill on those profits is much reduced under the Corporation Tax regime.

Reinvesting Profits Over a Number of Years

We now know that a property company can produce a significantly better outcome in the short term, year on year, when its profits are being reinvested.

In Example 'A', we assumed that the investors had built up identical portfolios over a period of time. However, in practice, it is likely that if both investors reinvest all or most of their profits, the company investor will eventually build up a larger portfolio of properties. This is because the lower Corporation Tax rates will leave the company investor with extra resources to invest in new properties.

The long-term effect of reinvestment through a property company is best illustrated by way of the example that follows (Example 'C'). In this example, we will have to make many assumptions, including rates of return, interest rates and the rate of growth of property values. Here again we will follow the hypothetical long-term trend for the reasons discussed in Section 11.1.

Whilst the real outcome over the coming years will almost certainly be different from that which is predicted here, the example will still serve as a valid illustration because we will apply all of our assumptions equally to the company investor and the personal investor, thus revealing a difference in their two outcomes that is entirely due to their different tax environments.

The numbers will get quite messy in this example but please bear with me, as it is worth persevering to see the ultimate result.

Example 'C', Part 1

Lenny and Dawn each own identical rental properties, both worth £300,000. They each earn annual rents of £25,500 and, after deducting costs of £5,500, are left with annual profits of £20,000.

Lenny's property is owned personally and, because he is a higher rate taxpayer, he is left with after-tax profits of £12,000.

Dawn uses a company, Saunders Limited, to invest. Saunders Limited's rental profits will be subject to Corporation Tax at 20% (see Section 2.5). On a profit of £20,000 this will give rise to a Corporation Tax bill of £4,000, leaving the company with £16,000.

Each investor is using their property business to save for retirement, so all after-tax profits are saved and reinvested.

After three years, Lenny will have £36,000 available for reinvestment. With a 70% Buy-to-Let mortgage, this will enable him to buy a new property at a cost of £120,000. This brings in rental income of £10,200, less interest of £4,200 and other costs of £850, leaving him with an annual rental profit of £5,150.

Lenny's total annual rental profit for both properties is now £25,150 (£20,000 PLUS £5,150). After his higher rate Income Tax at 40%, this leaves him with after-tax profits of £15,090.

Dawn, the company investor, also buys a new property after three years, but she has £48,000 available (3 x £16,000). This enables her to buy a property for £160,000, which produces rental income of £13,600. After interest of £5,600 and other costs of £1,050, Dawn's company receives an additional annual rental profit of £6,950 from this property.

Saunders Limited's annual profits are now £26,950, giving rise to Corporation Tax, at 20%, of £5,390, leaving profits after tax of £21,560.

Analysis of Example 'C', Part 1

Already, we can see that Dawn is moving ahead of Lenny. Her company's second property purchase is worth £40,000 more and her after-tax profits are now almost £6,500 per annum greater (assuming she continues to keep them within the company).

For the sake of illustration, we have had to make a number of assumptions here, which are worth explaining:

- Rental income is assumed to be 8.5% of the property's value
- Mortgage interest is at 5%
- Other annual costs amount to a fixed element of £250 per property, plus a variable element equal to 0.5% of the property's value

We are now going to move forward many more years, assuming that Lenny and Dawn continue to reinvest all of their available after-tax profits in new property every three years using 70% Buy-to-Let mortgages.

The result in Part 2 will be based on all of the same assumptions as in Part 1 above, assuming, in turn, that these all remain valid throughout that period.

Additionally, and purely for the sake of simplicity, we will also assume that:

- The rentals are never increased on any of the properties
- There is no capital repayment of any of the mortgages (i.e. we assume that they are all interest-only mortgages)
- Lenny and Dawn's other taxable income amounts to £50,000 each
- Our forecast tax rates for 2014/15 (see Appendix B) apply throughout the relevant period

Example 'C', Part 2

After continuing in the same way for 15 years, Lenny and Dawn will each have a portfolio of six properties.

Lenny's properties now produce total annual rental profits of £63,894. After higher rate Income Tax (including an additional £2,779 due to the partial loss of his personal allowance), this leaves £35,558 of annual after-tax income.

Dawn's property company is now receiving annual rental profits of £90,515, leaving a sum of £72,412 after Corporation Tax.

Let us suppose that, at this point, both Lenny and Dawn wish to stop reinvesting, retire and start spending their rental profits privately. We already know how much net income Lenny will receive.

For Dawn, we now need to take account of the Income Tax that she will suffer when she withdraws her after tax profits from the company. The dividend itself (£72,412) will be taxed at an effective rate of 25%, i.e. £18,103, but she will also lose her personal allowance, adding a further £3,746 (£9,365 x 40%) to her tax bill and making a total cost of £21,849.

Dawn will therefore be left with net annual income from her property business of £50,563 (£72,412 - £21,849).

Analysis of Example 'C', Part 2

What this example shows is that the ability to reinvest a greater share of the annual rental profits over a number of years has ultimately provided Dawn, the corporate investor, with a greatly increased income.

In fact, in this example, **the company investor has an after-tax income 42% greater than that enjoyed by the personal investor!**

This example has shown that, in a long-term reinvestment scenario, a property investment company really can provide enormous tax benefits to those who build up a portfolio of properties and ultimately use it to generate income.

12.9   RETAINING THE WEALTH

So far, so good, but we still haven't tackled the issue of capital gains. Although Lenny and Dawn have now stopped reinvesting, they do still have the pressure of a property-letting business to worry about. To genuinely retire, they may, in fact, wish to now sell all of their properties.

To look at the final outcome on the ultimate sale of the property portfolios, let's move on one final three-year period and assume that Lenny and Dawn each then sell all of their properties.

We will also need to make three other major assumptions for this purpose:

i) Property values have increased at an average compound rate of 7.5% per annum (see Section 12.1).
ii) Inflation has averaged 3.5% per annum.
iii) There have been no changes to the tax system beyond our forecasts for 2014/15, other than an increase in the annual Capital Gains Tax exemption to £20,000.

Example 'C', Part 3

Eighteen years after we started, Lenny's property portfolio is worth a total of £2,927,533. The total cost of this portfolio was £1,303,209, thus giving him total capital gains of £1,624,324.

Let's assume that Lenny's disposals are spread over two tax years, with annual exemptions of £20,000 in each year.

Deducting these two annual exemptions leaves Lenny with total taxable gains of £1,584,324, thus giving rise to total Capital Gains Tax liabilities (at 28%) of £443,611.

After paying his Capital Gains Tax and also repaying all of his mortgages, Lenny will be left with net proceeds of £1,781,676.

Now let's look at Dawn.

The property portfolio in Dawn's company will now be worth a total of £3,919,426. The cost of the portfolio was £1,894,783, producing total capital gains of £2,024,643. Indexation relief will amount to a total of £729,555, leaving taxable indexed gains of £1,295,088.

We will again assume that the disposals are spread over two of Saunders Limited's accounting periods, so that almost £600,000 (2 x £300,000) of the company's capital gains will be subject to Corporation Tax at 20% and the remainder at an effective rate of 25% (see Section 2.5).

(Part of the £300,000 small profits rate band will, however, be used against the company's rental income in these last two years, estimated at £90,515 in total.)

The Corporation Tax on the company's capital gains therefore amounts to a total of £298,298.

After paying this Corporation Tax and repaying all of the mortgages that the company took out, the remaining funds in the company will be £2,504,780.

Dawn now winds up Saunders Limited in order to get these proceeds into her own hands.

Here, we will assume that Dawn originally invested £300,000 in the company (the value of her first property), meaning that she will have a capital gain of £2,204,780. (We are again ignoring the costs of the winding up as we did in Section 12.6.)

Dawn is entitled to an annual exemption of £20,000, leaving her with a taxable gain of £2,184,780. Her Capital Gains Tax liability at 28% on the winding up of her property investment company will therefore amount to £611,738, leaving her with net proceeds of £1,893,042 (£2,504,780 - £611,738).

Analysis of Example 'C', Part 3

So how much better off is the company investor compared with the private investor?

Ultimately, our corporate investor, Dawn, has emerged £111,366, or 6.25%, better off than Lenny, our personal investor.

This may not sound much, but it actually represents over 37% of the original amount invested by each investor!

Factor in the higher after tax income received by Dawn in the last few years before the winding up and **the total return on her original investment is over 57% more than the private investor**, Lenny.

In short, what this means is that, over a long period of time, the reinvestment of the additional net income receivable through the use of a company should eventually produce a sufficiently improved position to more than compensate for the disadvantages of realising capital gains in, and extracting them from, a company.

A Little Extra Tax Tip

As explained in Section 12.6, a dividend subject to Income Tax at an effective rate of 25% is preferable to a capital gain taxed at 28%.

Someone in Dawn's position could therefore save a little tax by extracting some additional dividends from the company before the winding up.

This will produce a saving to the extent that it brings the company owner's total taxable income up to £100,000 (just as Louise did in Section 12.6) or, where the owner's personal allowance has already been withdrawn, to £150,000.

I avoided this extra complexity in the example above, as it was already complicated enough and the extra saving for Dawn would have been relatively small. In practice, however, this small additional saving will be worth considering.

12.10 LONG-TERM REINVESTMENT CONCLUSIONS

After taking a long and detailed look at the possible outcomes for two investors (one corporate and one personal) over many years, we can still see that the fundamental position remains that companies are a good vehicle in which to build a portfolio, but do tend to suffer some drawbacks on its eventual disposal.

However, the last example does show that the accumulation and reinvestment of additional net profits within a company over many years may eventually produce a beneficial result, even after taking the capital gains position into account.

Just how long the reinvestment period needs to be to achieve this will depend on the circumstances prevailing. The company's tax position on the ultimate disposal of its properties is entirely dependent on the gap between retail inflation and the rate of growth in property values. The gap in this example was 4%, whereas, in reality, it will fluctuate greatly and may sometimes even be negative.

The same model as that used for our example in Sections 12.8 and 12.9 indicates an overall detrimental result for the company if the average annual rate of growth in property values exceeds 11% (with retail inflation remaining 3.5%), or if the retail inflation rate drops below 0.63% (with an average annual growth rate in property values of 7.5%).

In other words, our model indicates that the company only remains beneficial on the ultimate sale of the property portfolio if the average annual rate of growth in property values does not exceed the rate of retail inflation by more than around 7% to 7.5%.

Clearly, in reality, things will never be exactly the same as any prediction that we may try to make. It is impossible to generalise the true position for every single property investor's likely outcome. Investors must therefore consider their own plans and their own view of the probable outcome in order to decide how this illustration best applies to them.

What is fairly clear, however, is that a property investment company used as a vehicle in which to reinvest profits with the aim of growing a portfolio over many years will produce a significantly higher level of net income after a long reinvestment period, if the portfolio is retained in the company.

If, however, the portfolio is ultimately disposed of and the company is wound up, the position may not always be so beneficial and may even prove detrimental if the rate of capital growth in the portfolio is far in excess of retail inflation rates.

12.11 THE BENEFITS OF REINVESTMENT FOR A TRADING COMPANY

The one thing that we have not yet covered is the situation where the profits from a property *trade* are being reinvested over a long period.

I did hint in Section 12.2 that this was almost a 'no-brainer', with a property company being the obvious winner in most cases. However, I feel that this stance does warrant an illustrative example to back up my assertions!

In this case, we will start with the current position, using 2011/12 tax rates. As the example progresses, however, we will move on to the forecast future tax rates set out in Appendix B, including the forecast rates for 2014/15 which we have used for most of the calculations in the last two chapters.

Example 'D' Part 1

Nick and Ann are both property developers. Each of them acquires a derelict property in Fife at a cost of £180,000, which they plan to renovate and convert into flats which they will then sell. Nick is going to carry on his business as a sole trader. Ann, on the other hand, forms a property development company, Rainbow Developments Limited.

Neither Ann nor Nick has any other income, so each will need £10,000 each year out of their net profits to cover modest living expenses.

In the year ending 31st March 2012, their first year of trading, each of them manages to develop their property and sell all of the flats. After building costs, interest costs and other trading expenditure, each makes a total profit of £100,000 which they plan to reinvest in their business, together with their original capital of £180,000.

At 2011/12 tax rates (Appendix A), Nick will have a total Income Tax liability of £30,010. He will also have to pay Class 2 National Insurance at £2.50 a week and Class 4 National Insurance totalling £4,323.

All in all, Nick's total tax bill will amount to £34,465, leaving him only £65,535 of net, after-tax profit. £10,000 of this goes on living expenses, leaving £55,535 available to reinvest, plus his original capital of £180,000, making a total of £235,535.

Ann, on the other hand, pays herself a salary of £7,225: the National Insurance primary threshold for 2011/12). This gives rise to a small employer's National Insurance liability of £21, and leaves a taxable profit in the company of £92,754.

After Corporation Tax of £18,551 (at 20%), the company is left with a net profit of £74,203. From this, Ann pays herself a dividend of £2,775, to cover the rest of her living expenses, leaving the company with £71,428 to reinvest plus Ann's original capital of £180,000, making a total of £251,428.

Analysis of Example 'D' Part 1

Already we can see that Rainbow Developments Limited, the property development company, has an extra £15,894 available for reinvestment. This is because the company has been able to retain almost 29% more of its profits than Nick was able to keep himself.

Example 'D' Part 2

In April 2012, Nick and Ann both reinvest their available profits and capital in a new development. In each case, they double the amount available by borrowing the same sum as they are investing themselves.

After all relevant expenditure, each development yields a profit of 25% before interest costs at 7.5%.

Throughout the rest of this example, I'm also going to assume that Ann and Nick's requirements for living expenses will each increase by £2,000 per annum. For future personal tax rates and allowances, we will follow the principles explained in the Foreword and Section 11.2 and illustrated in Appendix B. Future Corporation Tax rates are set out in Section 2.5 and we will assume that they will remain unchanged from the year ending 31st March 2015 onwards.

On the basis of the above assumptions, Nick will make a profit of £100,102 in the year ending 31st March 2013 and will have total Income Tax and National Insurance costs of £34,385. After living expenses of £12,000, he will have total profits and capital left for reinvestment the next year of £289,252.

In the same year, Rainbow Developments Limited will make a net profit before tax of £106,857, which is £6,755 more than Nick, owing to the greater amount of profit available for reinvestment from the previous year.

Rainbow Developments Limited will then pay Ann a salary of £7,485 (the estimated National Insurance primary threshold for 2012/13) and employer's National Insurance of £22. The Corporation Tax at 20% on the remaining £99,350 profit will be £19,870, and Ann will take out a dividend of £4,515 to top up her salary to the level required to cover her living expenses for the year.

This will leave the company with net retained profits of £74,965 which, this time, is £21,248 more than Nick had left for reinvestment. Rainbow Developments Limited's total funds available for reinvestment in April 2013 are £326,393. This is over £37,000, or almost 13%, more than Nick is able to invest.

In fact, by using a company, Ann has experienced 34% more growth than Nick when compared to the original £180,000 of capital which they each invested originally.

Analysis of Example 'D' Part 2

After only two years of trading, the property development company is producing almost 7% higher profits before tax and has accumulated 34% more after-tax profit for reinvestment. Through her company, Ann is already seeing the twin benefits of:

- Having greater funds available for reinvestment, whilst

- Being able to do so within a lower tax environment.

Example 'D' Part 3

Ann and Nick both continue trading for several years in exactly the same vein.

By 31st March 2016, Nick will be making profits after tax of £106,386 and will have accumulated funds available of £514,182.

*By the same point in time, Rainbow Developments Limited will be making profits after tax of £182,003, even after paying Ann a salary of £8,325. The total funds being generated will therefore be £190,328, which is almost **80% more** than Nick's business.*

At the beginning of April 2016, Rainbow Developments Limited will have total accumulated funds available of £727,280, over £213,000, or 41%, more than Nick!

Analysis of Example 'D' Part 3

After five years of trading, the property development company is clearly substantially more successful than the sole trader property developer. All of this simply because of the ability to reinvest a greater proportion of each year's profits.

As with property investment companies, however, we must also now consider the position on a final dissolution of each business.

Example 'D' Part 4

In April 2016, Ann and Nick each reinvest their available funds in one last new development.

By the time he has completed and sold his last development, Nick will be left with a sum of £618,760 after tax and his usual living expenses.

What about Rainbow Developments Limited and Ann, though?

Rainbow Developments Limited **started** in April 2016 with funds available for investment of £727,280, already over £213,000 ahead of Nick.

Let us suppose that the company then invests in a new development in the usual way. On completion, the new development will be worth £1,818,201.

After accounting for borrowings, including accumulated interest, the net worth of the company will be £1,036,374. Even if Ann takes out a salary of £8,625 and her maximum tax free dividend of £34,763, it will still be worth £992,959.

By this point, a business like Rainbow Developments Limited's property development trade could have some substantial goodwill value, although we are going to ignore that here for the sake of illustration.

Nevertheless, by selling the company, rather than the property development within the company, Ann may effectively be able to avoid suffering the Corporation Tax on the profit from her last development, which would have amounted to £60,110.

At this stage, therefore, Ann might potentially be able to sell the company for the net value of its assets, i.e. £992,959.

After deducting her original investment of £180,000, Ann would therefore have a capital gain of £812,959 (£992,959 - £180,000). At this point (2016/17), the annual Capital Gains Tax exemption should be around £12,800, leaving Ann with a taxable gain of £800,159.

Ann's shares in the company will qualify for entrepreneurs' relief, so her gain will be subject to Capital Gains Tax at just 10%, giving her a tax bill of a mere £80,016.

This would leave Ann with net proceeds from her company sale of £912,943 (£992,959 - £80,016). Adding her salary of £8,625 and dividends of £34,763, and then deducting £20,000 to cover her usual living expenses, would leave her with a final sum of £936,331.

Analysis of Example 'D' Part 4

After one last development, Ann has been able to sell her company and retain over £317,500, or 51%, more than Nick, her sole trader rival.

In the final period, she was able to add the benefit of a Capital Gains Tax rate of just 10% (see Section 7.3) to the advantages that she had already accumulated over the preceding years.

And The Purchaser Can Save Money Too!

Readers may wonder, however, why a purchaser would be prepared to buy Rainbow Developments Limited for the value discussed above when a sale of the development within the company would produce a Corporation Tax bill which amounts to £60,110.

I have a few answers to give in defence of the approach taken in my example.

Firstly, even if the purchaser did demand a price reduction to reflect the potential Corporation Tax bill, Ann would still end up over £263,000 better off than Nick. (She would also obtain the same outcome if she sold the development first and then wound up the company.)

Secondly, as I mentioned above, as a well-established property development company, Rainbow Developments Limited could have a goodwill value which more than compensates for the latent Corporation Tax bill.

Most of all though, the answer is Stamp Duty Land Tax!

If a purchaser acquired the new development directly, the Stamp Duty Land Tax bill would be £72,730. Instead, they can purchase the company at a Stamp Duty cost of only £4,965, giving them a saving of £67,765, which makes up for the potential Corporation Tax charge.

Note to the Example

Here again I must stress the warnings given in Section 11.17, although in Rainbow Developments Limited's case, there were clearly ample profits to cover the proposed dividends each year.

Wealth Warning

The VAT position on the final development held by Rainbow Developments Limited would also need to be considered, as there is some risk of a 'claw back' of any VAT claimed by the company on this last project, depending on the purchaser's future intentions for the company.

Chapter 13

The Importance of Interest Relief

13.1 INTRODUCTION

A property company which borrows to finance property purchases or other aspects of its property business obtains Corporation Tax relief for interest and other finance costs.

Relief may follow either the special rules explained in Section 4.7, or the general principles for any trading deduction explained in Chapter 5, depending on the type of property business which the company has. Either way, however, as long as the interest or other finance costs are incurred for business purposes, the company does get Corporation Tax relief.

Investors themselves will obtain Income Tax relief for interest on borrowings invested in the property company, provided that it is a 'Close Company', but not classed as a 'Close Investment Holding Company'. Both of these terms are explained in Section 16.1.

To obtain relief, the investor must also either have a 'material interest' in the company, or must hold <u>some</u> ordinary shares in the company <u>and</u> work for the greater part of their time in the actual conduct or management of the company's business.

A 'material interest' is broadly defined as more than 5% of the company's share capital and shares held by 'connected' persons (see Appendix D) may usually be counted for this purpose, as long as the individual concerned does hold some of the shares personally.

In the case of most private property companies, the investor will qualify as having a 'material interest', although, for a large property company, it may be that some new investors come on board who qualify for relief through the second criterion instead.

Where the investor qualifies for relief, they are equally eligible for interest relief on funds borrowed to purchase shares in the company or funds borrowed to lend to the company.

Top Tax Tip

The important point to note, therefore, is that, in most cases, an investor who borrows funds to invest in their own property company can claim tax relief for their interest against their other income.

For this purpose it does not matter what form the investor's other income takes and it does not have to be in any way related to the property business.

We will look at an illustration of the potential benefits of interest relief claimed directly by the investor personally later in this chapter.

Combining the potential for personal interest relief for the investor with the beneficial regime enjoyed by the company itself (see Section 4.7) makes a property investment company very attractive whenever there is a possibility, or indeed a probability, that interest costs will exceed net rental income (after deducting other allowable expenses, including the 10% wear and tear allowance – see Section 4.5).

Again, we will look at an illustration of the benefits of a property investment company in this situation later in this chapter.

13.2   WHO SHOULD BORROW THE FUNDS?

When investing in property through a company, there are three possible approaches to the financing structure:

i) Borrow the funds personally and then invest them in shares in the company.
ii) Borrow the funds personally and then lend them to the company.

iii) Borrow the funds within the company.

These three different structures make several important differences to the overall tax situation:

- Tax relief on the interest paid.
- Additional tax arising due to the need to extract funds to service personal debt held outside the company.
- The Capital Gains Tax position on an ultimate winding up or sale of the company.
- Stamp Duty on a sale of the company's shares.

They do not, however, make any difference to the capital gains position on property disposals made by the company itself.

An additional non-tax issue is the impact on the investor's ability to withdraw the sums invested back out of the company.

Over the next few sections, we will take a look at the implications of each structure in turn. In each case, we will assume that the company is a Close Company, but not a Close Investment Holding Company.

We will also assume that the rate of interest charged will be unaffected by the funding method used. In practice, this may not be the case and investors will therefore also need to weigh up the impact of any differences in interest rates.

13.3   BORROWING TO INVEST IN SHARES

The individual will obtain interest relief on the borrowings. This can be highly advantageous if the individual is a higher rate taxpayer, as relief is being given at a higher effective rate than the Corporation Tax paid by the company on its profits.

If the individual is able to service the debt from other resources then this is all well and good and in Section 13.8 we will take a look at the significant benefits which this can produce.

In many cases, however, it will be necessary to extract funds from the company in order to service the debt.

Example

Gill, a higher rate taxpayer, borrowed £100,000 to invest in her own property company. She pays annual interest totalling £7,000, thus providing her with effective relief of £2,800 (at 40%).

However, in order to pay this interest, Gill has to take a dividend of £7,000 out of her company. This costs her an additional £1,750 (25%) in Income Tax, meaning that her effective relief for the interest is only £1,050 (15%).

Clearly, if personal debt needs to be serviced through the withdrawal of funds from the company, this will generally eliminate any apparent advantage of obtaining interest relief personally: Gill's effective rate of relief is only 15%; the company would obtain Corporation Tax relief at 20% or more if it were paying the interest.

If Gill had total income in excess of £150,000 and was thus paying 'super tax' at 50%, the overall effective rate of relief if she were taking dividends to service her interest payments would be just 13.9% (50% - 36.1%).

Note that we have only considered the payment of interest here and have ignored capital repayments. These would, of course, only serve to further increase the Income Tax cost on the withdrawal of the necessary funds from the company.

Basic rate taxpayers would not have the problem of Income Tax arising on the sums withdrawn from the company by way of dividend. However, the rate of relief for their interest payments, 20%, would never exceed the relief which the company would obtain if it were paying the interest directly.

Hence, corporate borrowings will generally provide better tax relief than individual borrowings invested in property company shares in most circumstances.

On a winding up where borrowings have been invested in company shares, the individual will have a high base cost in the shares, thus reducing the potential Capital Gains Tax impact (as was the case for Louise in Example 'B', Part 3 in Section 12.6).

A sale of the company's shares could give rise to a fairly substantial Stamp Duty bill for the purchaser, as much of its value will be held as non-distributable share capital.

Another big drawback to this structure is the difficulty in withdrawing the funds invested. This requires a winding up, corporate restructuring or company purchase of own shares. We have covered winding up in Section 12.6. While in some cases they can prove worthwhile, the other possible methods are likely to prove costly in terms of both the tax charges arising and the professional fees which will inevitably be incurred.

13.4   BORROWING TO LEND TO THE COMPANY

Lending funds to the company will produce the same interest relief as in Section 13.3 above, as long as the loan is structured properly.

All of the same issues regarding withdrawal of the necessary funds to service the debt, etc, apply here in equal measure except that the investor can, if desired, also charge the company interest on the outstanding loan from them to the company.

Provided that the interest charged does not exceed a normal commercial rate, the company will obtain Corporation Tax relief on interest paid to the investor, although the investor will, of course, be taxed on this income. This is a useful third alternative for 'profit extraction' (see Chapter 10), as Corporation Tax relief is obtained without any National Insurance costs arising.

A slight cashflow disadvantage does arise due to the fact that the company must deduct 20% Income Tax at source from payments of interest to the individual investor and account for this to HM Revenue and Customs on a quarterly basis. The tax deducted can later be set off against the individual's Income Tax liability under Self-Assessment, but this can leave investors 'out of pocket' when they have to service personal borrowings whilst only receiving 80% of the interest due from the company.

The major advantage of this structure (over Section 13.3) is that the funds invested can be withdrawn from the company at any time (with no tax liability), if the cash is available.

On a winding up, the amounts due to the investor can be repaid without any tax implications. This would leave the same level of Capital Gains Tax as in Section 13.3 above.

On a sale of the company, the funds due to the investor would effectively be deducted from the value of the company's shares, thus reducing the amount of Stamp Duty payable by the purchaser.

All in all, lending funds to the company is generally to be preferred to borrowing to invest in shares and still has the potential to produce the significant benefits which we will explore in Section 13.8 at the end of this chapter. The company will, of course, need some share capital but this can be kept at a minimal level in most private companies (e.g. £100).

13.5   CORPORATE BORROWINGS

Where the company obtains funds through its own direct borrowings, this will, of course, mean that it is the company which claims relief for the interest costs. However, it also means that there will be no need to extract funds from the company in order to service the debt.

Whether this is better than the position which results through personal borrowings invested into the company will depend on whether the investor is a higher rate taxpayer and whether they would have had to withdraw funds from the company to service any private debt.

For higher rate taxpayers like Gill in our example in Section 13.3, borrowings in the company will generally produce a better overall effective result for interest relief where it would otherwise be necessary to pay out dividends in order to service personal debt.

Where, however, a higher rate taxpayer is able to service the debt from other resources, a better rate of tax relief is obtained by borrowing funds personally for investment into the company.

As discussed in Section 13.3, where the investor is a basic rate taxpayer, personal borrowings can never produce a better rate of relief than corporate borrowings.

Where the company pays interest to any investor to enable them to service personal debt, the position regarding interest relief is effectively the same as for corporate borrowings, except for the slight cashflow disadvantage discussed in Section 13.4.

The position on a winding up where corporate borrowings have been used will depend on whether the borrowings are still in place at that time. If, at that time, there are still loans to be repaid out of property disposals, then the total sums to be distributed on the winding up will be reduced.

Hence, if all of the borrowings were still in place, the position would again be much the same as in Example 'B', Part 3 in Section 12.6. However, if the borrowings have been repaid, this means that the sum distributed on the winding up is increased.

Example 'B', Part 4

Returning to our earlier example in Sections 12.5 and 12.6, let us now suppose that Louise set Dawson Limited up with only a small nominal sum in share capital (so small, in fact, that we will ignore it for the sake of illustration). Dawson Limited borrowed £250,000 to finance the property purchase and these borrowings have now been completely repaid out of rent received by the company.

As before (see Section 12.6), we will assume that Louise first takes sufficient dividend to bring her total taxable income up to £100,000. We will again assume that this equates to a dividend of £50,400, leaving net proceeds of £419,600 in Dawson Limited.

This sum is then distributed to Louise on the winding up (once more ignoring professional fees, etc). Again, this represents a capital disposal by Louise but, this time, she has no (or very little) base cost to set off. She will therefore have a capital gain of £419,600. Even after deducting her future estimated annual exemption of £15,000, her taxable gain will be £404,600.

Louise's Capital Gains Tax bill on this gain, at 28%, will therefore be £113,288, meaning that the total tax burden on this property disposal would be £155,888! (Including the Corporation Tax paid by Dawson Limited on the property sale, £30,000, and the Income Tax paid by Louise on her dividend, £12,600.)

Analysis of Example 'B', Part 4

Clearly, this is a very poor result for Louise.

However, we must bear in mind that the company has repaid its borrowings from rental profits. To repay £250,000 out of after tax profits will have required pre-tax profits of at least £312,500 (based on Corporation Tax at 20%).

If Louise had received rental profits of £312,500 personally, she would have suffered at least £125,000 in additional Income Tax (at 40%). Hence, by using a company, Louise has achieved a cumulative tax saving on her rental income of at least £62,500 (£125,000 - £62,500).

If we factor in this cumulative tax saving, the actual overall net cost of the property disposal becomes £93,388 (£155,888 - £62,500).

Nevertheless, this is still £7,500 more than the overall cost achieved in Part 3 of this example (see Section 12.6), indicating that using corporate borrowings which are then repaid out of rental profits can have severe long-term financial drawbacks.

This situation has arisen because Louise has used the company's rental profits to repay its borrowings rather than extract them from the company or reinvest them.

In Section 12.4, we saw that reinvestment was a good strategy for a property company from an income perspective. In that case, however, the reinvestment strategy was designed to grow the company's property portfolio.

In this example, we can see that 'reinvestment' in the form of mere repayment of existing debt has only led to problems at a later stage. Inevitably, this result is bound to arise where the eventual intention is simply to realise gains on existing properties and then extract the proceeds from the company for personal use. This is not true reinvestment, but merely the deferral of profit extraction.

We must contrast this outcome with the position which arose in Example 'C' in Sections 12.8 and 12.9, where we saw that the accumulation of additional after-tax resources through reinvestment in new property could eventually compensate for the greater tax burden on the ultimate capital gains.

As usual, it is for individual investors to weigh up the conflicting factors in order to decide which approach is best for them.

Of course, in practice, the investor does not always have the luxury of being able to choose which financing structure is wanted, as banks will very often only be prepared to lend to the individual.

13.6   DEEDS OF TRUST

As explained in Section 1.3, it is sometimes difficult for a company to be able to borrow funds for the purchase of investment property at the same level as the personal investor.

Whereas a loan to value ('LTV') of 85% may sometimes be possible for an individual investor, the maximum borrowing afforded to corporate investors is often just 70%. This, in effect, means having to raise twice as much deposit money if investing via a company.

One way to resolve this dilemma is for the individual investor to take legal title to the property in their own name, thus enabling borrowings to be made at the desired level.

The investor then enters into a 'Deed of Trust' with the company. This is effectively a legal agreement under which the investor agrees that the beneficial ownership of the property actually lies with the company and the company agrees to recompense the investor for any costs incurred in relation to the property.

The effect of the Deed of Trust is therefore to put both the company and the individual investor into the same position as they would have been if the company had purchased the property, whilst allowing a more favourable level of borrowings to be obtained.

As long as the Deed of Trust is prepared and executed correctly and its terms actually adhered to in practice, the position for most tax purposes will be just as if the company had legal title to the property. One exception to this, however, is that a Stamp Duty Land Tax charge could arise on a later transfer of the legal title in the property to the company due to the market value rule explained in Section 15.12.

13.7 ROLLING UP INTEREST IN A COMPANY

As explained in Section 4.7, a property investment company can effectively 'roll up' its accumulated interest costs and set them off against the capital gains arising on the sale of its investment properties.

This is clearly much better than the position for individual investors, for whom any surplus interest costs simply form part of rental losses which can generally only be set against future rental profits.

To see what an enormous advantage this provides in practice, let's look at an example.

Example

Brian and Jason both buy a portfolio of investment properties for £1m each. They each borrow £750,000 to fund their purchases, on which the interest charge, at 6%, is £45,000 per annum.

Each investor has other allowable costs relating to his portfolio of £40,000 per annum and each portfolio yields annual rental income of £70,000. Each portfolio is therefore making an overall profit of £30,000 per annum before interest costs.

Brian makes his investments through his company, Habana Properties Limited. The company sets £30,000 of its annual interest cost against its rental profits each year and carries the excess (£15,000) forward. (If the company had other sources of income it could set this excess cost against them.)

Jason makes his investments personally and therefore has an overall rental loss of £15,000 each year which he can only carry forward to set against future rental profits from UK property (assuming his current portfolio is all made up of UK property).

After ten years, Habana Properties Limited has unrelieved interest costs carried forward of £150,000 and Jason has rental losses of £150,000.

We will assume here that both Habana Properties Limited and Jason have had to borrow a further £150,000 to fund the deficit in their rental income over this ten year period, bringing their total borrowings to £900,000 each. (We will, however, ignore the additional interest costs arising for the sake of simplicity.)

At this point, both investors decide to sell off their portfolio. They each sell their properties for a total sum of £1.6m making total capital gains of £600,000 before any reliefs.

Jason deducts his annual exemption of, say, £15,000 and is left with taxable gains of £585,000. He is a higher rate taxpayer, so his Capital Gains Tax liability at 28% amounts to £163,800 leaving him with net proceeds of £536,200 after repaying his borrowings (£1.6m - £900,000 - £163,800).

Habana Properties Limited claims indexation relief at, say, 40%, leaving a taxable gain of £200,000 (£600,000 - £1m x 40%). The company is then able to set its unrelieved 'rolled up' interest costs of £150,000 against this gain leaving just £50,000 chargeable to Corporation Tax. The company's Corporation Tax bill, at 20%, therefore amounts to just £10,000.

At this stage, we see that the company has saved over £150,000 compared with the individual investor!

But what if the investor now wishes to wind the company up so that he can obtain his net sale proceeds?

Taking account of its borrowings, the company's remaining net funds amount to £690,000 (£1.6m - £900,000 - £10,000). Of this, £250,000 represents the original equity invested by Brian ten years previously and can therefore be returned to him tax free. Hence, if Brian winds up Habana Properties Limited at this point, he will have a capital gain of £440,000 (£690,000 - £250,000).

After deducting his estimated future annual exemption of £15,000, Brian is left with a taxable gain of £425,000 which, as a higher rate taxpayer, gives him a Capital Gains Tax liability, at 28%, of £119,000.

Hence, deducting his Capital Gains Tax bill from his net proceeds of £690,000 (ignoring the costs of the winding up as usual) we see that Brian eventually keeps a net sum of £571,000, or almost £35,000 more than Jason.

(Note that Brian may have been able to reduce his tax bill by paying himself some dividends prior to the winding up. I have ignored this option here for the sake of simplicity, but it would only serve to improve his position still further. See Sections 12.6 and 12.9 for further details.)

As we can see from this example, the ability to 'roll up' interest in the company provides the opportunity to make enormous Corporation Tax savings. In this case, the Corporation Tax bill on a gain of £600,000 was slashed to less than 1.7%!

Where sale proceeds are being retained in the company for reinvestment, this will therefore provide a massive advantage over individual investors.

Admittedly, as we can see from the last part of the example, a large part of the initial Corporation Tax savings may effectively be lost if the proceeds are returned to the individual investor but, even then, a reasonable saving may still arise.

Note that, in the above example, Jason's accumulated rental losses of £150,000 simply go to waste. In practice, an investor such as Jason would be well advised to keep at least part of his portfolio in order to be able to utilise these losses. More advice on getting value out of rental losses is contained in the Taxcafe.co.uk guide *'How to Avoid Property Tax'*.

13.8 PERSONAL INTEREST RELIEF

Finally, to finish off this chapter, it is worth taking a look at the benefits of personal Income Tax relief for interest on funds invested in a property company.

As we saw in Section 13.4, it will generally be sensible to lend borrowed funds to the company rather than use them to purchase company shares.

In Section 13.3, we saw that borrowing to invest in a property company is not beneficial where the debt has to be serviced by paying dividends to the investor.

Where the personal debt can be serviced by paying interest to the investor, the position is effectively neutral, since the taxable income matches the personal interest relief obtained (subject to the cashflow issue discussed in Section 13.4).

What we have not yet looked at, however, is the position where interest relief is being obtained personally without the need to extract funds from the company to service the debt.

Here again, the use of a property investment company will provide enormous advantages over the personal investor due to the more beneficial interest relief situation.

Example

Patrick and Francois both have large salaries of £100,000. Each of them borrows £1m to invest in property and incurs annual interest charges, at 5%, of £50,000.

Patrick invests his borrowed funds directly into his own personal property portfolio. Patrick's properties yield a rental profit of £40,000 before interest. After deducting his interest costs, however, Patrick is left with a rental loss of £10,000 which he can only carry forward.

Francois lends his borrowed funds to his company, Wadyamin Fudpoiznin Limited, and the company invests the funds in a property portfolio. The company's properties also yield a rental profit of £40,000 before interest.

Wadyamin Fudpoiznin Limited therefore pays Corporation Tax at 20% on its rental profits, i.e. £8,000.

Meanwhile, Francois claims interest relief for £50,000. As he is a higher rate taxpayer, this will provide him with a tax repayment of £20,000 (£50,000 x 40%).

*In net terms therefore, Francois and his company receive an overall tax **refund** of £12,000 (£20,000 - £8,000).*

Remarkably, this net refund actually exceeds the overall deficit of £10,000 on Wadyamin Fudpoiznin Limited's property portfolio (i.e. the deficit which arises after taking Francois' interest costs into account: £50,000 - £40,000).

*In other words, Francois' interest relief has turned an effective **loss** before tax of £10,000 into an effective **profit** after tax of £2,000 (£12,000 - £10,000).*

The Government is therefore effectively funding Francois' property portfolio and adding a little extra too!

As we can see from this example, where a higher rate taxpayer borrows to lend funds to their property company, the tax relief on the interest arising is highly beneficial.

The example also demonstrates that, where rental income is insufficient to cover interest costs, using a company can actually enable the investor to recover their deficit from the Government!

Even when rental profits are being made, the fact that tax relief can be obtained at 40% or even 50% on interest when company profits are being taxed at only 20% will continue to provide a significant benefit.

Chapter 14

How to Set Up Your Own Property Company

14.1 WHO CAN HELP AND HOW MUCH DOES IT COST?

If you do decide to go ahead and form a property company, it is pretty easy to do. Most lawyers can form a company for you, as well as many accountants. Some have so-called 'off-the-shelf' companies available for use at a moment's notice.

Alternatively, if you feel confident about tackling the 'paperwork' yourself, there are specialist company formation agents you can use, which will generally work out cheaper than using another intermediary. I say 'paperwork', but much of it can be done online these days.

The typical cost of forming a company through a formation agent is around £100 to £250. If you use a lawyer or accountant to assist with the task, or need to set up a specialised share structure, however, the costs may well be significantly more, perhaps as much as £500 to £1,500 in some cases.

Whoever you use to form your company, you will find that they ask a great many questions about the prospective officers of the company for the sake of 'security'. This is all in the name of the 'anti-money laundering' regulations. Details requested have been known to include eye colour, mother's maiden name and certain digits from National Insurance numbers.

14.2 THE COMPANY'S CONSTITUTION

The company's constitution is embodied in two documents:

- The company's Memorandum of Association, and
- The company's Articles of Association

223

The Memorandum covers what the company is empowered to do and sets out the framework for its share structure. Most modern Memorandums of Association empower the company to do pretty much anything. For a property company, it is important to ensure that the company has the power to:

- Borrow money,
- Buy or sell land and property, and
- Rent out, or grant leases over, property

As well as anything else that you are expecting to need the company to do.

The Articles of Association govern the rights of the holders of each class of shares (there only needs to be one class, but there can be more), as well as the power to appoint or remove directors or auditors (where necessary) and the conduct of general meetings of the company's members.

The company will need a registered office address, which must be occupied and cannot be a mere P.O. box. The company's name should be displayed prominently at the registered address and its statutory books and records should be kept there.

A UK company can be registered in Scotland, in Northern Ireland or in England and Wales, depending on where its registered office is located.

You will need to appoint at least one person to serve as a director. You may also need to appoint a company secretary if required by your company's Articles of Association. From April 2008, a company secretary is no longer a mandatory requirement but many company's constitutions will still require one.

Directors and company secretaries are referred to as the company's 'officers'. You will need to provide Companies House with a home address for each officer. You can also provide a 'service address' for each officer. The service address will appear on the public record and can therefore be used to keep the officers' home addresses private. If you do not provide a service address, the officer's home address will be made public!

The company's registered office address can be used as the service address for one or more of the company's officers, if desired. A service address must again be occupied and not a mere P.O. box.

The owners of shares in the company are referred to as 'members'. A company must have at least one member. Until a few years ago, companies had to have at least two members.

A UK company may either be a private company or a public limited company (PLC). Most companies are private companies and there is little point in being a PLC unless you are seeking a stock-market quotation.

It is also possible to form a 'Societas Europaea' (or 'SE' for short), a new form of European company available throughout the European Union. The tax treatment of a 'Societas Europaea' will depend entirely on where it is resident and hence, if you form one of these companies, and base it in the UK, it will be subject to Corporation Tax in exactly the same way as any other UK company.

The act of forming a company is often referred to as 'incorporation' and the day on which the company is formed is known as its date of incorporation.

Once you have formed your company, it can go ahead and borrow money or purchase new properties. Provided, of course, that the lenders are willing to co-operate!

14.3   OTHER COMPANY FORMATION FORMALITIES

Shortly after you register your company with Companies House, you will receive a letter from them congratulating you on your new company and advising you of some of your responsibilities as a company director.

You will also receive a form CT41G from HM Revenue and Customs. You should complete and return this form in order to get the company into the Corporation Tax system. It is important to do this within three months of when the company commences any business activities, as penalties will be imposed if you do not return the completed form within this timescale.

You will usually need to register the company as an employer for PAYE purposes. Remember that paying yourself, or your spouse or partner, a small salary will be enough to mean that the company must register as an employer. You may also need to register the company for VAT, if applicable (see Chapter 9).

In some cases, you will also need to submit a 'Form 42' to HM Revenue and Customs by 6th July following the end of the tax year in which the company's shares are issued. This form provides details of shares issued to a company's employees, including directors, and may also need to be submitted again following any further subsequent issues of shares by the company.

14.4   CHANGING YOUR COMPANY'S ACCOUNTING DATE

Initially, the company's accounting date will automatically be set as the date falling twelve months after the end of the month in which the company was incorporated.

However, a company's accounting year-end date does not need to permanently remain as the same calendar date and can generally be changed.

Generally speaking, in order to change the company's accounting date, you will simply need to submit a form AA01 to Companies House any time before the earlier of the filing deadline for the accounts based on its original accounting date and the filing deadline based on the revised accounting date which you are now requesting.

See Section 14.6 for details of Companies House accounts filing deadlines. Take note of the additional requirement in respect of the company's first accounting period, which is particularly relevant here.

Subject to a few restrictions, a company may change its accounting date at any time. However, this generally happens most often at the beginning of a company's life due to the application of the initial rule explained above.

Naturally, where a change is made to the accounting date, for whatever reason, the company will have a short or long accounting period (i.e. a period other than a year).

This has some important consequences for the company's Corporation Tax position and we will look at these in Section 16.5.

14.5   DEALING WITH COMPANIES HOUSE

Once your company is set up, you will need to advise Companies House of any changes in the company's:

- Directors (or their particulars – i.e. their name, home address or service address)
- Company Secretary (or their particulars)
- Registered Office
- Accounting Date (as explained in Section 14.4)
- Issued share capital
- Charges (i.e. mortgages and other secured loans)

The last point is particularly significant for property companies and it is important to ensure that any charges over the company's property are registered with Companies House and that these details are kept up to date.

There are also two things that Companies House will require from you on an annual basis:

- Statutory Accounts (see Section 14.6) and
- An Annual Return

The annual return provides details of the company's share capital and shareholders. The return will be sent to the company's registered office address a few weeks in advance of the filing deadline.

The filing deadline for the return will usually be 28 days after each anniversary of the company's date of incorporation.

As with taxation, there are penalties for late filing of either the accounts or the annual return. Extensions to the filing deadlines are, however, sometimes granted. You must apply to Companies House directly (preferably in advance), for these.

Wealth Warning

Do not confuse the Companies House requirements with HM Revenue and Customs' requirements.

Both institutions require a set of accounts and a return from you each year, with different deadlines. Complying with one institution's requirements will not satisfy the other institution and you will suffer penalties if you make the mistake of thinking that it does.

14.6   STATUTORY ACCOUNTS

Every company must prepare a set of statutory accounts for each of its accounting periods. These accounts must adhere to a standard format specified by Company Law and generally accepted accounting practice (sometimes referred to as 'GAAP').

The full set of statutory accounts must always be submitted to HM Revenue and Customs together with the company's Corporation Tax Return, as explained in Section 2.8.

Small and medium-sized companies (see below) may, however, file a set of abbreviated statutory accounts with Companies House. These abbreviated accounts must be prepared on the same basis as the full statutory accounts but provide less detail on the company's activities. This is to ensure that smaller companies do not need to make too many of their business dealings public.

Remember that accounts held at Companies House are part of the public record and can be seen by anyone, so I would generally recommend that abbreviated accounts are filed whenever possible.

Broadly speaking, a company is 'Small' for these purposes if it meets at least two of the following three tests:

i)   Turnover (i.e. gross income) does not exceed £5,600,000 per annum.
ii) Total asset value does not exceed £2,800,000.
iii) It has no more than 50 employees.

Most property companies will tend to qualify as 'Small' on the basis that they meet tests (i) and (iii).

A 'Medium-Sized' company is one which fails to meet the 'Small' company test but which does meet at least two out of the following three tests:

i)   Turnover (i.e. gross income) does not exceed £22,800,000 per annum.
ii) Total asset value does not exceed £11,400,000.
iii) It has no more than 250 employees.

Statutory accounts are usually prepared on an annual basis, although other accounting periods, up to a maximum length of 18 months, may sometimes be used. We will return to the Corporation Tax consequences of this in Section 16.5.

Where it has been necessary to prepare additional, more detailed, accounts for Corporation Tax purposes, these do not need to be filed with Companies House.

Whether abbreviated accounts are used or not, private companies must generally file the appropriate statutory accounts at Companies House within nine months of their accounting date. The company's **first** set of accounts must, however, be filed by the **earlier** of nine months from the accounting date or 21 months from the date of incorporation.

14.7   CHOOSING AN ACCOUNTANT OR AUDITOR

Not every company requires an audit. Generally speaking, the company's accounts will only need to be audited if the company meets one of the following criteria:

- Turnover exceeds £5,600,000 per annum, or
- Total gross asset value exceeds £2,800,000.

'Turnover' is an accounting term for gross sales or rental income (but does exclude VAT, where applicable).

Very few property investment companies will exceed the first limit, but the second limit will quite often be exceeded as it is based on **gross** asset values (i.e. the total value of all the company's properties and other assets, with no deduction in respect of borrowings and other liabilities).

The first limit (turnover), however, will be of more concern to property development companies.

Exceeding one of the above limits makes an audit mandatory, but there is nothing to stop you having your company audited even if you do not meet these criteria. You might wish to do this, for example, if you have left the running of your company in the hands of managers and would like some independent verification of the company's financial results.

An audit of the company's accounts *must* be carried out by a firm of qualified accountants registered to carry out audit work.

Most other people operating a business through a company will usually also find that they need the services of an accountant, even if they don't need an audit.

In this case, there are no legal requirements regarding the type of accountant you must use. Nevertheless, whilst there are some very good unqualified accountants, I would generally recommend that you use a qualified firm of accountants who are members of one of the major recognised accountancy bodies, such as the Institute of Chartered Accountants in England and Wales ('ICAEW') or the Institute of Chartered Accountants of Scotland ('ICAS').

Furthermore, as property is a specialised area, you should try to find a firm with experience in the property sector.

You might also like to ask your prospective accountant where your accounts will actually be prepared. Some accountancy firms are now adopting the rather reprehensible habit of sending client files half way around the world for processing, without even telling the client what they are doing!

Chapter 15

How to Put Existing Property into a Company

15.1 INTRODUCTION

The basic problem with transferring anything into your company is the fact that you and the company are 'connected'. As explained in Section 6.2, this means that, in principle, any transfers of assets between you and the company will be deemed to take place at market value for Capital Gains Tax purposes. Furthermore, as explained in Section 8.3, any transfer of property to a connected company will also be deemed to take place at market value for Stamp Duty Land Tax purposes.

Potentially, therefore, you could face a huge tax bill if you try to transfer existing properties into a company.

We will return to the issue of Stamp Duty Land Tax on transfers to your own property company in Section 15.12.

As far as Capital Gains Tax is concerned, there are two important reliefs available which may potentially resolve the problem in some cases. Careful use of these reliefs may even create additional tax advantages for those with the 'right kind' of property business.

These important Capital Gains Tax reliefs are:

- Relief for 'Gifts Of Business Assets', and
- So-called 'Incorporation Relief'.

Whether either or both of these reliefs are available, and the extent to which they may be used to defer, or even reduce, your potential Capital Gains Tax liabilities, will depend on the exact nature of your property business in the past, the present and the future.

Tax Tip

Both of these Capital Gains Tax reliefs are available when the business qualifies for them at the time of the transfer of the assets. The business does not need to continue to qualify for any particular period after the transfer.

This creates some significant tax-planning opportunities, which we will explore later in this chapter.

I would, however, suggest that the business needs to continue for some period after the transfer, or else the qualifying activity would probably be regarded as no more than an artificial sham.

Where the business qualifies for one of the above reliefs, the relief is equally available to transferor individuals, partnerships or trusts. However, for the rest of this chapter, I will refer just to individual transferors for the sake of simplicity.

15.2   GIFTS OF 'BUSINESS ASSETS'

The first of the two potential Capital Gains Tax reliefs available is something of a misnomer since, in fact, the relief will generally only apply to trading assets, rather than what the average person would regard as a business asset. Within tax legislation, 'business' is a much wider term than 'trade' and, as we have discussed already, property investment or property letting is not usually considered to be a 'trade' for tax purposes.

Hence, this relief is unlikely to be available to a property investment or property letting business, although we will return to this subject in Section 15.9.

The relief for 'Gifts Of Business Assets' will, however, be available to a property development business or a qualifying furnished holiday letting business. It should, in fact, be available to any business classed as a 'trade' (see Chapter 3), although we will return to this point in Section 15.6.

The relief for 'Gifts Of Business Assets' works where you transfer qualifying 'trading' properties to your company for no consideration, or for a consideration less than market value.

For this relief, it is not necessary to actually transfer the whole business, as the relief can be claimed in respect of any asset used in a qualifying trade. Hence, for example, an individual who used both an office and a warehouse in their property development business could claim relief on a 'gift' of the warehouse to a company while still retaining personal ownership of the office.

The relief works by allowing the capital gain that arises on the transfer under the normal rules to be 'held over'. This means that the individual making the transfer has no Capital Gains Tax liability, but it also means that the assets transferred to the company have a lower base cost (see Section 6.3). The assets' base cost is reduced by the amount of gain 'held over'.

Where the asset is only partly used in the qualifying trade, or has been used in the qualifying trade for only part of the transferor's period of ownership, the amount of gain that may be 'held over' is proportionately reduced. This will usually mean that some Capital Gains Tax liability will still arise on the transfer.

Note that this relief is not automatic and a claim must be made jointly by the transferring taxpayer and the recipient company. Under self-assessment, the claim must be made using the form provided with Helpsheet IR295, obtainable online from: www.hmrc.gov.uk/helpsheets/ir295.pdf

The relief cannot be used to transfer shares in one company from an individual's ownership into the ownership of another company.

Example

Tom runs a property development business from his office in Glasgow. He decides that he would like to transfer the whole business, including his office, into a new company, Smith Developments Limited.

Tom bought his office for £100,000 in March 2000 and has used it as

his trading premises ever since. Its current market value is £250,000, but Tom 'gifts' the property (i.e. transfers it for no consideration) to Smith Developments Limited in March 2012.

Under the normal rules, Tom would have had a capital gain of £150,000. However, if Tom and his company jointly elect to 'hold over' the gain, Tom will have no chargeable capital gain. Smith Developments Limited's base cost in the office property will be its market value, £250,000, less the 'held over' gain of £150,000, i.e. £100,000.

As we can see, the company ends up with the same base cost for the office property as the individual owner had. (Plus the additional Stamp Duty Land Tax cost, which I have ignored here for the sake of illustration.)

Note that Tom's actual capital gain (had he not elected to 'hold over') would have qualified for entrepreneurs' relief and therefore would probably have been subject to Capital Gains Tax at just 10% (see Section 7.3). Hence, assuming that his annual exemption of £10,600 (estimated for 2011/12) was available, his actual potential Capital Gains Tax bill may therefore have been as low as £13,940.

Against this, we must weigh the fact that a sale of the property by the company after the transfer would give rise to a Corporation Tax bill of at least £30,000 (depending on the date of sale and the level of the company's profits and once again ignoring the Stamp Duty Land Tax cost for the sake of illustration).

It's a case of a small amount of tax now versus a much greater amount of potential tax in the future. This presents us with a bit of a dilemma and we will return to this point in Section 15.5.

Tax Tip

Rather than 'gifting' assets to the company for no consideration, it is often worth selling them for a small sum in order to utilise the transferor individual's available reliefs.

The 'Gifts Of Business Assets' relief can still be used to 'hold over' the element of the gain that arises only due to the 'deemed' sale proceeds at market value rule, with the individual's Capital Gains Tax calculation then proceeding on the basis of the actual consideration.

With many new companies, this is often done by agreeing a sale price for the asset and allowing that sum to be left outstanding as a loan from the transferor to the company.

The loan may be paid back to the transferor as the company's funds permit, giving the transferor what is, to all practical intents and purposes, a tax-free income from the company until the loan is paid off.

Example Revisited

In the above example, Tom could have transferred the office property to Smith Developments Limited for £110,600. After electing to 'hold over' the amount representing the difference between market value and actual consideration (£139,400), this would leave him with a capital gain of £10,600.

This gain would then be covered by his annual Capital Gains Tax exemption, leaving him with no tax to pay and a 'tax-free' sum of £110,600, which he can draw upon as funds permit.

Meanwhile, Smith Developments Limited's base cost is £10,600 more than it would have been and this will save at least £2,120 in Corporation Tax on a sale of the property.

15.3 INCORPORATION RELIEF

Technically, this relief should be available whenever any 'business' is transferred to a company wholly or partly in exchange for shares.

A huge area of difficulty arises, however, in determining exactly what constitutes a 'business' for this purpose. Certainly, anything that may be deemed to be a 'trade' (see Chapter 3) must also qualify as a 'business', as will any qualifying furnished holiday letting businesses.

Beyond this, however, matters become unclear. There is no statutory definition of what constitutes a business for the purposes of Incorporation Relief and, to date, there is not any truly relevant case law to fall back on either.

We will return to the tricky question of what constitutes a qualifying business for this purpose in Section 15.10.

In the meantime, however, let's just concentrate on how the relief works. Incorporation Relief works along similar principles to the relief for 'Gifts Of Business Assets', except that:

- The transferor must transfer the whole of their business as a 'going concern'.
- The assets transferred only need to be in use in the business at the point of transfer. Unlike the relief for 'Gifts Of Business Assets', there is no restriction to the relief if the assets have not been in business use throughout the transferor's ownership (but see the 'Tax Tip' in Section 15.1).
- The transfer must be made wholly or partly in exchange for shares in the transferee company (the relief will only apply to the part of the sale consideration which is satisfied in shares).
- The gain 'held over' is deducted from the transferor individual's base cost in the shares and not from the value of the underlying assets transferred. In effect (where the transfer is made wholly in exchange for shares), this means that the transferor's Capital Gains Tax base cost for those shares becomes the same as the base cost which the transferor previously had for the underlying assets.
- It also follows that the new base costs which the company has in the business assets transferred to it are those assets' market values at the date of transfer. This provides a unique opportunity to 'step up' the base cost of those assets and thus save a fortune on their ultimate sale. We will look at this further in Section 15.8.
- Where the necessary conditions apply, the relief is given automatically. The transferor may, however, elect to disapply the relief. (Why would they want to disapply it? – see the warning below.)

Wealth Warning

Incorporation relief will eliminate, or at least reduce, the Capital Gains Tax arising on the transfer of an individual's qualifying business to a company.

However, it is essential to remember that this will mean that any available entrepreneurs' relief is not claimed.

Usually, of course, where entrepreneurs' relief was available on the business, then it will also be available on the company shares and it is only necessary to hold the shares for one year for this purpose.

In some cases, however, there may be a risk that the company will not qualify as the transferor's 'personal company' for entrepreneurs' relief purposes (see Section 7.3) and the chance to claim entrepreneurs' relief will effectively have been lost. In these cases, it may therefore sometimes be better to disapply this relief.

There is, of course, also the possibility that the transferor ends up selling their shares within less than a year after the transfer. Again, in such cases, an election to disapply incorporation relief will often be beneficial.

An election to disapply incorporation relief must normally be made by the second anniversary of the 31st January after the tax year in which the transfer took place. *For example, for a transfer made during 2011/12, the normal deadline to elect to disapply is 31st January 2015.*

However, if the transferor has disposed of all of the shares received as consideration for the transfer by the end of the next tax year after the transfer, the deadline is accelerated by a year.

15.4 WHICH RELIEF IS BEST?

In some cases, the relief for 'Gifts of Business Assets' and Incorporation Relief may both potentially be available to prevent any Capital Gains Tax liability from arising on the transfer of a property business into a company.

In such cases, it is generally possible to choose which one of the two reliefs you wish to use. Actually, when I say it is possible to 'choose' which relief is used, this choice is generally made by the way in which you structure the transaction used to transfer your business.

In essence, by making the transfer of your whole business wholly or partly in exchange for shares, you will effectively be 'choosing' Incorporation Relief (as it is then automatic). Alternatively, by transferring qualifying trading properties into a company for no consideration, or a consideration that is less than market value (and, if you are transferring your whole business, does not consist wholly or partly of shares), you will be able to claim relief for 'Gifts of Business Assets'.

All of this assuming that you do have a business which qualifies for the reliefs of course!

The best choice will depend on your future plans and expectations for the properties and business being transferred.

In general, however, the relief for 'Gifts of Business Assets' offers far greater flexibility, both in terms of the assets that are to be transferred and in the choice of the level of Capital Gains Tax to be paid.

Furthermore, the ability to use the relief for 'Gifts of Business Assets' to create what is effectively a source of tax-free income, as we saw in Section 15.2, means that this is often the preferred route.

In the second part of the example in Section 15.2, we looked at a situation where the consideration was fixed at the maximum level that still left the transferor with no Capital Gains Tax to pay.

In practice, however, where entrepreneurs' relief is available, many transferors will choose to pay some Capital Gains Tax at just 10%, in order to increase the level of the loan account, which they can later draw upon tax free. This is because the 10% Capital Gains

Tax bill is far less than the tax arising on withdrawals made by way of salary or dividend (see Chapter 10).

Hence, in effect, by using the relief for 'Gifts of Business Assets' (where available) you can actually choose how much Capital Gains Tax you want to pay on the transfer and you can effectively 'bank' the sum which has been taxed and withdraw it later with no further tax to pay.

Admittedly, similar results can be achieved with Incorporation Relief, by using a mixture of shares and cash as consideration for the transfer of the business, but it is much more difficult to judge this correctly in order to achieve the optimum, or desired, result.

The relief for 'Gifts of Business Assets' also enables you to keep the share capital in your company at a low level, thus enabling you to withdraw your investment far more easily. By contrast, to use Incorporation Relief, you will generally need to issue large amounts of share capital, making it difficult for you to withdraw your investment from the company.

Incorporation Relief also requires you to transfer your whole business. This could mean having to transfer properties and other assets that you did not wish to transfer and it also maximises your Stamp Duty Land Tax exposure (see Section 15.12).

By using the relief for 'Gifts of Business Assets' you can effectively 'cherry pick' the properties and other assets that you wish to transfer. Note, however, that entrepreneurs' relief is only available where the assets transferred constitute a distinct part of the business which is capable of being operated as a going concern in its own right. This should not present any difficulties in the case of qualifying furnished holiday lettings, but will need careful consideration in the case of a property development business.

Incorporation Relief does, however, have two major advantages over relief for 'Gifts of Business Assets'.

Firstly, as explained in Section 15.3, with Incorporation Relief there is no reduction in the amount of gain that may be 'held over' if the assets have not been used in the business throughout the transferor's ownership. In some cases, this may enable the owner of business property to obtain relief for their whole capital gain, rather than just part of it.

Secondly, of course, there is the ability for the company to get a 'step up' in the base cost of the assets transferred to their current market values.

In some cases, however, the 'step up' in base cost will be of limited value when the business is eligible for entrepreneurs' relief and the maximum Capital Gains Tax exposure for the transferor is thus only 10%.

Add to this the fact that most property business transfers will attract Stamp Duty Land Tax at rates of up to 5% (see Section 15.12) and we can see that the benefit of the 'step up' may sometimes be quite doubtful when entrepreneurs' relief is also available.

Nevertheless, there are occasions when the 'step up' in base cost offered by Incorporation Relief will be valuable, especially when the use of the properties being transferred is expected to change.

We will explore some opportunities for tax planning with Incorporation Relief in Section 15.8.

In general, however, it is fair to say that where both reliefs are available, most people will benefit more from the relief for 'Gifts of Business Assets'.

15.5   PAY NOW, SAVE LATER

As we have already discussed, where a property business, or a part of a property business capable of operating as a going concern in its own right, is eligible for entrepreneurs' relief, the Capital Gains Tax rate which the owner will suffer on a transfer into a company is just 10% (on the first £5m of capital gains per person).

There is therefore a strong argument for saying that, in these circumstances, it is better not to claim either of the two major hold over reliefs discussed in the previous section since, by paying tax at 10% now, the transferor may achieve far greater tax savings in the future.

Furthermore, as we discussed in the previous section, this will allow the transferor to withdraw substantial sums from the company tax free.

Example

Scott is a higher rate taxpayer and has a qualifying furnished holiday letting business in the Scottish Borders. In September 2011, Scott transfers several furnished holiday letting properties into Murray Lettings Limited, a new property investment company which he has just set up. Scott bought the properties many years ago for a total of £200,000 and, at the time of the transfer, they are worth a total of £1,200,000.

If Scott does not claim to hold over his gain arising on the transfer of the properties, his Capital Gains Tax liability will be as follows:

	£
Deemed sale proceeds (market value on transfer)	1,200,000
Less:	
Original cost	200,000

	1,000,000
Less:	
Annual exemption	10,600

Taxable gain	989,400
	=========

Capital Gains Tax payable at 10%:   £98,940

Whilst Scott is not exactly happy to pay this tax, he nevertheless appreciates that, at less than 10%, it does represent a very good rate of tax. He therefore decides to transfer his properties for a sum of £1,200,000, which he can leave outstanding on loan account, rather than attempt to hold over the gain arising.

Over the next few years, Scott is therefore able to take £1,200,000 out of the company tax free (although he has to use the first £98,940 to pay his Capital Gains Tax bill).

If he took this sum out of the company by way of dividends, he would have had to pay a total of at least £300,000 in Income Tax.

By paying £98,940 in Capital Gains Tax up front, Scott has therefore been able to save at least £201,060 in the long run.

Furthermore, the company will also have a base cost of £1,200,000 for the properties rather than the £200,000 that it would have had if Scott had 'held over' his capital gains. On a sale of the properties, this higher base cost will save the company at least £200,000 (at 20%).

Hence, the £98,940 'up front' payment of Capital Gains Tax could eventually save Scott and the company together a total of over £400,000!

Note that, in this example, Murray Lettings Limited would also have a Stamp Duty Land Tax bill, at either 4% or 5% (i.e. either £48,000 or £60,000), on the transfer of Scott's properties. This would actually increase the company's base cost in the properties although, once again, I have ignored this in the example for the sake of illustration.

We will look at Stamp Duty Land Tax on property transfers in more detail in Section 15.12, but the important point to note here is that it makes no difference to the Stamp Duty Land Tax liability whether or not Scott holds over the capital gain arising on the transfer of his properties.

The 'pay now save later' strategy will be even more beneficial when the availability of entrepreneurs' relief is about to be lost. So beneficial sometimes, in fact, that it can make the transfer of property into a company a tax saving strategy in itself.

Example

Frank has a small villa which he purchased a few years ago for £100,000 and which is currently worth £250,000. He used the property as qualifying furnished holiday accommodation until 5th April 2009 and then changed over to long-term residential lettings. This means that the property will cease to qualify for entrepreneurs' relief after 5th April 2012.

In March 2012, however, Frank transfers his property to a new company, Hadden Lettings Limited.

Frank has a capital gain of £150,000. He deducts his 2011/12 annual exemption of £10,600 (estimated), leaving £139,400 which is subject to Capital Gains Tax at just 10%, i.e. £13,940.

The company also has a Stamp Duty Land Tax liability of £2,500 on the property, bringing its total base cost up to £252,500.

Five years later, in March 2017, Hadden Lettings Limited sells the property for £300,000, thus producing a capital gain of £47,500. After indexation relief of £47,391 (based on the company's base cost for the property of £252,500 and assuming inflation at 3.5% per annum), Hadden Lettings Limited has a chargeable gain of just £119, which is then subject to Corporation Tax at 20%, i.e. £24.

Frank then winds up Hadden Lettings Limited and his net proceeds of £297,476 (£300,000 LESS £24 Corporation Tax and £2,500 Stamp Duty Land Tax) give him a capital gain of £47,476. As Hadden Lettings Limited was not a trading company, Frank will not be eligible for entrepreneurs' relief on this occasion.

After deducting Frank's estimated 2016/17 annual exemption of £12,800, his taxable gain is reduced to £34,676. He is a higher rate taxpayer so this leaves him with a Capital Gains Tax bill, at 28%, of £9,709.

Frank's total tax costs on the property are thus:

£13,940 (Capital Gains Tax) + £2,500 (Stamp Duty Land Tax) + £24 (Corporation Tax) + £9,709 (Capital Gains Tax) = £26,173.

If Frank had still held the property personally at the time of sale, he would have had an overall capital gain of £200,000. As the property had been used for long-term lettings for the previous eight years, no entrepreneurs' relief would have been available.

After deducting his 2016/17 annual exemption of £12,800, Frank would therefore have had a taxable gain of £187,200 and a Capital Gains Tax liability at 28% of £52,416.

*Hence, by transferring the property into a company in 2012 and paying a small Capital Gains Tax bill of £13,940, Frank has ultimately reduced his overall tax bill by £26,243, or **over 50%!***

This example shows that an incorporation of a business that qualifies for entrepreneurs' relief on the transfer may ultimately be beneficial when a change in use of the property (or properties) has occurred, or is anticipated in the future.

This will, however, depend on the relative length of time and growth in value of the property in private ownership and qualifying business use, as compared with the length of time and growth in value of the property in company ownership and non-qualifying use. In practice, it will be necessary to prepare forecasts of the expected final sale position in order to decide if this route is beneficial.

15.6 'TRADING' BUSINESSES

If your business is regarded as 'trading' for tax purposes (see Chapter 3), then both the relief for 'Gifts of Business Assets' and Incorporation Relief should be available to deal with the problem of capital gains arising on the transfer of assets into your company.

Wealth Warning

When considering the transfer of a property trade, it is important to remember that there will also be other tax issues involved.

Such a transfer will be regarded as a cessation of trade for Income Tax purposes. It will also be necessary to make appropriate elections relating to trading stock, development work-in-progress and capital allowances, in order to prevent unwanted and unnecessary tax liabilities from arising.

The transfer will probably also give rise to Stamp Duty Land Tax liabilities, as explained in Section 15.12.

Transfers of trades will also mean a change in the 'taxable person' for VAT purposes and this will lead to a few formalities which will need to be observed (see Section 15.13).

Each of the two key Capital Gains Tax reliefs should readily be available to a property development or property management business, although, in the latter case, there may not be many assets to transfer.

As for a property dealing, or property trading, business (see Section 3.4), the Capital Gains Tax reliefs are theoretically available but:

- Will be of little benefit, as the properties held by the business represent trading stock and not capital assets,
- Could potentially be denied by HM Revenue and Customs who may argue that the business is actually one of property investment.

In most cases, it will make more sense to simply start up a new property dealing business within a company, rather than attempt to transfer the existing business.

15.7 FURNISHED HOLIDAY LETTINGS

As usual, furnished holiday letting businesses (see Section 4.6) have a privileged status and transfers of such businesses are eligible both for the relief for 'Gifts Of Business Assets' and for Incorporation Relief.

As explained in Section 15.4, where both reliefs are available, the best choice will depend on future plans and expectations and the choice will generally be made through the structure used for the transfer transactions.

As also explained in Section 15.4, relief for 'Gifts Of Business Assets' is usually preferable where entrepreneurs' relief is available.

In the next section, however, we will look at some situations where the 'step up' in base cost provided by Incorporation Relief can be used to produce significant tax savings on qualifying furnished holiday letting property.

Whilst qualifying furnished holiday letting properties do enjoy a number of advantages for Capital Gains Tax and Income Tax purposes, they are unfortunately still subject to Stamp Duty Land Tax in the usual way on a transfer into a company (see Section 15.12).

Where a furnished holiday letting business is registered for VAT (see Section 9.3), the transfer of the business to a company will again mean a change in the 'taxable person' for VAT purposes. We will look at some of the formalities which need to be dealt with in this situation in Section 15.13.

When transferring a furnished holiday letting business, it may also be necessary to make appropriate capital allowances elections, in order to prevent any balancing charges from arising.

15.8   TAX PLANNING WITH INCORPORATION RELIEF

In this section, we will look at some tax planning opportunities with Incorporation Relief which are suitable for qualifying furnished holiday letting properties (see Section 4.6) and other properties used in a qualifying trade, such as hotels and guest houses, for example.

Incorporation Relief not only allows assets to be transferred into a company free of Capital Gains Tax, but also enables the base cost of the transferred assets to be increased to their current market value.

Where the Stamp Duty Land Tax burden is not too significant, there may sometimes be an opportunity to benefit from this advantage.

This might occur, for example, where properties stand at significant capital gains but have a total value not far below one of the Stamp Duty Land Tax thresholds (see Section 8.3).

Example

Many years ago, Sean purchased three small cottages for £8,000 each. Since then, he has operated the properties as a furnished holiday letting business and each cottage is currently worth £83,000.

Sean is getting a little tired of the furnished holiday letting business and would like to sell the cottages after the next summer season and reinvest the proceeds in long-term residential letting properties. Sean has also decided that he would like to run his future investments through a limited company.

As Sean has held the properties for more than a year and operates each of them as a qualifying furnished holiday let, he would be entitled to entrepreneurs' relief on a sale of the properties.

Nevertheless, a straightforward sale of the three properties would still give Sean a total capital gain of £225,000 (three times £83,000 less three times £8,000). After deducting his (estimated) annual exemption of £10,600, he would be left with a taxable gain of £214,400 which, even at just 10%, would give him a Capital Gains Tax bill of £21,440.

Instead, therefore, Sean forms a company, Lamont Holidays Limited, and transfers his holiday letting business into it in exchange for shares plus £11,731 in 'cash'. (The 'cash' element is initially left outstanding as a director's loan account until the funds are available to pay Sean.)

The total value of Sean's properties was £249,000. He received £11,731 in cash, so his shares must be worth £237,269.

Sean's total capital gain, based on the market values of his properties, is £225,000. This gain is attributed as follows:

To shares:	*£225,000 x £237,269/£249,000 =*	*£214,400*
To cash:	*£225,000 x £11,731/£249,000 =*	*£10,600*

Sean will be eligible for Incorporation Relief in respect of the gain attributed to his shares. This means that he can 'hold over' this part of his gain. The base cost of his shares thus becomes £22,869 (£237,269 LESS £214,400).

The gain of £10,600 attributed to 'cash' will be taxable but will be covered by Sean's annual exemption, leaving him with no tax to pay.

The company will have to pay Stamp Duty Land Tax at 1% on the value of the properties at the date of transfer, i.e. £2,490. It does not matter that each property's value was below the £125,000 threshold (see Section 8.3), as the three were transferred together as 'linked transactions' and the 1% rate therefore applies.

After the summer season, the company is able to sell the three cottages. As the company has a base cost of £83,830 for each property (including the Stamp Duty Land Tax paid), there is likely to be little or no Corporation Tax payable on the sale.

Sean can, if he so chooses, remove £11,731 of the sale proceeds tax free from the company, by way of repayment of his director's loan. Add to this the usual ability to take a blend of salary and dividends tax free (see Section 11.17) and Sean may be able to extract over £50,000 of Lamont Holidays Limited's sale proceeds without having to pay a penny in tax.

The remaining balance is available to invest in Sean's new venture and the only amount lost in tax was a modest £2,490 of Stamp Duty Land Tax.

The formation of Lamont Holidays Limited and subsequent transfer of Sean's business has produced a net saving of £18,950 (£21,440 saved in Capital Gains Tax less £2,490 paid in Stamp Duty Land Tax). Sean has also been able to enjoy up to more than £50,000 of the sale proceeds tax free and may even have some further Income Tax savings on his last summer season profits, as we saw in Chapter 11.

If Sean had formed his company through the 'Gift of Business Assets' route, he would have had a Corporation Tax liability of £44,502 (£222,510 at 20%) on the company's sale of the properties, as the base cost of each property would have then been a mere £8,830 (including the Stamp Duty Land Tax paid by the company on the transfer).

15.9 TURNING INVESTMENT PROPERTY INTO 'TRADING' PROPERTY

In previous sections of this chapter, we have seen the benefits of the two Capital Gains Tax 'hold over' reliefs when transferring qualifying trading properties or furnished holiday lettings into a company.

Unfortunately, the relief for 'Gifts Of Business Assets' is strictly restricted to businesses which also qualify as 'trading' for entrepreneurs' relief purposes (see Chapter 3 and Section 7.3).

On the face of it, therefore, it would appear that a property investment business could never be eligible for relief for 'Gifts Of Business Assets'.

Partial relief may, however, be available where the business qualifies as a 'trade' at the point of the transfer. One way to qualify as a 'trade' for this purpose would be to use the property as qualifying furnished holiday accommodation (see Section 4.6).

Example

Anne has a house in Edinburgh which she has held as an investment property since buying it for £500,000 in April 2008. In April 2011,

Anne starts to let the property out as qualifying furnished holiday accommodation.

In April 2014, Anne transfers the property into her company Patron SRU Limited. The property's value at this point is £700,000.

Anne is deemed to have made a capital gain of £200,000. However, as she has used the property for a qualifying purpose for three years out of a total period of ownership of six years, Anne may claim to 'hold over' 3/6ths of her capital gain, i.e. £100,000.

As can be seen from the example, changing an existing property's use provides some scope to reduce the Capital Gains Tax liability arising on a transfer into a company by claiming relief for 'Gifts of Business Assets', but the relief is only partial.

Incorporation Relief may provide a better solution under these circumstances since, as explained in Section 15.3, there is no reduction in the amount of gain which may be 'held over' when the property has not always been used in a qualifying business.

All that is required in order to claim Incorporation Relief without restriction is that the property is used in a qualifying business at the point of transfer. (Although, in practice, qualification for a reasonable period both before and after the point of transfer is probably necessary, for the reasons explained in Section 15.1.)

In the next section, we will look at whether a property investment business may itself be a qualifying business for Incorporation Relief purposes, without any need to change the nature of the business.

What is more certain, however, is that if we can change the use of investment property so that it qualifies as furnished holiday letting property (as defined in Section 4.6) or as other qualifying trading property, then it will be eligible for Incorporation Relief, or for partial relief for 'Gifts of Business Assets', on a transfer to a company.

Unfortunately, not every property is suitable for the 'commercial letting of furnished holiday accommodation' – a term which must be met in order for it to qualify as a furnished holiday letting for the purposes of the two Capital Gains Tax 'hold over' reliefs.

So, can other investment properties ever become trading assets?

To achieve this will require the landlord to provide a significant level of additional services to tenants.

Generally speaking, merely ancillary services, such as cleaning the common stairwell of a block of flats, will not usually be regarded as sufficient to give the landlord trading status.

What is usually required is some form of services to individual rooms or tenants, such as the provision of meals, cleaning bedrooms or making up beds. Where a range of services are provided to individual tenants or their rooms, trading status should be assured and, in these cases, the landlord need not carry out the work personally, but may employ others to do it.

In the middle ground, there are those who provide an intermediate level of services to their tenants, such as window-cleaning and small property repairs. Where the landlord is engaged virtually full-time in managing properties and is providing many of these services personally, HM Revenue and Customs may sometimes accept that he or she is trading, although the position is far from certain.

Another useful indicator of trading status is the length of the average tenant's stay in the premises. The shorter the better from this point of view and average stays measured in days are more likely to indicate a trade than those measured in months.

In short, to achieve trading status generally requires the landlord to be running their property more like a guest house or a hostel than a normal letting business.

If this can be achieved, however, then either Incorporation Relief or partial relief for 'Gifts of Business Assets' should be available on a transfer of property into a company.

At a later date (say a year or two after the transfer), the company could then cease providing the additional services and revert to a pure property investment business.

Wealth Warning

It must be remembered that running the business as a trade prior to the transfer will lead to liabilities for both Class 2 and Class 4 National Insurance (see Section 11.11).

Significant levels of ancillary services will also lead to a requirement for the business to be registered for VAT.

Holiday accommodation businesses will also need to be registered for VAT if total annual sales exceed £70,000.

15.10 PROPERTY INVESTMENT BUSINESSES & INCORPORATION RELIEF

Theoretically, the requirements for Incorporation Relief are not as strict as for relief for 'Gifts of Business Assets' and only require a 'business' rather than a 'trade'. However, some of the case law on the subject states that the "mere passive holding of investments and collection of rent does not amount to a business" for this purpose.

There is other case law, however, which holds that a 'business' need not be an active one and that such a thing as a 'passive business' might exist.

Unfortunately, none of the case law on the subject is really decisive. There are no decided cases to tell us what the courts think that 'business' means in the context of Incorporation Relief and we are left scrabbling around trying to find some sort of definition within the many asides made by judges during cases on other areas of tax law.

Certainly, if the business can be adapted to achieve trading status in the manner described in Section 15.9, then Incorporation Relief should be available.

Whether Incorporation Relief might be available for other property investment businesses remains uncertain.

Whilst, in theory, any property investment business must be regarded as a 'business' and would therefore appear to be eligible for Incorporation Relief, in practice I am not aware of any case where the relief has been claimed for such a business.

The stance taken by HM Revenue and Customs, as one might expect, is to follow the criterion that the mere holding of investment property and collection of rent does not constitute a business for Incorporation Relief purposes. (Whilst happily continuing to collect Income Tax on the profits generated from this 'non-business' activity!)

One of the major problems, of course, is that to get the relief, one must transfer the entire business to the company. If relief is not then forthcoming, there could well be a substantial Capital Gains Tax bill. Furthermore, whether relief is obtained or not, Stamp Duty Land Tax will usually be payable at rates of up to 5% on the total value of all of the properties transferred.

So, the stakes are high and the outcome is uncertain!

Before even considering whether to attempt an Incorporation Relief claim, it would be necessary to take a very detailed look at the particular circumstances of the property business in question and establish whether it amounts to more than 'the mere passive holding of investments'.

But just how much more than passive investment does the business need to be in order to qualify?

In theory, it doesn't need to be any more than passive investment, but that's not how HM Revenue and Customs sees it. Not that they are the final authority on the matter – that's the job of the courts; but who among us really wants to go 'head to head' with them over such a 'cause celebre'?

But that is just what this situation needs – a proper test case to decide the matter!

What Can We Do In The Meantime?

In the meantime, it may still be possible to claim Incorporation Relief where the owner has a well-established business and is actively involved in the day-to-day running of it, so that HM Revenue and Customs could not possibly say that the properties were mere 'passive' investments.

Nevertheless, as I say, the position remains uncertain and I would not like to rely on a claim for Incorporation Relief for any property investment business other than a furnished holiday letting business.

But What If You Could Get The Relief?

Anyone who did successfully obtain Incorporation Relief would achieve a tax-free uplift in the base cost of all of their properties to current market value.

Well, not exactly 'tax-free', there is Stamp Duty Land Tax to worry about. But even at rates of up to 5%, this could be a price worth paying in some cases.

As investment properties would be subject to Capital Gains Tax at 18% or 28% in the transferor's own hands, the uplift in base costs could provide the potential to make massive savings.

Once in the company, properties could generally be sold with a Corporation Tax exposure of just 20% of the future increase in their value above the rate of retail price inflation. The company could then reinvest the vast majority of the sales proceeds, having suffered only a minimal level of tax exposure.

Yes, the stakes are high indeed!

Example

Jim has a large property investment portfolio with a total current market value of £1.5m. Jim has built the portfolio up over many years and several of the older properties stand at substantial capital gains. Jim has a substantial and well-established property business and is actively involved in running his business on a day-to-day basis. We will assume, therefore, that he can successfully argue that he does indeed have a 'business' for the purposes of Incorporation Relief.

Within his portfolio, Jim has ten houses in Essex which he purchased for just £15,000 each and which are now worth £100,000 each. This will give Jim a gain of £85,000 on the sale of each house.

A sale of all ten houses would thus leave Jim with a Capital Gains Tax bill of £238,000 (10 x £85,000 x 28%). (Jim is a higher rate taxpayer and has already used his annual Capital Gains Tax exemption.)

Jim would like to sell off his old houses and reinvest the money in some new properties which, he anticipates, will yield higher rental returns. He is not, however, happy at the prospect of losing almost £240,000 of his proceeds in Capital Gains Tax.

Instead, therefore, Jim transfers his entire property investment business to a new company, Telfer Limited, in exchange for shares. Jim then holds over his capital gains under Incorporation Relief.

Whilst Telfer Limited will have to pay Stamp Duty Land Tax of £75,000 (£1.5m at 5% - but see Section 15.12), the old houses in Essex can now be sold with little or no tax liability arising, leaving a net sum of almost £1,000,000 available for Jim to reinvest, or £163,000 more than he would have had if he had simply sold the houses in Essex himself.

Furthermore, all of Jim's remaining properties will now have a base cost of 105% of their current market value, thus significantly reducing any exposure to tax on sale.

15.11 OTHER INVESTMENT PROPERTIES

So, what happens if we transfer investment properties to a company and cannot claim either of the two Capital Gains Tax reliefs which we have already explored?

Without the availability of any special Capital Gains Tax relief, the owner of investment properties faces the problem of separate capital gains calculations on the transfer of each individual property. In each case, the owner faces a Capital Gains Tax bill based on a 'deemed' sale at market value.

Stamp Duty Land Tax liabilities will also arise in the usual way for any transfers with a total value in excess of £125,000 (or £150,000 in the case of commercial property).

Sometimes, with careful timing and the use of annual exemptions, it is, however, still possible to make the transfers at little or no tax cost, especially where a couple own properties jointly.

The possible availability of principal private residence relief on some properties should also be borne in mind when considering this type of strategy. (But see Section 16.2 regarding the pitfalls of private use of property after putting it into a company.)

Tax Tip

A former principal private residence may usually be transferred into a property investment company at any time up until at least three years after it ceased to be your main residence (and possibly much later in some circumstances) without incurring any Capital Gains Tax liability.

Be careful, however: if the property was not always your main residence throughout the period from purchase up until when you finally moved out of it, there might be some exposure to Capital Gains Tax.

Remember also that Stamp Duty Land Tax will be payable as usual in the case of any property with a market value in excess of £125,000.

Nevertheless, generally speaking, unless you have the confidence to attempt an Incorporation Relief claim, it remains difficult to get an existing property investment business into a company without running the risk of incurring a large Capital Gains Tax bill.

In most cases, therefore, it is safer to look to the company as a vehicle only for your future investments and to keep your existing properties in your own hands.

The 'Backdoor Route'

Borrowings secured on your existing personal property portfolio could be invested in the company to enable it to acquire new property. You, in turn, would be eligible for Income Tax relief on the interest on such borrowings, as the funds are being invested in a 'Close Company' (see Section 16.1). This would minimise your personal tax exposure on your own personal portfolio whilst enabling you to build up a new portfolio within your company.

Another Possibility

Another possibility which might be worth exploring in these circumstances is the use of a property management company (see Section 17.1).

Yet Another Possibility

Or maybe think about leasing your properties to your own company?

This is far from simple and, like any other tax planning, will require detailed professional advice.

15.12 STAMP DUTY LAND TAX ON TRANSFERS

Transfers of property to your company will give rise to Stamp Duty Land Tax liabilities based on the greater of the amount of consideration actually paid by the company for the transfer, or the market value of the properties transferred. (See Section 8.3 for the rates of Stamp Duty Land Tax applying.)

'Consideration' for this purpose will include not only any amount actually paid, or payable, by the company, but will also include the amount of any mortgages or other loans over the properties which the company takes over. 'Consideration' also includes the value of any shares issued in exchange for the properties transferred.

Worst of all, where a whole business is transferred (e.g. to obtain Incorporation Relief or entrepreneurs' relief), all of the property transfers will amount to 'linked transactions' and the Stamp Duty Land Tax will be calculated on the total value.

However, Stamp Duty Land Tax only applies to the transfer of land and property so the value of other assets can be disregarded for these purposes. Hence, when transferring a whole business it will be necessary to make an apportionment.

Example

Chris transfers his property development business, worth £1m, to Paterson Developments Limited in exchange for shares. The business value is made up as follows:

	£
Office premises	*100,000*
Work-in-progress & Land bank	*300,000*
Building materials in stock	*50,000*
Plant and machinery	*100,000*
Motor vehicles	*50,000*
Debtors	*550,000*
Goodwill	*100,000*

	1,250,000
Less Creditors	*250,000*

	1,000,000
	========

Of these, only the office premises and work-in-progress would be subject to Stamp Duty Land Tax. This gives a total value of £400,000 which is subject to Duty.

The Stamp Duty Land Tax payable on this transfer would therefore be just £12,000 (£400,000 at 3%).

Tax Tip

When transferring a property development business to a company, it is worth trying to time the transfer at a point when the business has as little work-in-progress on hand as possible, including its land bank. This will help to reduce the amount of Stamp Duty Land Tax arising on the transfer.

Alternatively, by using the 'Gifts of Business Assets' route, the transferor could refrain from transferring any work-in-progress, thus reducing their exposure to Stamp Duty Land Tax.

The New 5% Rate

As discussed in Section 8.3, the Government is proposing to introduce a new Stamp Duty Land Tax rate of 5% for purchases of residential property with a consideration of more than £1m after 5th April 2011.

What is not yet clear is whether this rate will apply in a case where it is only the 'linked transactions' rule which takes the total consideration over £1m (i.e. where none of the individual properties are worth in excess of £1m but the total value of all properties transferred exceeds £1m).

It is also unclear whether the 5% rate will apply in the case of transfers to a company where the actual consideration is not in excess of £1m but the 'deemed' consideration (i.e. market value of the properties) is.

It is for this reason that I referred to a rate of '4% or 5%' in the example (Murray Lettings Limited) in Section 15.5.

In the example in Section 15.10 (Telfer Limited), I did use a rate of 5%, but this is again uncertain.

15.13 VAT AND BUSINESS TRANSFERS

Whole Businesses

If the whole business is transferred and is registered for VAT, this will mean that there is a change in the 'taxable person' for VAT purposes.

The transferor will need to cancel their VAT registration or apply to transfer it to the company. The transferee company will need to register for VAT.

It is important that the business is transferred as a going concern or there may be VAT charges arising on the assets transferred.

Where some assets are retained, VAT charges may also arise on these. VAT charges may also arise if the transferee company does not register for VAT.

Partial Transfers

If only part of the business is transferred, the transferor may need to charge the company VAT on the assets transferred if any of the transfers amounts to a taxable supply (see Chapter 9).

The transfer will not represent a taxable supply, however, if the part of the business transferred amounts to a 'going concern' in its own right (e.g. ten furnished holiday letting properties, together with an office and staff, out of a total portfolio of twelve properties) **and** the transferee company registers for VAT.

If the transferor is not left with a taxable business after the transfer then they will need to cancel their VAT registration and this may lead to VAT charges on the assets retained.

Commercial Properties

If a commercial property on which the option to tax has been exercised (see Section 9.4) is transferred, a VAT charge will arise unless:

i) The transfer is part of the transfer of a business as a 'going concern', and

ii) The transferee company notifies HM Revenue and Customs **_on or before the date of the transfer_** that it also opts to tax the property.

Chapter 16

Some Other Important Tax Issues

16.1 CLOSE COMPANIES AND CLOSE INVESTMENT HOLDING COMPANIES

Broadly speaking, a company is a 'Close Company' if it is under the control of five people or less. The vast majority of private property companies will therefore be Close Companies.

This is good news since additional reliefs are available in respect of shares and other investments in Close Companies, including interest relief, as discussed in Chapter 13.

Close Investment Holding Companies

Any close company which does not exist wholly or mainly for a 'qualifying purpose' is a Close Investment Holding Company. Fortunately, 'qualifying purposes' include carrying on a trade <u>and</u> renting property to unconnected persons.

Hence, a property business will generally represent a qualifying purpose and a property company will <u>not</u>, therefore, usually be a Close Investment Holding Company.

This is very important because Close Investment Holding Companies must pay Corporation Tax at the **_main rate_** on all of their profits and gains. Furthermore, investors are not eligible for interest relief on investments in Close Investment Holding Companies.

Most property companies, however, do remain eligible for the full range of effective Corporation Tax rates set out in Section 2.3 and their investors are eligible for interest relief, as explained in Chapter 13. Unless, that is, they fall foul of the matters which we are about to discuss in Section 16.2 below.

16.2 THE DANGERS OF PRIVATE USE

It is generally not advisable to hold properties through a company where there is some private use. For these purposes, 'private use' would include:

- Using it as your own private residence (whether or not your main residence).

- Allowing your spouse, partner or any other member of your family to use it as a private residence.

- Letting the property to any 'connected' person.

Private use of a property held through a company could result in:

- The company becoming a Close Investment Holding Company and therefore having to pay the main rate of Corporation Tax on **all** profits.

- Loss of interest relief on sums invested in the company.

- Loss of entrepreneurs' relief on company shares (where they might otherwise qualify).

- Income Tax Benefit-in-Kind charges on the company's directors.

- Class 1A National Insurance liabilities for the company.

- Deemed distributions of income which are taxable on the shareholders as if they were dividends.

Furthermore, where a property with private use is owned personally, there is scope to make use of the principal private residence exemption, private letting relief and rent-a-room relief. The scope to use these reliefs is lost if the property is held in a company.

Certainly therefore, as far as UK property is concerned, any private use of property held by a company is best avoided.

The position for foreign property is somewhat different since there are often good reasons for holding a second home abroad through a company. Furthermore, in 2007, HM Revenue and Customs confirmed that the owners of a company which exists solely to hold a private residence overseas will be exempt from any Benefit-in-Kind charges in the UK in respect of their personal use of the property.

The exemption only applies, however, if the company exists solely to hold foreign property. If the company has any other activities, the Benefit-in-Kind charge for personal use by the company owners will continue to apply under normal principles.

The company must also be held directly by individuals. The exemption is not available, for example, where a company is held by a trust or another company.

Hence, whilst this exemption may be useful in some cases, it will generally make sense to ensure that any company formed to hold a second home abroad is kept entirely separate from any other company owned by the same person or persons.

We will return to the issue of multiple companies in Section 16.4.

16.3   SELLING THE COMPANY

Very often a property company will continue in the same ownership (or at least the same family) until its usefulness has expired, when it will be wound up. We looked at this in Section 12.6. Sometimes, however, a property company may be sold with its existing business intact. This is particularly likely in the case of a property development company, as we saw in Section 12.11.

Another time when a property company may be sold with its existing business intact is when the purchaser wishes to acquire a ready-made portfolio held by a property investment company.

The sale of the company represents a capital disposal and the individual investor making the sale will therefore have a Capital Gains Tax liability in much the same way as that arising on a winding up.

Example

Isabel started her property investment company, Angel Limited, in 1985 with an investment of just £10,000 share capital.

In December 2011, Isabel decides to sell Angel Limited to Big Properties PLC for £1m. Her capital gain on the sale is therefore £990,000. After deducting her annual exemption of £10,600 (estimated) she is left with a taxable gain of £979,400. She is a higher rate taxpayer, so she will pay Capital Gains Tax, at 28%, i.e. £274,232.

Stamp Duty

A huge advantage for the purchaser of a property company is the ability to make large Stamp Duty savings, as only 0.5% will need to be paid on the purchase price of the shares. Not only is this considerably less than the Stamp Duty Land Tax rate of up to 5% applying to property purchases, but also the actual amount of consideration to which the duty applies will often be reduced.

Example

Di Rollo Properties Limited owns a portfolio of residential properties with a total value of £5m. The company also has borrowings and other liabilities totalling £2m, giving it a net value of £3m.

Marcus is interested in acquiring the Di Rollo Properties Limited portfolio. If he buys the property portfolio from the company, he will have to pay Stamp Duty Land Tax at 5% on £5m, i.e. £250,000 (see Section 15.12).

Alternatively, if Marcus buys the company, he will only have to pay Stamp Duty at 0.5% on £3m, i.e. £15,000 – a saving of £235,000!

Given the commercial advantages of acquiring an existing, well-run property portfolio and the potential Stamp Duty savings, a well-packaged property company can be a very attractive target for potential purchasers. Naturally, one can expect this to be reflected in the sale price!

266

16.4 BENEFITS AND DANGERS OF MULTIPLE COMPANIES

"Great," you might be thinking. "I'll form one company to take the first £300,000 of profits and another to take the rest. That way, I'll never pay more than 20%."

Sorry, no, that won't work. In fact, in some cases it would be absolutely disastrous!

This is because the Corporation Tax profit bands described in Section 2.3 must be divided up where there are any associated companies. The bands are divided equally between all of the relevant associated companies, meaning that the more companies you have, the higher your effective rates of Corporation Tax in each company are going to be.

What is an Associated Company?

An associated company is another company under the control of the same persons and <u>their</u> associates. (A person's associates are other persons with whom they are 'connected' – see Appendix D.)

Hence, in the simplest case, if you form two companies and own all of the shares in both of them, then these companies are associated with each other.

Example

Marie has a property company, Morgan Limited, which has a 31st March year end and makes annual profits of £200,000. As things stand, Morgan Limited's annual Corporation Tax bill (from the year ending 31st March 2012 onwards) will be £40,000 (£200,000 at 20%).

Marie's property business is expanding, so she decides to form a second company, Cody Limited. In its first year, the new company just manages to break even. However, because there are now two associated companies, the Corporation Tax profit bands must now be divided in two. Each of Marie's companies therefore gets half of the relevant tax bands.

Morgan Limited's Corporation Tax bill for the year ending 31st March 2012 is therefore now £44,375 (£150,000 at 20% plus £50,000 at 28.75%).

If Marie had kept her whole property business in just one company, its Corporation Tax liability would have remained £40,000.

Hence, whilst Cody Limited has no tax to pay (as it has not yet made a profit), its mere existence has cost Morgan Limited an extra £4,375!

The moral here is that a proliferation of companies is generally a bad idea!

When Must A Company be Counted as an Associated Company?

A company does not need to be counted as an associated company if it is not carrying on a business. (The term 'business' is defined very widely here and might include, for example, a company holding a portfolio of stock market investments. However, a company which simply had an interest-bearing bank account, and no other assets, has been held <u>not</u> to be carrying on a business for this purpose.)

Readers may feel that there is some inconsistency between the interpretation of the term 'business' which is being used here and the interpretation used for Incorporation Relief purposes (see Section 15.10). And you'd be right – this is a prime example of HM Revenue and Customs having their cake and eating it!

Fortunately, however, a company which exists only to hold property and which is not actively seeking to rent out any property does not usually need to be counted as an associated company. Amongst other things, this means that a company formed purely to hold a second home overseas may usually be excluded from the associated company rules.

For accounting periods ending after 31st March 2011, it is proposed that any companies controlled by relatives or business partners will not need to be counted as associated companies unless there is a substantial commercial relationship between the companies or the companies form part of a tax planning arrangement designed to extend the availability of the small profits rate of Corporation Tax.

This exception also generally applies to earlier accounting periods except in the case of companies controlled by spouses or minor children.

Subject to the above exceptions, however, <u>any</u> associated company must be taken into account, regardless of what country it is based in or registered in.

Trading Companies

It should be noted that <u>any</u> associated company carrying on <u>any</u> kind of business will have this same effect on the Corporation Tax rates applying to your property company. This remains the case even if your other company carries on an entirely different kind of business.

Conversely, of course, the creation of a property company will have an equally detrimental effect on the Corporation Tax position of any existing trading company which you might have.

You might be tempted, therefore, to think that it would be a good idea to make your property investments through another existing company (thus avoiding the kind of problems which Marie experienced in the example above).

Here though, great care needs to be exercised. If your other company is carrying on a business which is regarded as a 'trade' within the UK tax system, your shares in that company will be eligible for entrepreneurs' relief and holdover relief for Capital Gains Tax purposes (see Chapter 7) and also for business property relief for Inheritance Tax purposes.

Putting non-qualifying property investments into such a company could jeopardise the 'business asset' status of your shares in that company and could eventually cost you dearly in Capital Gains Tax or Inheritance Tax.

In this type of scenario, you would need to weigh your annual Corporation Tax costs against your eventual Capital Gains Tax or Inheritance Tax position in order to determine the best course of action overall.

16.5 SHORT AND LONG ACCOUNTING PERIODS

For a variety of reasons, companies sometimes prepare accounts covering periods other than a year. This often occurs at the beginning or end of a company's life, although it will also occur in the event of a change of accounting date. (We saw one reason why you might wish to consider changing your company's accounting date in Section 2.7.)

As shorter or longer accounting periods will often occur at the beginning of a company's life, it is worth us spending a little time on the Corporation Tax implications of such periods.

Longer Accounting Periods

For Corporation Tax purposes, periods of over one year must be divided up into two periods:

- The first twelve months, and
- The remainder.

Trading profits may be divided between the two periods on a pro-rata basis, although a strict 'actual' basis may be used if there is reasonable justification for doing so.

Rental income should strictly be allocated on an 'actual' basis, although a pro-rata basis will often be acceptable.

Other investment income and capital gains should be allocated to the period in which they arose.

Each of the two periods is then taxed separately in its own right. The first period is taxed under the normal principles applying to a period of a year. The second period is dealt with as a short accounting period.

Short Accounting Periods

Where a company has a short accounting period, the profit bands given in Section 2.3 must be reduced accordingly.

Example

Lansdowne Road Limited draws up accounts for the period ending 31st March 2012, showing a profit of £250,000. If this were the profit of a twelve month period, Corporation Tax would be payable at 20%, and would amount to £50,000.

However, let us suppose that these accounts cover the nine-month (or 275 day) period from 1st July 2011 to 31st March 2012.

The Corporation Tax calculation is therefore now as follows:

£225,410 (£300,000 x 275/366) x 20% =	*£45,082*
£24,590 (Remainder) @ 28.75% =	*£7,070*
Total Tax Due:	*£52,152*

Starting Business

It is also important to understand that a new accounting period for Corporation Tax purposes starts when the company starts business. This will generally be some time after the date of incorporation.

Example

Webster Limited is a property investment company. The company was incorporated on 12th May 2011 but does not rent out its first property until 15th September 2011.

Webster Limited changes its accounting date to 30th June and prepares its first set of accounts for the period from 12th May 2011 to 30th June 2012.

For Corporation Tax purposes, however, the company is regarded as having one accounting period as a dormant company, from 12th May to 14th September 2011 and then a second accounting period, as a property investment company, from 15th September 2011 to 30th June 2012.

If Webster Limited prepared its first set of accounts to a date more than twelve months after it commenced business, it would have three accounting periods for Corporation Tax purposes.

Ceasing Business

For Corporation Tax purposes, an accounting period is also deemed to come to an end when the company ceases business.

Tax Returns & Tax Payments

In any case where a company's accounting period must be divided up into more than one period for Corporation Tax purposes, each period will require its own Corporation Tax Return.

The filing deadline for each Return will usually remain twelve months from the company's accounting date, except in the case of periods in excess of 18 months, when returns are due within 30 months of the beginning of the accounting period.

The due date for payment of Corporation Tax (except for large companies under the instalment system – see Section 2.6) is always nine months and one day after the end of each period.

Example

Hastings Limited draws up accounts for the fifteen months ending 31st December 2011.

The company will need to prepare a tax return for the year ending 30th September 2011 and pay the Corporation Tax due for that period by 1st July 2012.

The company will also need to prepare a tax return for the three-month period ending 31st December 2011 and pay the Corporation Tax due for that period by 1st October 2012.

As a general rule, I would advise all company owners to keep HM Revenue and Customs informed of any changes which affect their company's Tax Return periods, including any changes of accounting date, the setting up of new companies and commencement of business.

Most important of all is to advise HM Revenue and Customs if the company ceases all business activity and becomes inactive.

In this way, one hopes that HM Revenue and Customs will issue notices requiring the company to deliver Tax Returns for the right periods.

There are detailed rules governing the position where notices are issued requiring the company to deliver a Corporation Tax Return for a period which does not correspond to one of its actual accounting periods. In most cases, such notices will result in a requirement to submit at least one Corporation Tax Return and penalties (as detailed in Section 2.9) will arise for failure to do so.

The important point to note is that you cannot afford to ignore a notice to deliver a Corporation Tax Return just because it has been issued for the wrong period!

16.6 BECOMING NON-RESIDENT

Throughout this guide, we have been looking at the implications for UK resident property investors using a UK resident property company. Space does not permit a detailed examination of the position for non-residents, but it is worth making a few brief observations.

Tax Residence for Companies

Subject to any applicable Double Tax Treaty, a company is treated as UK resident if:

i)   It is UK registered, or
ii) It has its place of central management and control in the UK.

A detailed examination of (ii) would take too long to fit in here, but it is fair to say that if you are UK resident, it is very difficult for any property company which you run not to be regarded as UK resident also.

Emigration for Companies

Generally speaking, a UK registered company cannot 'emigrate' – i.e. it cannot cease to be UK resident. This may, however, in some cases, be overridden by the terms of a Double Tax Treaty between the UK and another country.

If a UK resident company does succeed in 'emigrating', i.e. becoming non-UK resident, then, unless it does so with the specific consent of Her Majesty's Treasury, it must pay an 'exit charge'. The 'exit charge' is basically a sum equal to the Corporation Tax which would arise if the company were to sell all of its assets at their market value.

In view of these points, any UK resident individual who ultimately intends to emigrate should think very carefully before using a property company.

Non-resident Companies

In the same way as for non-resident individuals, subject to any applicable Double Tax Treaty, a non-UK resident company is liable for UK tax on income from UK property, but is exempt from tax on capital gains unless connected with trading activities in the UK.

However, if a non-UK resident company is under the control of a UK resident individual, then the individual is personally liable for Capital Gains Tax on the capital gains made by that company.

Hence, overseas (non-resident) companies are generally of little use to UK resident individual investors buying UK property.

Even for non-UK resident individuals investing in UK property, the situation is not exactly clear-cut.

Wealth Warning

If attempting to run a UK property portfolio through an overseas company, it is essential to ensure that the company's 'place of central management and control' is outwith the UK.

Otherwise, the company will be deemed to be UK resident, thus bringing all of its properties into the UK tax net for capital gains purposes, etc.

This can be very difficult (and costly) to achieve in practice and detailed professional advice should always be sought before attempting to rely on this strategy.

Non-UK Resident Individuals

By using a UK resident company, a non-UK resident individual property investor would effectively be bringing properties into the UK tax net.

As explained in Section 3.4, however, where a non-UK resident is investing substantially in UK property, there is often a risk that HM Revenue and Customs will argue that the individual has a taxable UK trading activity rather than falling under the capital gains regime and therefore being exempt on their UK property gains.

A UK property company may be useful in such a case, as there is less difference in the amount of tax payable *within* a company between a property 'trading' business and a property 'investment' business. Although this does effectively mean 'admitting defeat' and accepting that the business will be taxable in the UK, it is nevertheless a case of 'damage limitation', as the Corporation Tax rates applying will generally be lower than the Income Tax which is potentially at stake.

Furthermore, since the income from UK properties is always taxable in any case, the use of a UK company may often remain advantageous.

Nevertheless, the major drawback for a non-resident in using a UK company remains the fact that the company will be subject to UK Corporation Tax on its capital gains, whereas the individual would be exempt from UK tax on those gains.

The only way to avoid any tax on the properties' capital growth in the company would be for the non-resident individual to sell the company itself, rather than the properties held within it. Nevertheless, even then, one might reasonably expect the purchaser to take the potential Corporation Tax liability on capital gains in the company into account when negotiating a purchase price! (Although, against this, there are also Stamp Duty advantages to be considered, as explained in Section 16.3.)

Chapter 17

Specialised Property Companies

17.1 PROPERTY MANAGEMENT COMPANIES

We have looked at the taxation status of property management companies a few times throughout this guide and it is now worth taking a look at how these companies might be used as a planning tool.

The objective of this type of planning is to reduce the tax burden on the income from your properties without having the problems inherent in putting the properties themselves into a company.

Example

Jonah has a large property portfolio generating annual gross rents of £500,000 and a taxable profit of £100,000. His other taxable income for 2011/12 will total £50,000, so he can expect pay £42,990 in Income Tax on these profits.

Instead, however, from 1st April 2011, he decides to sub-contract the management of his properties to a new property management company, Lomu Property Services Limited.

Lomu Property Services Limited charges Jonah 15% of the gross annual rents on the properties (£75,000) as a service charge for managing the portfolio. Naturally, the company also ends up bearing some of the expenses in running the property portfolio and these amount to £10,000.

Jonah will now have a taxable annual rental income of £35,000 (£100,000, as before, less the £75,000 service charges from Lomu Property Services Limited, but add back the costs of £10,000 now borne by the company). This reduces his annual Income Tax bill to £14,000.

Meanwhile, Lomu Property Services Limited will have an annual profit of £65,000 (the £75,000 service charge less £10,000 expenses), giving it a Corporation Tax bill, at 20%, of £13,000.

The total tax paid by Jonah and Lomu Property Services Limited is thus £27,000, which, for 2011/12 alone, is £15,990 less than Jonah would have otherwise paid: a saving of over 37%!

As usual, however, it doesn't work quite so well if the company's profits are extracted. If Jonah takes out the company's after-tax profit of £52,000 as a dividend, he will have additional Income Tax of £15,990 to pay, leaving him precisely back where he started!

Wealth Warning

This type of arrangement is likely to attract close HM Revenue and Customs scrutiny and it is essential to ensure that the commercial reality of the situation matches up to the tax planning.

Firstly, the amount of service charge levied by the company must not exceed a normal commercial rate for those services.

Secondly, for Jonah to be able to claim a valid Income Tax deduction for these charges, he must be able to show that they were incurred wholly and exclusively for the benefit of his property rental business. In other words, there must be a genuine provision of services by the company.

Thirdly, the company itself must be carrying on a trade on a commercial basis. Otherwise, the company would be classed as a Close Investment Holding Company and much of the potential tax saving would be lost. To satisfy this requirement, the company should be managing other properties as well and not just those of the owner.

The arrangement will work best if there is a full-blown property management business, managing properties for a number of unconnected landlords on a fully commercial arm's length basis.

The service charges levied on the owner's property business from the company should be on the same basis as those for other landlords using the same services.

Tax Tip

Subject to the points set out above, even greater tax savings may be possible if the property management company is owned by and/or employs the investor's spouse, partner or other adult family members. (But do bear the warnings given in Section 10.4 in mind here.)

17.2 THE EIS PUB COMPANY

An individual's own Capital Gains Tax liabilities may be deferred by reinvesting some or all of the underlying capital gain in Enterprise Investment Scheme shares. To obtain relief, the investment must take place within the period beginning a year before, and ending three years after, the date of the disposal which gave rise to the gain.

When the investor is not 'connected' with the company issuing the shares, qualifying investments in Enterprise Investment Scheme shares also carry an Income Tax credit of up to 20% of the amount invested. Hence, combining the Income Tax credit with the potential for Capital Gains Tax deferral outlined above, gives a potential for immediate tax savings of up to 48% of the amount invested.

Enterprise Investment Scheme shares must be Ordinary Shares, as defined in tax legislation, must be issued wholly for cash and must be held for at least three years (sometimes longer). The issuing company must also continue to carry on a 'qualifying trade' throughout this period. All tax relief given on the initial investment will be withdrawn if any of these conditions are breached.

Any capital gain arising on the sale of Enterprise Investment Scheme shares which initially qualified for Income Tax relief, as described above, is exempt from Capital Gains Tax. This exemption is also lost if the Income Tax relief is withdrawn.

Note that it is only the capital gain on the Enterprise Investment Scheme shares themselves which may be exempt. Gains held over on reinvestment into Enterprise Investment Scheme shares will become chargeable to Capital Gains Tax on a sale of those shares at any time.

An annual limit applies to the amount invested in Enterprise Investment Scheme shares which is eligible for Income Tax relief. The current annual investment limit is £500,000.

However, from 2009/10 onwards, all Enterprise Investment Scheme investments may be carried back for Income Tax relief in the previous tax year.

In effect, this means that a person who did not make any Enterprise Investment Scheme investments in the previous year can get tax relief on an investment of up to £1,000,000.

So far, so good, but there are two major hurdles which we have to negotiate before we can make any use of an Enterprise Investment Scheme company for a property business.

Qualifying Trades

Firstly, we have the problem that companies engaged in any form of property business are generally ineligible to issue Enterprise Investment Scheme shares.

As explained above, the company must carry on a qualifying trade for a minimum period which will be at least three years. Not only is property investment excluded, even furnished holiday letting, but also most property-based trades, including property development, property dealing, property management, hotels, guest houses and many similar trades.

What is permitted, however, is a trade which is run from a property without the provision of any accommodation, such as a pub or restaurant.

Hence, a company formed to run a chain of pubs or restaurants might therefore qualify for the Enterprise Investment Scheme.

Severing the Connection

For the purposes of the Enterprise Investment Scheme, a person is connected with the company if:

i)   They are an employee of the company
ii) They hold more than 30% of the company's ordinary share capital, loan capital or voting power
iii) There are any circumstances under which they may come to hold more than 30% of the company's ordinary share capital, loan capital or voting power
iv) There are any circumstances under which they may be entitled to more than 30% of the company's assets on a winding up

Tests (iii) and (iv) above are very wide so great care is required here.

As for test (i), the investor can still be a director of the company, but this is subject to some very strict conditions which must be observed faithfully.

As usual, the holdings, rights, powers or employment status of 'connected persons' (see Appendix D) are taken into account in determining whether any of the above conditions are breached. However, for the purposes of the Enterprise Investment Scheme, brothers and sisters need not be counted as connected persons.

The EIS Pub Company

So, after examining all of the rules, we can conclude that four or more friends or siblings, or two or more unmarried couples, can get together to run a pub through an Enterprise Investment Scheme company.

And they only need to run the pub for a minimum period which may be no more than three years.

After that, the company can do (almost) whatever it likes and our investors will still keep their initial savings of up to 48% and the Capital Gains Tax exempt status of their shares.

Example

In October 2011, four friends, Martyn, Peter, Keith and David meet for dinner. The conversation turns to tax and each of them bemoans the bill which they will face the following January. It turns out that each friend made a substantial capital gain during 2010/11 and has to stump up the resultant Capital Gains Tax in just a few months' time.

"I've got a great idea" announces Martyn, "why don't we form an Enterprise Investment Scheme company! We can all defer £280,000 in Capital Gains Tax and also get an Income Tax credit of £200,000 each." He goes on to explain that his suggestion involves each of them investing £1,000,000 from their earlier gains into a new company in exchange for ordinary shares to be issued under the Enterprise Investment Scheme.

The other three friends are delighted by this idea and the quartet proceed to form 'Inglenook Pubs Limited'. Each friend invests £1,000,000 in ordinary shares in the company, getting a 25% stake in return.

Taking the £4m invested by the four friends, Inglenook Pubs Limited then purchases a small chain of public houses, which it proceeds to run with moderate success for just over three years. (Technically, a profit is not essential for this exercise, but the company must be engaged in a genuinely commercial venture in order to qualify for the Enterprise Investment Scheme.)

By early 2015, the company is free to close the pubs and perhaps convert the properties into flats. By 2017, the pubs have all been converted into flats which the company can either keep as an investment portfolio, or sell for profit.

Either way, the company is now worth, say, a total of £7.2m and each investor could potentially sell their shares to one of the other investors or to a third party.

Each friend therefore has a chance to realise a tax-free capital gain of £800,000 (£7.2m/4 = £1.8m LESS £1m invested). They can also keep their original £200,000 Income Tax credit.

The only fly in the ointment is that the original 'held over' capital gains will become taxable on the sale of the Enterprise Investment Scheme shares.

Even here, however, there is at least the benefit that the tax has been deferred for several years, plus the possibility that the Capital Gains Tax rate may have been reduced again by this stage (although there is also a risk that it may have been increased).

All-in-all, if anyone can succeed in meeting the necessary (and complex) conditions, the EIS Pub Company has the potential to generate massive tax savings and enable the investors to accumulate additional wealth free from the fear of Capital Gains Tax.

There's just one problem which I, for one, find a little objectionable: it involves closing pubs!

Chapter 18

In Conclusion

18.1 WEIGHING IT ALL UP

Now that we have carried out a detailed examination of the tax implications of using a property company, what conclusions can we draw?

- A property company's usefulness will depend on the type of property business that you have. Property development, trading and management businesses will all generally benefit from being carried out through a company. The position for property investment businesses, where long-term capital growth tends to be an integral part of the business plan, is less clear.

- A company will usually save you tax on your annual income.

- Basic rate taxpayers will not, however, benefit from using a property investment company.

- For higher rate taxpayers, any tax saving achieved by using a company will generally be eliminated when profits are always being withdrawn from the company.

- The greatest savings are achieved when the company's profits are continually reinvested. This, in turn, leads to a significant growth in pre-tax income and the total capital value of the company.

- A company provides greater scope to obtain tax relief for rental losses, interest and finance costs.

- Greater tax liabilities will arise on property disposals if the investor wishes to extract the proceeds from the company.

- Capital growth retained in the company, however, may ultimately be sold at a lesser tax cost.

- A successful property company is attractive to purchasers.

- Properties held in companies should not generally be used privately (although exceptions sometimes arise for foreign holiday homes).

- Transferring existing investment properties into a company is extremely hazardous to your wealth!

- On the other hand, companies may sometimes be used as a means to save Capital Gains Tax on future property disposals.

- Forming additional companies will generally lead to increased Corporation Tax costs. However, there are sometimes good reasons why additional companies should be used.

- Property management companies may be considered as an alternative to property investment companies in the right circumstances.

- Non-residents and those intending to emigrate should generally not use UK companies.

- To be certain about the benefits of a property company requires a crystal ball.

- The decision whether to use a company is dependent on a great many factors and each property investor's position is unique.

18.2   FUTURE TAX CHANGES

In the eight years since I wrote the first edition of this guide, we have seen enormous changes to the UK tax system. In fact, if there is one thing which the last eight years have taught us, it must surely be to take nothing for granted!

When I wrote the first edition of this guide, we had an extremely beneficial Corporation Tax regime, with the first £10,000 of annual company profits being exempt and profits of up to £300,000 taxed at just 19%.

Since then, we have seen massive changes in both the corporate and personal tax regimes in the UK.

One might expect, therefore, that the changes we have seen over the last eight years would have made an enormous difference to the question of whether it is beneficial to use a property company or not.

Not so! My main conclusion eight years ago was that a property company was of only marginal benefit unless the investor was prepared to reinvest their profits within the company over a long period of time.

Eight years later, we still see that a property company is generally only beneficial if profits are reinvested within the company.

Admittedly, the 'balancing act' which we looked at in Section 11.3 means that basic rate taxpayers no longer benefit from a property investment company, even if they do retain all of the profits in the company.

Nevertheless, despite all of the changes over the last eight years, higher rate taxpayers remain in the same fundamental position: there are massive savings to be made by using a company as long as the investor is prepared to retain and reinvest their profits within the company over a substantial period of time.

The question for us now is this: if the tax changes made over the last eight years have not altered the basic rationale behind using a property company, what is the likelihood that future changes will?

The Government is currently reviewing the taxation of small businesses in the UK. This, of course, includes private 'owner-managed' companies, which have long been on HM Revenue and Customs' 'hit list'.

At present, we have no idea what changes this review might lead to, nor what impact they might have on property companies.

In the past, there have been concerns that the Government might try to levy National Insurance on private company dividends. There were also additional Corporation Tax charges on small company dividends between 2004 and 2006.

As we saw in Section 10.4, we also have the threat of potential 'income shifting' legislation in the near future.

There is speculation that the private company as we know it may even be replaced by a different form of business entity. Exactly how such an entity might be taxed and whether existing companies will be forced to adopt such a new regime is, however, extremely unclear. I tend to suspect that such an entity may prove as elusive as the Holy Grail.

In summary, though, most of the pressure to reform the taxation of small companies seems to be focused on the extraction of profits by company owners.

Generally speaking, what the Government seems most intent on attacking is not small companies themselves, but rather small company owners who simply use their company as a means to save tax on what, in reality, is effectively just personal income.

Hence, whilst we cannot be certain what the future may hold, it nevertheless seems to me that any further changes which we may see in the near future are likely to simply reinforce the conclusion that a property company is not generally beneficial where all of its profits are being extracted by the owner every year.

Whilst the Treasury can be expected to eat into your tax savings to some extent, my feeling is that, whatever changes we may see, property companies are still likely to remain beneficial to higher rate taxpayers who wish to make long-term property investments and build up a property business over a number of years.

And long may it continue!

Appendix A

UK Tax Rates and Allowances: 2009/10 to 2011/12

	Rates	2009/10 £	2010/11 £	2011/12 £
Income Tax				
Personal allowance		6,475	6,475	7,475
Basic rate band	20%	37,400	37,400	35,000
Higher rate/Threshold	40%	43,875	43,875	42,475
Personal allowance withdrawal				
Effective rate/From	60%	n/a	100,000	100,000
To		n/a	112,950	114,950
Super tax rate/Threshold	50%	n/a	150,000	150,000

Starting rate band applying to interest and other savings income only

	10%	2,440	2,440	2,560
National Insurance				
Class 1 – Primary		11%	11%	12%
Class 4		8%	8%	9%
Primary threshold		5,715	5,715	7,225
Upper earnings limit		43,875	43,875	42,475
Additional Rate		1%	1%	2%
Class 1 – Secondary		12.8%	12.8%	13.8%
Secondary threshold		5,715	5,715	7,075
Class 2 – per week		2.40	2.40	2.50
Small earnings exception		5,075	5,075	5,315
Class 3 – per week		12.05	12.05	12.60
Pension Contributions				
Annual allowance		245,000	255,000	50,000
Lifetime allowance		1.75m	1.8m	1.5m
Capital Gains Tax				
Annual exemption		10,100	10,100	10,600*
Basic rate		18%	18%	18%
Higher rate		n/a	28% (1)	28%
Entrepreneurs' relief:				
Lifetime limit		1m	2m/5m (1)	5m
Rate of relief/Tax rate		4/9ths	4/9ths/10%(1)	10%
Inheritance Tax				
Nil Rate Band		325,000	325,000	325,000
Annual Exemption		3,000	3,000	3,000

Age-related Allowances, etc.

Age allowance: 65-74	9,490	9,490	9,940
Age allowance: 75 and over	9,640	9,640	10,090
MCA: born before 6/4/1935 (2)	6,965	6,965	7,295
MCA minimum	2,670	2,670	2,800
Income limit	22,900	22,900	24,000
Blind Person's Allowance	1,890	1,890	1,980

* - Estimated on basis of Budget Statement on 22ᵈ June 2010, with inflation (per RPI Sept 2010) at 4.6%.

Notes
1. Capital Gains Tax changes were introduced with effect from 23ᵈ June 2010.
2. The Married Couples Allowance, 'MCA', is given at a rate of 10%.

Appendix B

Forecast Future Tax Rates and Allowances

The use of these forecast future rates and allowances within this guide is explained in the Foreword. Further details are also given in Section 11.2.

	Rates	Bands, allowances, etc.		
		2012/13	**2013/14**	**2014/15**
		£	£	£
Income Tax				
Personal allowance		8,105	8,735	9,365
Basic rate band	20%	34,370	33,740	34,635
Higher rate/ Threshold	40%	42,475	42,475	44,000
Personal allowance withdrawal				
Effective rate/ From	60%	100,000	100,000	100,000
To		116,210	117,470	118,730
Super tax rate/ Threshold	50%	150,000	150,000	150,000
Starting rate band applying to savings income only				
	10%	2,650	2,750	2,850
Capital Gains Tax				
Annual exemption		11,000	11,400	11,800
Inheritance Tax				
Nil Rate Band		325,000	325,000	325,000
Age-related Allowances				
Age allowance: 65 -74		10,290	10,660	11,040
Age allowance: 75 & over		10,450	10,820	11,200
MCA maximum		7,555	7,825	8,105
MCA minimum		2,900	3,010	3,120
Income limit		24,900	25,800	26,800

National Insurance

Class 1 Rate	12%	12%	12%
Class 4 Rate	9%	9%	9%
Additional Rate	2%	2%	2%
Primary Threshold	7,485	7,755	8,035
Secondary Threshold	7,325	7,585	7,855
Upper Earnings Limit	42,475	42,475	44,000
Class 2 per week	£2.60	£2.70	£2.80

Marginal Corporation Tax Rates 2009 to 2015

Year Ending:	Company Profits: Up to £300,000	£300,000 to £1.5M	Over £1.5M
31-Mar-2009 to			
31-Mar-2011	21.000%	29.750%	28.000%
30-Apr-2011	20.918%	29.668%	27.918%
31-May-2011	20.833%	29.583%	27.833%
30-Jun-2011	20.751%	29.501%	27.751%
31-Jul-2011	20.666%	29.416%	27.666%
31-Aug-2011	20.581%	29.331%	27.581%
30-Sep-2011	20.499%	29.249%	27.499%
31-Oct-2011	20.414%	29.164%	27.414%
30-Nov-2011	20.332%	29.082%	27.332%
31-Dec-2011	20.247%	28.997%	27.247%
31-Jan-2012	20.162%	28.912%	27.162%
29-Feb-2012	20.085%	28.835%	27.085%
31-Mar-2012	20.000%	28.750%	27.000%
30-Apr-2012	20.000%	28.648%	26.918%
31-May-2012	20.000%	28.542%	26.833%
30-Jun-2012	20.000%	28.439%	26.751%
31-Jul-2012	20.000%	28.333%	26.667%
31-Aug-2012	20.000%	28.227%	26.582%
30-Sep-2012	20.000%	28.125%	26.500%
31-Oct-2012	20.000%	28.019%	26.415%
30-Nov-2012	20.000%	27.917%	26.333%
31-Dec-2012	20.000%	27.811%	26.249%
31-Jan-2013	20.000%	27.705%	26.164%
28-Feb-2013	20.000%	27.606%	26.085%
31-Mar-2013	20.000%	27.500%	26.000%
30-Apr-2013	20.000%	27.397%	25.918%
31-May-2013	20.000%	27.291%	25.833%
30-Jun-2013	20.000%	27.188%	25.751%
31-Jul-2013	20.000%	27.082%	25.666%
31-Aug-2013	20.000%	26.976%	25.581%
30-Sep-2013	20.000%	26.873%	25.499%
31-Oct-2013	20.000%	26.767%	25.414%
30-Nov-2013	20.000%	26.664%	25.332%

31-Dec-2013	20.000%	26.558%	25.247%
31-Jan-2014	20.000%	26.452%	25.162%
28-Feb-2014	20.000%	26.356%	25.085%
31-Mar-2014	20.000%	26.250%	25.000%
30-Apr-2014	20.000%	26.147%	24.918%
31-May-2014	20.000%	26.041%	24.833%
30-Jun-2014	20.000%	25.938%	24.751%
31-Jul-2014	20.000%	25.832%	24.666%
31-Aug-2014	20.000%	25.726%	24.581%
30-Sep-2014	20.000%	25.623%	24.499%
31-Oct-2014	20.000%	25.517%	24.414%
30-Nov-2014	20.000%	25.414%	24.332%
31-Dec-2014	20.000%	25.308%	24.247%
31-Jan-2015	20.000%	25.202%	24.162%
28-Feb-2015	20.000%	25.106%	24.085%
31-Mar-2015	20.000%	25.000%	24.000%

Connected Persons

The definition of 'connected persons' differs slightly from one area of UK tax law to another. Generally, however, an individual's connected persons include the following:

i) Their husband, wife or civil partner
ii) The following relatives:
   o Mother, father or remoter ancestor
   o Son, daughter or remoter descendant
   o Brother or sister

iii) Relatives under (ii) above of the individual's spouse or civil partner
iv) Spouses or civil partners of the individual's relatives under (ii) above
v) The individual's business partners
vi) Companies under the control of the individual or of any of their relatives under (i) to (iv) above
vii) Trusts where the individual, or any of their relatives under (i) to (iv) above, is a beneficiary

Retail Prices Index

	1982	1983	1984	1985	1986	1987	1988	1989
Jan		82.61	86.84	91.20	96.25	100.0	103.3	111.0
Feb		82.97	87.20	91.94	96.60	100.4	103.7	111.8
Mar	79.44	83.12	87.48	92.80	96.73	100.6	104.1	112.3
Apr	81.04	84.28	88.64	94.78	97.67	101.8	105.8	114.3
May	81.62	84.64	88.97	95.21	97.85	101.9	106.2	115.0
Jun	81.85	84.84	89.20	95.41	97.79	101.9	106.6	115.4
Jul	81.88	85.30	89.10	95.23	97.52	101.8	106.7	115.5
Aug	81.90	85.68	89.94	95.49	97.82	102.1	107.9	115.8
Sep	81.85	86.06	90.11	95.44	98.30	102.4	108.4	116.6
Oct	82.26	86.36	90.67	95.59	98.45	102.9	109.5	117.5
Nov	82.66	86.67	90.95	95.92	99.29	103.4	110.0	118.5
Dec	82.51	86.89	90.87	96.05	99.62	103.3	110.3	118.8

	1990	1991	1992	1993	1994	1995	1996	1997
Jan	119.5	130.2	135.6	137.9	141.3	146.0	150.2	154.4
Feb	120.2	130.9	136.3	138.8	142.1	146.9	150.9	155.0
Mar	121.4	131.4	136.7	139.3	142.5	147.5	151.5	155.4
Apr	125.1	133.1	138.8	140.6	144.2	149.0	152.6	156.3
May	126.2	133.5	139.3	141.1	144.7	149.6	152.9	156.9
Jun	126.7	134.1	139.3	141.0	144.7	149.8	153.0	157.5
Jul	126.8	133.8	138.8	140.7	144.0	149.1	152.4	157.5
Aug	128.1	134.1	138.9	141.3	144.7	149.9	153.1	158.5
Sep	129.3	134.6	139.4	141.9	145.0	150.6	153.8	159.3
Oct	130.3	135.1	139.9	141.8	145.2	149.8	153.8	159.5
Nov	130.0	135.6	139.7	141.6	145.3	149.8	153.9	159.6
Dec	129.9	135.7	139.2	141.9	146.0	150.7	154.4	160.0

	1998	1999	2000	2001	2002	2003	2004	2005
Jan	159.5	163.4	166.6	171.1	173.3	178.4	183.1	188.9
Feb	160.3	163.7	167.5	172.0	173.8	179.3	183.8	189.6
Mar	160.8	164.1	168.4	172.2	174.5	179.9	184.6	190.5
Apr	162.6	165.2	170.1	173.1	175.7	181.2	185.7	191.6
May	163.5	165.6	170.7	174.2	176.2	181.5	186.5	192.0
Jun	163.4	165.6	171.1	174.4	176.2	181.3	186.8	192.2
Jul	163.0	165.1	170.5	173.3	175.9	181.3	186.8	192.2
Aug	163.7	165.5	170.5	174.0	176.4	181.6	187.4	192.6
Sep	164.4	166.2	171.7	174.6	177.6	182.5	188.1	193.1
Oct	164.5	166.5	171.6	174.3	177.9	182.6	188.6	193.3
Nov	164.4	166.7	172.1	173.6	178.2	182.7	189.0	193.6
Dec	164.4	167.3	172.2	173.4	178.5	183.5	189.9	194.1

	2006	2007	2008	2009	2010
Jan	193.4	201.6	209.8	210.1	217.9
Feb	194.2	203.1	211.4	211.4	219.2
Mar	195.0	204.4	212.1	211.3	220.7
Apr	196.5	205.4	214.0	211.5	222.8
May	197.7	206.2	215.1	212.8	223.6
Jun	198.5	207.3	216.8	213.4	224.1
Jul	198.5	206.1	216.5	213.4	223.6
Aug	199.2	207.3	217.2	214.4	224.5
Sep	200.1	208.0	218.4	215.3	225.3
Oct	200.4	208.9	217.7	216.0	225.8
Nov	201.1	209.7	216.0	216.6	226.8
Dec	202.7	210.9	212.9	218.0	

Short Leases

(See Section 4.10)

Proportion of the original cost of a lease of 50 or more years' duration allowed as a deduction for capital gains purposes on a disposal of that lease.

Years Remaining	%	Years Remaining	%
50	100	25	81.100
49	99.657	24	79.622
48	99.289	23	78.055
47	98.902	22	76.399
46	98.490	21	74.635
45	98.059	20	72.770
44	97.595	19	70.791
43	97.107	18	68.697
42	96.593	17	66.470
41	96.041	16	64.116
40	95.457	15	61.617
39	94.842	14	58.971
38	94.189	13	56.167
37	93.497	12	53.191
36	92.761	11	50.038
35	91.981	10	46.695
34	91.156	9	43.154
33	90.280	8	39.399
32	89.354	7	35.414
31	88.371	6	31.195
30	87.330	5	26.722
29	86.226	4	21.983
28	85.053	3	16.959
27	83.816	2	11.629
26	82.496	1	5.983

Disclaimer

1. Please note that this Tax Guide is intended as general guidance only for individual readers and does NOT constitute accountancy, tax, investment or other professional advice. Neither Taxcafe UK Limited nor the author can accept any responsibility or liability for loss which may arise from reliance on information contained in this Tax Guide.

2. Please note that tax legislation, the law and practices by government and regulatory authorities (e.g. HM Revenue and Customs) are constantly changing. We therefore recommend that for accountancy, tax, investment or other professional advice, you consult a suitably qualified accountant, tax specialist, independent financial adviser, or other professional adviser. Please also note that your personal circumstances may vary from the general examples given in this Tax Guide and your professional adviser will be able to give specific advice based on your personal circumstances.

3. This Tax Guide covers UK taxation only and any references to 'tax' or 'taxation' in this Tax Guide, unless the contrary is expressly stated, refer to UK taxation only. Please note that references to the 'UK' do not include the Channel Islands or the Isle of Man. Foreign tax implications are beyond the scope of this Tax Guide.

4. Whilst in an effort to be helpful, this Tax Guide may refer to general guidance on matters other than UK taxation, Taxcafe UK Limited and the author are not experts in these matters and do not accept any responsibility or liability for loss which may arise from reliance on such information contained in this Tax Guide.

5. Please note that Taxcafe UK Limited has relied wholly on the expertise of the author in the preparation of the content of this Tax Guide. The author is not an employee of Taxcafe UK Limited but has been selected by Taxcafe UK Limited using reasonable care and skill to write the content of this Tax Guide.